Diary of an Enlisted Man

Your very truly
L. Van Alstyne

LAWRENCE VAN ALSTYNE

Diary of an Enlisted Man

The Recollections of a Union Soldier of
"Bostwick's Tigers," 128th New York Volunteers
During the American Civil War

Lawrence Van Alstyne

LEONAUR

Diary of an Enlisted Man
The Recollections of a Union Soldier of "Bostwicks Tigers," 128th New York Volunteers
During the American Civil War

by Lawrence Van Alstyne

First published under the title
Diary of an Enlisted Man

Leonaur is an imprint of Oakpast Ltd

ISBN: 978-1-78282-070-3 (hardcover)
ISBN: 978-1-78282-071-0 (softcover)

http://www.leonaur.com

Publisher's Notes

The views expressed in this book are not necessarily
those of the publisher.

Contents

With Loving Regard
For the Memory of My Parents
Who Watched for and Eagerly Read the Diary
As from Time to Time It Came to Them
And to My Comrades-in-Arms
Whether Living or Dead
This Volume is Affectionately Dedicated.

Preface

In the multitude of books written about the Civil War, very little is said of the enlisted man. His bravery and his loyalty are admitted and that is about all. Of his every-day life, the very thing his family and friends cared most to know about, there is hardly anything said. It is to remedy this omission in some degree that the following pages are published. They were written by an enlisted man and are mostly about enlisted men. They are filled with details that history has no room for, and for that reason may have an interest quite their own.

They were written at different times, in different places, and under a great variety of circumstances and conditions. Some were written as the line halted for rest while marching from place to place, some while waiting for trains or other modes of transportation, but the most were written by the light of a candle or a smouldering camp-fire while my comrades, no more weary than I, were sleeping about me. All were written amid scenes of more or less confusion, and many times of great excitement. They were written because of a promise made to my parents that I would make notes of my wanderings and of the adventures I met with.

At first I found it an irksome task, taking time I really needed for rest; but as time went on the habit became fixed, and I did not consider the day's work done until I had written in my diary of the events that came with it.

The diary was kept in small pocket notebooks, of a size convenient to carry in my pocket, and be ever ready for use. There was never a lack of subjects to write about. Events crowded upon each other so fast that each day furnished plenty of material for the time I could give it. I had never been far from home. The sights I saw were new and strange to me and made deep impressions. These, as best I could, I transferred to the pages of my diary, so the friends at home could, in a way, see the sights I saw and that seemed so wonderful to me. When pages enough were written for a letter, I cut them out and sent them home to be read by any who cared to, after which they were strung together on a string and saved for me to read again, should I ever return to do it. When I did return I found the leaves had so accumulated as to make a large bundle. There was no need for me to read them at that time, for the story they told was burned too deep in my memory to be easily forgotten. So I tied them in a bundle and put them away in an unused drawer of my desk, where they lay, unread and undisturbed for the next forty-five years.

But while the old diary lay hidden in my desk a new generation had crept upon the stage. We no longer occupied the centre of it. One by one we had been crowded off, and our ranks were getting so thin we had to feel around for the touch of a comrade's elbow. Every year there were more comrades' graves to decorate, and every year there were fewer of us left to decorate them. At last we had met an enemy we could not even hope to conquer. With sadness we saw first one and then another called out, and they did not return. They had answered the last roll-call, and it was only a question of a little time when the last name would be called, and the muster-out rolls be folded up and filed away.

It was with a feeling of ever-increasing loneliness that I untied the bundle and began to read the long-forgotten diary. In a little while I was a boy again, one of that great company that helped to make history read as it does. Almost half a century had suddenly rolled back and I was with Company B—"Bostwick's Tigers" we were called, not altogether on account of our fighting qualities, but because of the noise we sometimes made. I was having my share of the fun that was going, and was taking my share of the hard knocks as well.

I was never so absorbedly interested. I even forgot my meals. For weeks I thought of little else and did little else than read and copy those dim old pages. I read from them to. any who would listen, and wondered why it did not stir their blood as it did my own.

But the reason is plain. To the listener it was hearsay. To me it was real. So it may be with the diary now it is printed. In the nature of things it cannot be to others what it is to me. It is a part of my life. My blood would not tingle as it does at the reading of another man's life. It is what historians had neither time nor space to write, the every-day life of an enlisted man in time of war.

October, 1910.   L.V.A.

CHAPTER 1

The Recruiting Camp

August 19, 1862.
Hudson Camp Grounds.

I have enlisted! Joined the Army of Uncle Sam, for three years, or the war, whichever may end first. Thirteen dollars per month, board, clothes and travelling expenses thrown in. That's on the part of my Uncle. For my part, I am to do, I hardly know what, but in a general way understand I am to kill or capture such part of the Rebel Army as comes in my way.

I wonder what sort of a soldier I will make; to be honest about it, I don't feel much of that eagerness for the fray I am hearing so much of about me.

It seems to me it is a serious sort of business I have engaged in. I was a long time making up my mind about it. This one could go, and that one, and they ought to, but with me, some way it was different. There was so much I had planned to do, and to be. I was needed at home, etc., etc. So I would settle the question for a time, only to have it come up to be reasoned away again, and each time my reasons for not taking my part in the job seemed less reasonable. Finally I did the only thing I could respect myself for doing,—went to Millerton, the nearest recruiting station, and enlisted.

I then threw down my unfinished castles, went around and bid my friends goodbye, and had a general settling up of my affairs, which, by the way, took but little time. But I never before knew I had so many friends. Everyone seemed to be my friend. A few spoke encouragingly, but the most of them spoke and acted about as I would expect them to, if I were on my way to the gallows. Pity was so plainly shown that when I had gone the rounds, and reached home again, I felt as if I had been attending my own funeral. Poor old father and mother! They had expected it, but now that it had come they felt it, and though they tried hard, they could not hide from me that they felt it might be the last they would see of their baby.

Then came the leaving it all behind. I cannot describe that. The goodbyes and the good wishes ring in my ears yet. I am not myself. I am some other person. My surroundings are new, the sights and sounds about me are new, my aims and ambitions are new;—that is if I have any. I seem to have reached the end. I can look backwards, but when I try to look ahead it is all a blank. Right here let me say, God bless the man who wrote *Robert Dawson*, and God bless the man who gave me the book. *Only a few drops at a time, Robert.* The days are made of minutes, and I am only sure of the one I am now living in. Take good care of that and cross no bridges until you come to them.

I have promised to keep a diary, and I am doing it. I have also promised that it should be a truthful account of what I saw and what I did. I have crawled off by myself and have been scribbling away for some time, and upon reading what I have written I find it reads as if I was the only one. But I am not. There are hundreds and perhaps thousands here, and I suppose all could, if they cared to, write just such an experience as I have. But no one else seems foolish enough to do it. I will let this stand as a preface to my diary, and go on to say that we, the first instalment of recruits from our neighbourhood, gathered at Amenia, where we had a farewell dinner, and a final handshake, after which we boarded the train and were soon at Ghent, where we changed from the Harlem to the Hudson & Berkshire R. R., which landed us opposite the gates of the Hudson Fair Grounds, about 4 p.m. on the 14th. We were made to form in line and were then marched inside, where we found a lot of rough board shanties, such as are usually seen on country fair grounds, and which are now used as offices, and are full of bustle and confusion. After a wash-up, we were taken to a building which proved to be a kitchen and dining room combined. Long pine tables, with benches on each side, filled the greater part of it, and at these we took seats and were served with good bread and fair coffee, our first meal at Uncle Sam's table, and at his expense. After supper we scattered, and the Amenia crowd brought up at the Miller House in Hudson. We took in some of the sights of the city and then put up for the night.

The next morning we had breakfast and then reported at the camp grounds ready for the next move, whatever that might be. We found crowds of people there, men, women and children, which were fathers and mothers, wives and sweethearts, brothers and sisters of the men who have enlisted from all over Dutchess and Columbia counties. Squads of men were marching on the race track, trying to keep step with an officer who kept calling out "Left, Left, Left," as his left foot hit the ground, from which I judged he meant everyone else should put his left foot down with his. We found these men had gone a step further than we. They had been examined and accepted, but just what that meant none of us exactly knew. We soon found out, however,

Every few minutes a chap came out from a certain building and read from a book, in a loud voice, the names of two men. These would follow him in, be gone a little while and come out, when the same performance would be repeated. My name and that of Peter Carlo, of Poughkeepsie, were called together, and in we went. We found ourselves in a large room with the medical examiner and his clerks. His salutation, as we entered, consisted of the single word, "Strip." We stripped and were examined just as a horseman examines a horse he is buying. He looked at our teeth and felt all over us for any evidence of unsoundness there might be. Then we were put through a sort of gymnastic performance, and told to put on our clothes. We were then weighed and measured, the colour of our eyes and hair noted, also our complexion, after which another man came and made us swear to a lot of things, most of which I have forgotten already. But as it was nothing more than I expected to do without swearing I suppose it makes no difference.

The rest of the day we visited around, getting acquainted and meeting many I had long been acquainted with. In the afternoon the camp ground was full of people, and as night began to come, and they began to go, the goodbyes were many and sad enough. I am glad my folks know enough to stay away. That was our first night in camp. After we came from the medical man, we were no longer citizens, but just soldiers. We could not go down town as we did the night before. This was Saturday night, August 17th. We slept but little,—at least I did not. A dozen of us had a small room, a box stall, in one of the stables, just big enough to lie down in. The floor looked like pine, but it was hard, and I shall never again call pine a soft wood, at least to lie on.

If one did fall asleep he was promptly awakened by someone who had not, and by passing this around, such a racket was kept up that sleep was out of the question. I for one was glad the drummer made a mistake and routed us out at five o'clock instead of six, as his orders were. We shivered around until roll-call and then had breakfast. We visited together until dinner. Beef and potatoes, bread and coffee, and plenty of it. Some find fault and some say nothing, but I notice that each gets away with all that's set before him. In the afternoon we had preaching out of doors, for no building on the grounds would hold us. A Rev. Mr. Parker preached, a good straight talk, no big words or bluster, but a plain man-to-man talk on a subject that should concern us now, if it never did before. I for one made some mighty good resolutions, then and there.

Every regiment has a chaplain, I am told, and I wish ours could be this same Mr. Parker. The meeting had a quieting effect on all hands. There was less swearing and less noise and confusion that afternoon than at any time before. After supper the question of bettering our sleeping accommodations came up, and in spite of the good resolutions above recorded I helped steal some hay to sleep on. We made up our minds that if our judge was as sore as we were he would not be hard on us. We spread the hay evenly over the floor and lay snug and warm, sleeping sound until Monday morning, the 18th.

The mill of the medical man kept on grinding and batches of men were sworn in every little while. Guards were placed at the gates, to keep us from going down town. I was one of the guards, but was called off to sign a paper and did not go back. Towards night we had to mount guard over our hay. Talk about "*honour among thieves*," what was not stolen before we found it out, was taken from under us while we were asleep, and after twisting and turning on the bare floor until my aching bones woke me, I got up and helped the others express themselves, for there was need of all the cuss words we could muster to do the subject justice. But that was our last night in those quarters.

The next day the new barracks were finished and we took possession. They are long narrow buildings, about 100 feet by 16, with three tiers of bunks on each side, leaving an alley through the middle, and open at each end. The bunks are long enough for a tall man and wide enough for two men provided they lie straight, with a board in front to keep the front man from rolling out of bed. There are three buildings finished, and each accommodates 204 men. We were not allowed either hay or straw for fear of fire. As we only had our bodies to move, it did not take long to move in. Those from one neighbourhood chose bunks near together, and there was little quarrelling over choice. In fact one is just like another in all except location.

Walter Loucks and I got a top berth at one end, so we have no trouble in finding it, as some do who are located near the middle.

These barracks, as they are here called, are built close together, and ordinary conversation in one can be plainly heard in the others. Such a night as we had, story-telling, song-singing, telling what we would do if the Rebs attacked us in the night, with now and then a quarrel thrown in, kept us all awake until long after midnight. There was no getting lonesome, or homesick. No matter what direction one's thought might take, they were bound to be changed in a little while, and so the time went on. Perhaps someone would start a hymn and others would join in, and just as everything was going nicely, a block of wood, of which there were plenty lying around, would come from no one knew where, and perhaps hit a man who was half asleep. Then the psalm singing would end up in something quite different, and for awhile one could almost taste brimstone. I heard more original sayings that night than in all my life before, and only that the boards were so hard, and my bones ached so badly, I would have enjoyed every minute of it.

But we survived the night, and were able to eat everything set before us, when morning and breakfast time came. After breakfast we had our first lesson in soldiering, that is, the men of what will be Captain Bostwick's company, if he succeeds in filling it, and getting his commission, did. A West Point man put us through our paces. We formed in line on the race track, and after several false starts got going, bringing our left feet down as our instructor called out, "Left, Left," etc. A shower in the night had left some puddles on the track, and the first one we came to some went around and some jumped across, breaking the time and step and mixing up things generally. We were halted, and as soon as the captain could speak without laughing, he told us what a ridiculous thing it was for soldiers to dodge at a mud puddle. After a turn at marching, or keeping step with each other, he explained very carefully to us the "position of a soldier," telling how necessary it was that we learn the lesson well, for it would be of great use to us hereafter. He repeated it, until every word had time to sink in.

Heels on the same line, and as near together as the conformation of the man will permit. Knees straight, without stiffness. Body erect on the hips, and inclining a little forward. Arms hanging naturally at the sides, the little finger behind the seam of the pantaloons. Shoulders square to the front. Head erect, with the eyes striking the ground at the distance of fifteen paces.

Every bone in my body ached after a little of this, and yet our instructor told us this is the position in which a well-drilled soldier can stand for the longest time and with the greatest ease. This brings my diary up to this date and I must not let it get behind again. There is so much to write about, it takes all my spare time; but now I am caught up, I will try and keep so.

August 20, 1862.

Capt. Bostwick came from Albany last night. He has his commission, and is to be captain of Company B, his being the second company filled. I can now style myself of Co. B, 128th N.Y. State Volunteers. He got us together and gave us quite a speech. Told us what he would do, and what he expected us to do. I imagine none of us know very well yet what we will do. He said if he had not got his commission he would have gone in the ranks with us. We gulped this down, but I doubt if many believed it. But at all events we are one family now, and Ed. Bostwick is the head of it. We have known him so long as just Ed. Bostwick, that it will take some time to get used to addressing him as Capt. Bostwick. One of our company, Jim Wasburn, who hails from Sharon, was put in the guard-house three times yesterday for fighting. He ought to make a good soldier, for he had rather fight than eat. He is a "mean dog," always picking at someone smaller than himself.

Today he pushed Eph. Hammond over, as he was getting some water from a pail. Eph. is one of our smallest men, but he gave the bully a crack on the jaw that sent him sprawling, and took the fight all out of him. One of the Poughkeepsie boys has gone on the war path too. He began Sunday night by running past the guard, and then waiting until arrested. Just as he got inside he gave his captor the slip and hid in the barracks until the search was given up. Then he came out and dodged past another guard and gave his pursuers a lively chase over the fields before they caught him. He might be going yet if he had not stopped and let them take him. He was brought in, put in the guard-house, and before ten o'clock was out and down town, where he got into some mischief and was locked up by the police. Yesterday he was brought back under guard and again put in the guard-house, which by the way is only a tent, with a soldier stationed by it. Last night, as I was coming from the city I met him going down, and probably by this time he is in jail again.

6 p.m. Have just drawn our coats, drawers, stockings and shoes. Ben Rogers is here. He belongs to a Kinderhook company. Jim Rowe and John Pitcher have just come. Twenty-five of the company are old acquaintances, all from the same neighbourhood. Besides, I have made lots of new acquaintances here. Men are coming every day and almost by every train, and the prospect of our regiment being soon filled seems good. The President's call for 300,000 volunteers is being nobly responded to here, and probably it is the same all over the North.

August 21, 1862.

Last night I was one of those detailed for guard, and was put at one of the gates. This morning at 8.30 was what they call "guard mount." The men so detailed are divided into three squads, called first, second and third reliefs. The first goes on at 8.30 and remains until 10.30. Then the second relief goes on and stays until 12.30, when the third relief, to which I belong, takes the place until 2.30. This goes on until each relief has had four turns of two hours each on duty, and four turns each of four hours' rest, when 8.30 a. m. again comes around and a new guard is put in place of the old. The next day after being on guard, no duty is required of them. Nothing very hard about that so far as I can see. I begin to like it, and I am glad it is so, for there is no such thing as calling the boss up to settle.

August 22, 1862.

I caught cold last night, and feel a little slim today. Lew Holmes got a pass for himself and me to go down town and that cured me. The run about in Hudson with the nice fresh air of today, together with a five-day furlough, which was given out tonight, has worked wonders for those that were lucky enough to get them. It seems the men are all to have a five-day furlough, but not all at once. The Amenia crowd drew first prize. I am delighted to go, and yet there will be the goodbyes to say again, and I don't know after all whether I am glad or sorry.

August 23, 1862.

Night. Home again. We left Hudson at 5 a. m. Were delayed in Chatham, waiting for the Harlem train, long enough to make quite a visit with brother William and his wife Laura. Uncle Daniel was there also. There is little else talked of but the war. Men are arranging their business so as to go, and others are "shaking in their boots" for fear they will have to go. I don't waste any sympathy on this latter class. There are some I would like to see made to go. They belong in the Southern army, where all their sympathy goes.

I found our folks well and glad to see me. I have no sort of doubt of that. Just as we had had supper, Obadiah Pitcher came with his buggy and offered to take me to call on some friends; this I thought too good a chance to lose, and we went south. We found so many, and there was so much talking, it was Sunday morning when we came back.

August 24, 1862.
Sunday at home.

Herman and John, Betsy and Jane came to dinner. Such a dinner, too, as mother cooked for us. Dear old soul, how I wished I could eat enough to last until the war is over. Daniel McElwee came up and wanted me to go with him to Mabbettsville and see Mr. and Mrs. Haight. I put the best side of soldiering out, as Mrs. Haight wanted to know how her boy was faring. This seems to me the saddest side of war. Those that go have excitement enough to live on, but those that are left can only wonder how it is with their loved ones, and imagine worse things than may ever happen. I reached home in time to visit with father and mother awhile and then went to bed tired out.

August 25, 1862.
Amenia Union, N.Y.

The days of my stay being numbered, I am improving the time as best I can. Have been to John Loucks's, Isaac Bryan's, Daniel McElwee's, Hugh Miller's, Jason Hull's (where I had another good dinner), and then came on to this place and put up at Mr. Dutcher's. Met John Van Alstyne, who was on his way to Sharon, and was told I was a fool for enlisting. Maybe I am, John, but I have lots of company.

August 26, 1862.

Mary and I took a long ride, and then I left for Millerton. Saw the effects of a railroad smash up at Cooper's Crossing. The engine and cars were scattered along the front of the embankment and many of them only good for kindling-wood. The carcass of a cow, the cause of the accident, lay in one place and her hide in another. Attended a meeting at Millerton, heard some patriotic speeches and saw lots of people who seemed glad to see me. Was paid the town bounty of $100 and towards night wended my way over the hills home again, and am writing about it in my diary. This is my last night home. Tomorrow we are due in Hudson again. I have seen none of the others who came home with me. I suppose each one, like myself, has crowded the time full of visiting, for who knows when we will have another chance? We each try to act as if we had no thought for the morrow, but it is hard work and not very successful.

August 27, 1862.

Off for Hudson. The goodbyes have been said again, maybe forever. We are at Pine Plains now. This time we go by horse power instead of the cars. By "we," I mean Walter Loucks and myself who are
chums in camp, as we have long been chums at home. Herman and
John[1] take us up. We have a good team, a beautiful day, and have been
stopped at nearly every house long enough to say "how are you?" and
"goodbye." As soon as we stopped here, out came my diary and pencil.
The habit is getting fixed, and there is little danger of my forgetting
it. The trouble is there is so much to write about I will fill my book
before I come to the real thing. May be someone will sometime be
glad I wrote so much. It is like blazing one's way through the woods.
My trail can be followed, and it behooves me to behave myself, for I
claim all I write in my diary is true.

Night. In camp at Hudson Fair Grounds again. We had dinner
at Blue Store, made several stops on the way, one at Wagonhagers
Churchyard, where Leah Loucks lies buried.

We had supper at Miller's Hotel, where we spent our first night in
Hudson, and where Herman and John stay tonight. It was just a little
bit hard to crawl up into our bare board bunk, after the nice soft beds
we had slept in, but it is part of the contract and we took the dose
with as good grace as possible.

August 28, 1862.

Have been down town and had my picture taken to send home by
Herman and John. Have also been drilling, and altogether have had a
busy day. The ladies of Hudson (God bless them) are going to give us
a supper tonight, and H. and J. are going to stay.

Later. It is all over, except an uncomfortable fullness. Biscuit and
butter, three kinds of cake, beef tongue, fruit of several kinds and *lem-
onade.* We gave the ladies three cheers that must have been heard across
the river. There are lots of people here now. It seems as if I knew half
of them, too. We entertained our visitors until they had to leave camp,
and then had a prayer meeting and after it a stag dance, both of which
I attended.

August 29, 1862.

Received $25.00 today, which is half the State bounty. Friends of
the soldiers are coming and going all the time. One day is much like
another, and yet there is an endless variety. We have guard mount in

1. Herman C. Rowley and John C. Loucks.

the morning and then drill for a couple of hours. Then we are free to visit with our friends. We have lots of them nowadays. No one seems to lack for them. It reminds me of how well people are apt to speak of the dead. While alive we say all sorts of mean things to them and about them, but when they are gone it all seems forgotten and we only remember their good qualities. Some way the very kind attention we receive reminds me of that.

August 30, 1862.

$25.00 more today. How the money comes in! Many people were here today, some from our neighbourhood. the time flies fast. The ladies of Hudson presented us with two beautiful flags today, and Colonel Cowles with a horse, saddle and bridle. It was estimated that five thousand visitors were in camp today. We are the 128th Regiment the State of New York has sent out. I wonder if such a time was made over each one. There was good speaking when the presents were made and accepted. We certainly are having a grand send-off.

Night. There is a circus in Hudson tonight, and the guards have their hands full keeping the 128th in camp. Many get out, and the guard-house is full of those who were caught making the attempt.

August 31, 1862.

Sunday.

Spent the day in camp and a very quiet day at that. A paper has been circulated among us asking that the Rev. Mr. Parker, who preached for us once, be sent with us as chaplain. I understand every regiment has a chaplain (a minister) to look out for the spiritual welfare of the regiment. Judging from this one, they must find plenty to do.

September 1, 1862.

A rumour is afloat that we leave here soon. The 128th is about full, and no doubt we will go soon. But often a report is started by someone without the least reason or foundation. They do it I suppose to see how fast a lie will travel. Just the ordinary camp routine is all that came along today.

September 2, 1862.

We are all togged out with new blue clothes, haversacks and canteens. The haversack is a sack of black enamelled cloth with a flap to close it and a strap to go over the shoulder, and is to carry our food in,—rations, I should say. The canteen is of tin, covered with gray cloth; in shape it is like a ball that has been stepped on and flattened down. It has a neck with a cork stopper and a strap to go over the shoulder. It is for carrying water, coffee or any other drinkable. Our new clothes consist of light blue pants and a darker shade of blue for the coats, which is of sack pattern. A light blue overcoat with a cape on it, a pair of mud-coloured shirts and drawers, and a cap, which is mostly forepiece. This, with a knapsack to carry our surplus outfit, and a woollen blanket to sleep on, or under, is our stock in trade. I don't suppose many will read this who do not know from observation how all these things look, for it seems as if all creation was here to look at them, and us.

September 3, 1862.

Heigho! I'm a corporal!—whatever that may be. The appointments were made today, and I just caught on to the bottom round of the ladder. As I did not expect anything I suppose I should feel pleased. May be I do, I am not sure how I feel now-a-days. There is such a hubbub, I wonder we don't all go crazy. Some say we leave Hudson tonight. None of us know when or where we go, but there is a lot of guessing.

Night. Laura Loucks was in camp today. She is on her way home from her sister's, in the western part of the state. She greeted me with "There's another fool!" A great many goodbyes were said today, and tears enough shed to drown a cat.

September 4, 1862.

We go today, sure; that is, if reports are true. The government bounty was paid today, and the oath of allegiance taken by the regimental officers, as well as the men. Every day the net is drawn a little tighter. No use in kicking now. We are bound by a bond none of us can break, and I am glad to be able to say, for one, that I don't want to break it. But it seems as if things dragged awfully slow. I suppose it is because I know so little about the many details that are necessary for the full organization of a regiment.

Night. Here yet. I wish we might go. We are all ready and the sooner we go the more patriotism will be left in us. Too much of it is oozing out through the eyes. People keep coming to have a last word, a last goodbye and usually a last cry over it. I am heartily glad my folks have sense enough to keep away, for it is all I can stand to see the others. No doubt for many it is a last goodbye. In the nature of things we cannot all expect to come back, but God is good, and he keeps that part hidden from us, leaving each one to think he will be the lucky one. To make matters worse, the change of water, food, and mode of living is having its effects on many, myself among the number, and I feel pretty slim tonight. I will spread my blanket on my soft pine board, and, if my aching bones will let me, will try what a good sleep will do, for we are of all men know not what tomorrow may have in store for us.

September 5, 1862.

Still in Hudson. Was routed out twice last night, for no particular reason as far as I can discover, unless it was to make a miserable night still more miserable. After forming in line and standing there, half asleep, for awhile, the order, "Break Ranks" would come and we would go back to our bunks, and so the night wore away. At 4.30 we were called again, marched out for our morning ablutions, and then marched back again, wide awake, but pretty cross and ugly. We signed receipts for one month's pay in advance, and then had breakfast. We did nothing more until dinner time and were then told to take our haversacks and canteens with us. After dinner we were each given a day's supply of bread and a canteen full of coffee, and told to be ready to march at any minute.

CHAPTER 2

The Journey South

Six p. m. On board the steamship *Oregon*, bound for New York City. We had a busy time getting off. Crowds upon crowds of people lined the way from the camp ground to the steamboat landing. The windows and the house tops were also full. I don't see where so many people came from. Men, women and children were waving flags, handkerchiefs or anything else that would wave. They cheered us until hoarse. Bands played, every steam whistle in Hudson was blowing, in fact ever thing that could make a noise did so. Through it all we marched, reaching out every little while for a final handshake, and a last goodbye. Everyone seemed to know everybody else. I presume I shook hands with a hundred that I never saw before and may never see again. But the heartiness of it all, and the sincerity showed so plainly, that by the time the landing was reached the tears were washing the dust from our faces. I am glad it is over. No matter what comes next, it cannot be more trying than that march through Hudson.

Later. The sail down the Hudson is glorious. It is all new to me. As soon as we were clear from the dock I got into the quietest place I could find and told my diary about it. I wish I could better describe the doings about me. This will do to remind me of it all, if I ever see these scribblings again, and if not those that do see them may turn their imagination loose, feeling sure that it cannot overdraw the picture. But there is no use trying to write any more. Confusion reigns, and I am going to put away my dairy and take a hand in it,

September 6, 1862.
New York City, and my first peep at it. We are in City Hall Park, but I must go back and tell of our getting here. We had an all night's ride, passing many large places. So many knew the names of them, we

greenhorns only had to listen to find out where we were all the time. Some did not want to sleep, and the rest were not allowed to. The boatmen must be glad to see the last of us. We passed laws for their observance as well as for our own. The officers kept out of sight. I suppose they were asleep somewhere. May be it is well for both them and ourselves that they did not interfere, for the devil in each man seemed to have got loose. We didn't try to run the steamer but we ran everything else in sight. We took turns riding the walking beam. Some wanted to and the rest had to, and the wonder is no one was killed, or at least crippled.

We landed at the foot of Harrison Street, and marched to the City Hall Park, where I am now seated on the front porch of a tremendous great building, writing about it in my diary. Everything is clean here, and everything to me is new. I have never been in New York before, and I don't suppose I shall see very much of it now. I am on business for the boss, and cannot fool away the time running around the city, even if I was allowed to, which I am not. The officers have us shut in here, with a high picket fence, made of iron, around us on every side. Soldiers,—real soldiers,—are on guard just outside, keeping a close watch that none of us crawl under or jump over. We first had a good wash, then a good breakfast, and then were let alone to read the papers, or write letters or do anything we chose. I had a good nap. The stone I lay on was but little harder than my bunk in the barracks at Hudson, and it was a great deal warmer. The papers say the Rebs are expected to attack Harpers Ferry today. Why couldn't they wait until we got there? Maybe they have heard of us and are improving the time before we get there. Captain Bostwick has gone home for a visit, saying he would meet us in Washington.

Night. On the cars in Jersey City. Part of the regiment has gone on another train, and we are to meet in Philadelphia. We marched on the ferry-boat in double file, and were made to kneel on one knee, leaving the other sticking up for the man ahead to sit on. If it was done for our comfort it was a complete failure, but if it was to keep us from running all over the boat it worked well. Before we left City Hall Park I got a fellow on the outside to get me a bottle of blackberry brandy, and when we were finally seated in the car I out with my bottle and gave it a swing around my head to let the fellows see what I had, when it slipped from my hand and went to smash on the floor. Much as some of us needed it, we could only get a smell, as the fumes rose up to aggravate us.

At Elizabeth, N. J. we halted for a few minutes. Crowds of people lined the track, and although all were strangers to each other, we talked as if we were old acquaintances, Henry House, of Company B, asked a young lady to write him, and they exchanged names and addresses, promising each to write to the other.[1]

September 7, 1862.
Philadelphia. Sunday.

We were too crowded in the cars to see much, or to do much, coming here. Most of us slept nearly all the way. I did for one, but I had dreams of being trod on, and no doubt I was, for there are some that never sleep, and are constantly on the move. We finally stopped and were ferried across a river and landed in this city.

We then marched to a large hall called "The Cooper Shop," why, I don't know. We were given a royal meal, breakfast I should call it, but it was so dark, and I was so sleepy I hardly knew whether it was supper or breakfast. Cold beef, sausage, bread and butter, cheese, and good hot coffee. It was far ahead of any meal we have had so far. I am told that the place is kept open night and day by some benevolent association, and that no regiment passes through without getting a good square meal. If soldiering is all like this I am glad I am a soldier. If the Rebs ever get as far North as Philadelphia, I hope the 128th New York may be here to help defend the "Cooper Shop." After breakfast we went out on the sidewalk and slept until after daylight. We soon after started for a railroad station, where we took a train for Baltimore.

Our ride so far has been one grand picnic. We have lots of fun. No matter what our condition may be, there are some that see only the funny side, and we have enough of that sort to keep up the spirits of all. All along the way the people were out, and the most of them gave us cheers, but not all, as was the case in Hudson. We are nearing the enemy's country. The change in sentiment begins to show, and the farther we go, I suppose, the less cheering we will hear, until finally we will get where the cheers will all be for the other fellow, and we will find ourselves among foes instead of friends.

Later. We are stuck on an upgrade. The engine has gone ahead with a part of the train, and we are waiting for it to come back. The train men say we are about forty miles from Baltimore. That means forty miles from our fodder, and I for one am hungry now. That meal at the

---

1. They did correspond, and after the war were married, and as far as I ever knew or heard lived happily ever after.

Cooper Shop was good, but not lasting enough for this trip. The boys are out on the ground having some fun and I am going to join them.

Baltimore, Md. We are here at last. Marched about two miles from where the cars stopped, and are sitting on the side-walk waiting to see what will happen next. I hope it will be something to eat, for I am about famished. Some of the men are about played-out. The excitement and the new life are getting in their work. The day has been very hot, too, and with nothing to eat since some time last night, it is not strange we begin to wonder where the next meal is coming from, and when it will come. Baltimore is not like New York. I know that much now, but I don't know enough about either city to tell what the difference is. A regiment, fully armed, escorted us here from the cars, and are either staying around to keep us from eating up the city, or to keep the city from eating us, I don't know which. Some act friendly, but the most of the people look as if they had no use for us.

Later.—We have finally had something to eat. My folks always taught me never to find fault with the victuals set before me, so I won't begin now. But for that I should say something right now. But whatever it was it had a bracing effect and we soon started and marched through the city to high ground, which I am told is "Stewart's Hill."

September 8, 1862.
Monday morning.
Our first night in Baltimore is over. We had roll-call, to see if we were all here, and then spread our blankets on the ground and were soon sound asleep. Walt. Loucks and I each having a blanket, we spread one on the ground and the other over us. With our knapsacks for a pillow, we slept as sound as if in the softest bed. The dew, however, was heavy, and only for the blanket over us we would have been wet through. As it was, our hair was as wet as if we had been swimming. Sleeping on the ground, in clothing already wet with sweat, and the night being quite cool, has stiffened our joints, so we move about like foundered horses. Had the Rebs come upon us when we first got up we couldn't have run away and we certainly were not in a condition to defend ourselves. But this wore off after a little, and we were ourselves again. As it was in Hudson, so it is here. All sorts of rumours as to what we do next are going the rounds. I have given up believing anything, and shall wait until we do something or go somewhere, and then, diary, I'll tell you all about it.

Night. We put in the day sitting around and swapping yarns, etc.

None of us cared to go about, for we were pretty tired, after our hard day yesterday. Shelter tents were given out today. One tent for every two men. They are not tents at all, nothing but a strip of muslin, with three sticks to hold them up. There are four pins to pin the corners to the ground. Then one stick is put in like a ridge pole, and the other two set under it. The ends are pinned down as far apart as a man is long, and then the middle raised up. They may keep off rain, if it falls straight down, but both ends are open, and two men fill it full. We have got them up, each company in a row. It is a funny sight to stand on the high ground and look over them. Lengthwise, it is like a long strip of muslin with what a dressmaker calls gathers in it. Looked at from the side it is like a row of capital A's with the cross up and down instead of crosswise,

September 9, 1862.
Tuesday.

About midnight, an officer of some sort rode into camp with some word that was the means of our being routed out by the "Long Roll," the first time any of us ever heard it. It appears the "Long Roll" is only sounded when the quickest possible getting into line in fighting trim is necessary, as when the enemy is about to pounce upon us, etc. But we didn't hurry. One after another got up and all the time the officers were shouting, and some of them swearing. I thought they had all gone crazy. But finally we understood, and then down came our tents. The quartermaster team rushed up with boxes of guns, which were broken open and the guns handed out as fast as possible. Ammunition, too, was passed out, and we were told to load up and defend ourselves. The excitement was so great, and the ammunition so new to us, about half the guns were loaded with the bullet end down. The cartridges are a charge of powder, a big long bullet and a piece of paper. The paper is rolled up with the powder in one end and the bullet in the other, and to us, in the dark, both ends looked alike.

But no great harm was done, for no enemy appeared. Just what it was all for I don't know now, and quite likely never will. We got a ration of bread and coffee and with our guns—great heavy, clumsy things—and our tents added to our already heavy load, started off on a brisk pace, which was kept up until some began to fall out, completely exhausted. These were picked up by the quartermaster and commissary wagons, and so we went for about six miles along the road that is said to lead to Frederick. Then we halted, and after the stragglers had caught up, started back again, soon turning off in another direction on another road, and marched for about the same distance, where we turned into a field, partly level, and the rest a side hill. We halted when a little way from the road and were told we were to go into permanent camp there. Baltimore is in plain sight, although it is some way off. We were so tuckered out by our long tramp in the hot sun and with the heavy loads on our backs, we were glad to get up our tents, and after a coffee and bread supper, to turn in and sleep.

CHAPTER 3

Camp Millington, Md.

September 10, 1862.
Camp Millington.

We were too tired last night to look about and see where we were. This morning we were ourselves again, and began to take stock of our surroundings. We are in a newly seeded field, sloping generally to the east, though the upper part of it is nearly level. The place is called Millington, so we have named our camp, "Camp Millington." We pitched our tents in such a hurry that it had not a very orderly appearance, and after breakfast we divided up into companies, and each has tried to beat the other in slicking up.

We have quite an extended view. Towards the east we can see for miles across a sandy plain clear to the waters of Chesapeake Bay. Baltimore lies to the north. In other directions little but trees can be seen. Right in front runs a large brook, which turns the wheels of a flour mill, from which loads of flour are constantly being taken. Back of the mill, and not far from it, runs a railroad, said to be the Baltimore and Ohio. All day long, trains have been running, and the most of them loaded with soldiers. Some go towards Baltimore and some the other way. If I knew what it all means I would tell, but we are all strangers to the place and there is no use asking questions. Guards are posted on every side of us, and outside of that another line of guards called pickets are posted. We were called up and talked to by Major Parker.

A whole lot of rules were given out, which, if they are observed, will make the 128th a model regiment and each member of it a gentleman. I have sewed on my corporal stripes today, having carried them in my pocket until now. The only difference I have yet found out between a corporal and a private soldier is that a corporal does not have to stand guard. If we are really going to stay here I expect the next thing will be learning how to march, taking up the lesson where we left off in Hudson. From the way the regiment that escorted us through Baltimore handled themselves, I can see we have a whole lot to learn yet.

September 11, 1862.

We heard heavy firing this morning, from the direction of the city, which we at first thought must be fighting going on there, but which we afterwards learned was practice for the gunners at Fort Henry, and on the gunboats, both of which lie somewhere off in that direction. We kept on cleaning up our camp ground today and it begins to look real nice. A running vine, which was all over the ground, has poisoned a great many, although some that handled it the most did not get any. Philip Allen's face looks like a bladder. The doctor has fixed up a wash that he says will soon cure it. We had just about enough to do today to give us a good appetite. A storm is brewing, and we are wondering what it will do to us with only a strip of muslin to keep it off'.

September 12, 1862.

The storm came. A soaking rain in the night; it soaked every one of us. I suppose the officers fared better, for they have tents like houses, but we, the shelter-tent brigade, certainly took all that came. I got up from a puddle of water. The water ran down the hill, under our tents, and under us. This softened the ground so we sank right in. The ground is a red colour, and we are a sight to behold. By looking at a man's trousers it is easy to tell whether he slept on his back or on his side. In one case he has one red leg, and in the other, two. I think it would improve the appearance if the whole trousers were soaked in the mud. This sickly blue is about the meanest colour I can think of. I guess the government had more cloth than colour.

One fellow says there was only one kettle of dye. The officers' clothes were dipped first, then the privates' coats, and last the pantaloons. No matter what question comes up there are some who can explain and make it all clear. A part of Company B was sent out on picket duty today. I don't know where or what their duties are. All sorts of war stories are in the air. One paper tells of a great battle and the next one contradicts it. I guess it is done to make sale for papers. Newsboys rush into camp yelling *Extra* and we rush at them and buy them out. But it gives us something to talk about, and that is worth much to us.

September 13, 1862.

Saturday.

Washing day. All who are not on duty were let out to go in the stream below the mill and wash. We took off our clothes and rubbed and scrubbed them, until one colour, instead of several, prevailed, and then we sat around and waited for them to dry in the sun. From the looks of the wash-water, the clothes should look better than they do. They fitted rather snug when we got into them, but we will soon stretch them out again.

Night. A letter from father! So far as I know, he never wrote a letter before. I do not remember that I ever saw his handwriting until now. I expected to hear from him through others, but of getting a letter direct from him, I never even thought. Another was from my sister, Mrs. Loucks. They are all well, getting along first-rate without me. I guess I was not of so much account as I thought. However, I am delighted to hear about them. Captain Bostwick returned this p. m. and has told me all the home news. I almost feel as if I had been home, he told me so much about everything I wanted to know, and best of all brought me father's letter. I will answer that letter right off, now, and then go to bed, where many of the company already are.

September 14, 1862.

Sunday.

My first day on duty as corporal of the guard. Two hours on and four off duty gives me lots of time to write, and as it may interest our folks to know what guard duty really is, I will describe it as best I can. An officer of the guard, a sergeant of the guard, four corporals, and four times as many privates as there are posts to guard, are detailed the night before. In the morning at 8 a. m. the fife and drum sounds the call for guard-mount, and the whole detail reports at guard-head-quarters, which is wherever the call is sounded from. Three quarters of the detail go on duty and the other quarter, called supernumeraries, have nothing at all to do, unless a man on duty is taken sick, when a supernumerary takes his place. The corporal then on duty goes with the one just going on with the first relief, and marches to post No. 1, where the guard calls out, "Who comes there?"

The corporal says, "Relief."

"Advance Relief," says the guard on post, when he is replaced by a man from the new guard, and he takes his place in the rear, marching on to the next post, where the same ceremony is repeated until the last post is reached. The new guard is then on duty and the corporal marches the old guard to headquarters, where they are discharged and are free from all duty for the next twenty-four hours. The corporal of the relief now on post remains at guard headquarters for two hours, unless some trouble on the line happens, in which case the guard cries out "Corporal of the guard!" giving the number of post.

The corporal then goes direct to that post, and if the trouble be such as he cannot cope with, he calls "Sergeant of the guard!" In case it be too serious for the sergeant, the officer of the guard is called in the same way, and he is supposed to be able to settle the trouble, whatever it may be. At the end of two hours, the second relief goes on, and then the third in its turn, after which the first relief goes on again. This keeps on until 8 a. m. the next morning, when a new guard is mounted and the old one goes off. This gives each corporal and his relief four turns of duty of two hours each, and sixteen hours to lie around headquarters and do pretty much as he pleases. The sergeant and the officer of the guard rarely have anything to do but pass away the time in any lawful manner. But they must be ready, on call, at all times.

Train-load after train-load of troops keeps going past. The North must get empty and the South get full at this rate. Mosquitoes and flies are very troublesome. We must cover up head and hands at night, or if the blanket gets off we must scratch all the next day. Some don't mind it, but the most of us do, and if the pests would go where they are often told to go, they would get a taste of what they are giving us.

We have a sutler now. No peddlers are allowed on the camp grounds. It is buy of him now or go without. For change, he uses cards with his stamp on, good for from three to twenty-five cents, at his tent, and good for nothing at any other place. Report says we are to have a chaplain by next Sunday, and that it is the Rev. Mr. Parker, who preached for us at Hudson. I hope he will bring along all his patience and forbearance. He will need it. Bad as we are, I don't suppose we are worse than the average, but I think we must average pretty well up. We will know if he comes, and won't have to watch the almanac to tell when Sunday comes.

September 15, 1862.
Monday.
Two men in the guard-house. We are improving. Baltimore whiskey got into the camp some way and these men found it. At dress parade

tonight, a dispatch was read to us saying a great battle had been fought and a great victory won by McClellan. We gave three cheers that must have reached the scene of battle. It has set us up wonderfully.

September 16, 1862.
Tuesday.

We are getting right down to business now. Have company drill and will soon drill with the whole regiment together. Today we practiced the double-quick, which is nothing more than a run. The day was hot and these heavy clothes buttoned around us made us sweat, and one man gave out. He fell down and several fell over him, stopping the work long enough for us to catch breath. He was put under a tree, and by the time we were through was able to walk back to camp. I went into the mill today and asked for a job. The miller said he thought I had about all the job I could attend to. That is the nearest approach to a joke I have heard from a native. They are the dumbest set of people I ever met. At least they seem so to me. The country is queer, too. There are no roads here. They are all turnpikes. Many of the houses set so far back from the road, and shade trees are so plenty, that they are not seen unless one goes on purpose.

To the west and south the country looks like a forest, but there are no forests here, only scattering trees all over the fields and along the roads. The people are Dutch, mostly, and the rest are negroes,— "Niggers" they are universally called here. Money has another name, too. I bought a bundle of straw for a bed, which I was told was a "fip" for a bundle. I tied up a bundle and was then told it would be a "levy," all of which meant that if the man bound it up it was a "fip" and if I bound it it would be a "levy," which is two fips. I found out at last that a "fip" was sixpence and a "levy" was a shilling. Two fellows got too much of the sutler's whiskey today. They forged an order for it, and as a punishment each had a placard pinned to his back, with the nature of his offense printed in large letters, and were marched about the camp until sober.

September 17, 1862.

Two letters today, and two papers, all from home. Seems as if I had been there for a visit. I wonder if my letters give them as much pleasure? I expect they do. It is natural they should. I know pretty nearly what they are about, but of me, they only know what I write in my letters, and in this, my everlasting letter, as I have come to call my diary. It is getting to be real company for me. It is my one real confident.

I sometimes think it is a waste of time and paper, and then I think how glad I would be to get just such nonsense from my friends, if our places were changed. I suppose they study out these crow's tracks with more real interest than they would a message from President Lincoln. We are looking for a wet bed again tonight. It does not rain, but a thick fog covers everything and the wind blows it in one side of our tents and out the other.

Maybe I have described our life here before, but as no one description can do it justice I am going to try again. We are in a field of 100 acres, as near as I can judge, on the side of a hill, near the top. The ground is newly seeded and wets up quickly, as such ground usually does. We sleep in pairs, and a blanket spread on the ground is our bed while another spread over us is our covering. A narrow strip of muslin, drawn over a pole about three feet from the ground, open at both ends, the wind and rain, if it does rain, beating in upon us, and water running under and about us; this, with all manner of bugs and creeping things crawling over us, and all the while great hungry mosquitoes biting every uncovered inch of us, is not an overdrawn picture of that part of a soldier's life, set apart for the rest and repose necessary to enable him to endure several hours of right down hard work at drill, in a hot sun with heavy woollen clothes on, every button of which must be tight-buttoned, and by the time the officers are tired watching us, we come back to camp wet through with perspiration and too tired to make another move.

Before morning our wet clothes chill us to the marrow of our bones, and why we live, and apparently thrive under it, is something I cannot understand. But we do, and the next day are ready for more of it. Very few even take cold. It is a part of the contract, and while we grumble and growl among ourselves we don't really mean it, for we are learning what we will be glad to know at some future time.

Now I am about it, and nothing better to do, I will say something about our kitchen, dining room and cooking arrangements. Some get mad and cuss the cooks, and the whole war department, but that is usually when our stomachs are full. When we are hungry we swallow anything that comes and are thankful for it. The cook house is simply a portion of the field we are in. A couple of crotches hold up a pole on which the camp kettles are hung, and under which a fire is built. Each company has one, and as far as I know they are all alike. The camp kettles are large sheet-iron pails, one larger than the other so one can be put inside the other when moving. If we have meat and potatoes, meat is put in one, and potatoes in the other. The one that gets cooked first is emptied into mess pans, which are large sheet-iron pans with flaring sides, so one can be packed in another. Then the coffee is put in the empty kettle and boiled.

The bread is cut into thick slices, and the breakfast call sounds. We grab our plates and cups, and wait for no second invitation. We each get a piece of meat and a potato, a chunk of bread and a cup of coffee with a spoonful of brown sugar in it. Milk and butter we buy, or go without. We settle down, generally in groups, and the meal is soon over. Then we wash our dishes, and put them back in our haversacks. We make quick work of washing dishes. We save a piece of bread for the last, with which we wipe up everything, and then eat the dish rag. Dinner and breakfast are alike, only sometimes the meat and potatoes are cut up and cooked together, which makes a really delicious stew. Supper is the same, minus the meat and potatoes. The cooks are men detailed from the ranks for that purpose. Everyone smokes or chews tobacco here, so we find no fault because the cooks do both. Boxes or barrels are used as kitchen tables, and are used for seats between meals. The meat and bread are cut on them, and if a scrap is left on the table the flies go right at it and we have so many the less to crawl over us. They are never washed, but are sometimes scraped off and made to look real clean. I never yet saw the cooks wash their hands, but presume they do when they go to the brook for water.

September 18, 1862.

Mr. Parker came last night, and is to be our chaplain. He is the one who preached for us at Hudson Camp Ground, and the one we asked to have for chaplain of the 128th. He can sing like a lark, and we are glad he is here. There are many good singers in the regiment. There is talk of organizing a choir or club, and no doubt the dominie will join it. We have more good news from the front. McClellan seems to fit the place he is in. It is reported that George Flint and Elihu Bryan have been taken prisoners. I know them well, but don't remember the regiment they went out in.

September 19, 1862.

Reports are that a great battle has been fought at Antietam, and a great victory won. Do they tell us this to keep up our courage, or has the beginning of the end really come? Tomorrow we have the promise of going on picket duty. Good! anything for a change. It will give me something to write about in my diary, if nothing more. Things are getting rather monotonous, and any change will be good for us, provided it is not for the worse. Prayer meeting every night now. Chaplain Parker seems in dead earnest. He wants us all to be ready to die. Then, he says, if death don't come, we will be in better shape to live. Very few of the officers attend prayer meeting, though they encourage the men to do so.

September 20, 1862.

In spite of the fact that we are sumptuously fed, I have long longed for a good square meal off a clean table. This morning, early, I sneaked away to a farm house I had often looked at, and wondered if the people there would contract to fill me up for such a consideration as I could afford. I told them I was not begging, but would like to buy a breakfast. The lady was willing, and I was soon sitting in a chair at a clean table with a clean table-cloth and clean dishes on it. And such a breakfast! I forgot who or where I was. The smell of the victuals made me ravenous, and I ate until I could eat no more. They were pleasant people and seemed to enjoy seeing me eat. I felt guilty because I had not asked my friends to go with me, but I wanted first to investigate on my own hooky for I was not at all sure of getting anything when I set out, in which case I was going back to camp in time for breakfast, and say nothing about it. But when the hostess would not take anything for the hearty meal I had eaten, I was glad I had not brought my family with me. I gave them my heartiest thanks and returned to camp to find Company B getting ready for picket duty, and I was soon in my place ready for anything.

10 a. m. We are about six miles from Camp Millington, at a village called Catonsville. That is, the company is broken up into squads, and the one I am with is here, and in my charge as corporal. I am to keep one man on post and change him for another every two hours. Not a very hard job for any of us. The people seem very pleasant, and as the day is not very hot we are simply having a picnic. We are to pick up travellers who cannot give a good account of themselves and hold them until the officer of the guard comes round, and let him decide what to do with them. Coming here we passed Louden Park Cemetery, a beautiful place, and the largest of its kind I ever saw. Shade trees all over it, great fine monuments and vaults as large as small houses. I guess only rich people are buried there, for I saw no common headstones. But then I suppose we only saw a part of it, and the best part at that.

Night. The day has passed quietly. Nothing startling happened. The people have treated us royally, gave us all the peaches we could eat, and also gave us the credit of being the best behaved of any detail that has been here.

9 p. m. Some firing was heard on the post next ours, and which is the farthest out of any. I went out to learn what it meant. It seems a man came along and when halted, jumped the fence and ran for a piece of woods nearby. Mike Sullivan started out to capture him. They shot at each other, but the man got away. Mike got a lot of slivers stuck in his face by a bullet hitting a post he was passing as the shot was fired. This is the only excitement we have had up to this time, midnight.

September 21, 1862.

Sunday morning. Nothing happened during the night. We bought a good breakfast of a family who make a business of feeding the soldiers that come here, for I was told there is a detail here every day. I wish it might be us every time. As soon as the new guard arrives we are to go back to camp and camp fare again.

2 p. m. In camp again. It seems hotter and dirtier than ever after our day in the country. Before we left Catonsville we filled our haversacks with great luscious peaches. Those that ripen on the tree the people cannot sell, so they gave us all that would fall with a gentle shake of the tree. How I wished I could empty my haversack in your lap, mother. On the way to camp we met a drove of mules, said to be 400 of them, loose, and being driven like cattle. They were afraid of us and all got in a close bunch, and the 400 pairs of ears all flapping together made a curious sight. We were told they came from Kentucky, and are for use in the army. They were all bays, with a dark stripe along the back and across the shoulders, looking like a cross laid on their backs. It hasn't seemed much like Sunday. But Sunday doesn't count for much in the army. Many of our hardest days have been Sundays. But I am sleepy, having been awake all last night. It is surprising how little sleep we get along with. I, who have been such a sleepy-head all my life, get only a few hours' sleep any night, and many nights none at all. I suppose we will sometime get accustomed to the noise and confusion, that so far has had no end, night or day.

September 22, 1862.
Monday.

Knapsack drill today,—something new to me, though I am told it is to take place every Sunday morning when in camp. As we were not here yesterday, it was put off until today. We marched out to the drill ground with our knapsacks on, expecting to practice as usual, except that we were loaded that much heavier. As all our belongings were in our knapsacks, they were quite heavy. We formed in column by companies and were told to "unsling knapsacks." We all had to be coached, but we finally stood at attention with our knapsacks lying on the ground wide open before us. Then the colonel, the major and the captain of the company being inspected, marched along and with the tip of their swords poked over the contents, regardless of how precious they might be to us. And such a sight as they saw! Besides our extra underclothing, some clean and some unclean, there were Bibles, whiskey bottles, novels, packs of cards, love letters and photographs, revolvers and dirk knives, pen and ink, paper and envelopes and postage stamps, and an endless variety of odds and ends we had picked up in our travels.

As soon as the inspection was over with Company A, they were marched back to camp and so all along the line until Company B, the last of all, was reached. When we got back to camp some of the companies had been there long enough to get asleep. Nothing more was required of us, and we put in the time as we chose, provided always that we observed the camp regulations.

I may never have so good a chance, so I will try and explain some of the things we have learned to do and how we do it. Begin with roll-call. The orderly sergeant, Lew Holmes, has our names in a book, arranged in alphabetical order in one place, and in the order in which we march in another. If it is simply to see if we are all here, he sings out "Fall in for roll-call" and we get in line, with no regard to our proper places, and answer to our names as called from the alphabetical list. If for drill, "Fall in for drill!" and then we take our places with the tallest man at the right, and so on, till the last and shortest man is in place on the left. We are then in a single line, by company front. The orderly then points at the first man and says "One," which the man repeats. He then points to the second man and says "Two," which is also repeated. So it goes down the line, the one, two, being repeated, and each man being careful to remember whether he is odd or even.

When that is done, and it is very quickly done, the orderly commands, "Right face!" The odd-numbered men simply swing on the left heel one quarter of the way around and stand fast. The even-numbered men do the same, and in addition step obliquely to the right of the odd-numbered man, bringing us in a double line and one step apart, which distance we must carefully keep, so that when the order "Front!" is given, we can, by reversing the movement of "Right face!" come to our places without crowding. When coming to a front, the line is not apt to be straight and the order "Right dress!" is given, when the man on the right stands fast and the one next to him puts himself squarely by his side. The next moves back or forth until he can just see the buttons on the coat of the second man to his right,— that is, with his head erect, he must look past one man and just see the buttons on the coat of the second man from him. That makes the line as straight as you can draw a string. "Left face!" is the same thing reversed.

In marching, one has only to keep step with the one irregular time all comes upon the file leaders, which are the two in front; they must keep step together. If Company B is going out to drill by itself it is now ready. If, however, the entire regiment is to drill together, as it has a few times, Company A marches out first, and as the rear passes where Company F is standing the latter falls in, close behind; and so each company, until Company B, which is the left of the line, and the last to go, falls in and fills up the line, Why the companies are arranged in the line as they are is a mystery I have so far failed to find out. From right to left they come in the following order: A, F, D, I, C, H, E, K, G and B. A is said to have the post of honour, because in marching by the right flank it is ahead, and meets danger first if there be any. Company B has the next most honourable position, because in marching by the left flank it is in the lead. There is a great advantage in being in the lead.

On a march the files will open, more or less, and when a halt is ordered the company in the lead stops short. The other companies keep closing up the files, and by the time the ranks are closed "Attention!" may sound, and another start be made. The first company has had quite a breathing spell, while the last has had very little, if any. If I were to enlist again, I would try hard to get in Company A, for all the marching we have so far done has been by the right flank. Company A at the head and Company B bringing up the rear. When we reach the field we are generally broken up into companies, each company drilling in marching by the front, wheeling to the right and left, and finally coming together again before marching back to camp.

September 22, 1862.
Tuesday.
Another inspection today. This time our guns and accoutrements

were inspected, and much fault was found because we had not kept our guns from rusting. Only a few got off without a scolding, and these were some that seem to love a gun and care for it as they would a baby. This, with our everyday drill, and a general cleaning and scouring up of our guns and the brass on our belts and cartridge boxes, has kept us busy all day long. I had kept the inside of my gun clean, so I only had the outside to scour up. Little by little we learn our lesson, learn to put the best on top, and little by little the screws of discipline are turned on.

September 24, 1862.
Wednesday.

New tents were given us today. "A" tents they are called; I suppose because they are in the shape of a letter A. They are like the roof of a house cut off at the eaves, and one gable split open for us to enter, with strings sewed fast to one side and buttonholes in the other so we can close them up tight. A detail from each company has been clearing up the ground and laying out for an all winter stay. The officers have moved back to the more level portion of the field, which brings our lines of tents on much better ground than before. A long and wide street has been laid out and is being graded off, on the west side of which the officers' tents are ranged, the colonel's tent in the middle and a little in the rear of the tents of the captains and lieutenants, which are directly in front of their respective companies. On a line with Colonel Cowles' tent are those of the lieutenant colonel (which by the way has no occupant yet, he being oft' somewhere on detached service), the major, quartermaster, adjutant, surgeon and chaplain.

Back of these is a big tent called the Hospital, which so far has not been of much use. Then in front of all these are the companies' quarters, the ten company streets running off at right angles to the broad street along which the company officers' tents are now being placed. A wide space is left in front of Colonel Cowles' tent, and runs clear through camp, nothing being on it but a flag-pole, which is to stand directly in front of the colonel's tent and in line with the tents of the company officers. So many hands make light work of any job, but I am only telling how it is to be, for only the laying out is completed and the grading begun.

We that were not detailed for the work were taken out to the great sandy plain toward what I am told is Chesapeake Bay and given a lesson in battalion-drill.

The 135th N.Y. was with us, and from the crowds of people who were there I suppose battalion drill is something worth seeing. But it was anything but fun for us, and we came back to camp hungry, tired, and with as much dust on us as would stick. We were glad enough to crawl into our old shelter tents. It is well I wrote the most of the day's doings before we went out, for it is hard work to put this little finish to it. Goodnight, diary.

September 25, 1862.
Thursday.

On picket duty at Catonsville again. The people and the peaches are just as good as ever. We are glad enough of this outing, after our hard day yesterday. The six-mile walk has given us good appetites and the prospects of a good feeding when dinner time comes makes us feel like colts turned out to grass.

Night. Some of my squad, when off duty, went visiting the posts farther out, and having found some whiskey, got gloriously drunk. The sober ones have to do double duty, and the drunks are locked in an empty omnibus which stands beside the road. What sort of punishment will fit their offense I don't know. They have been so happy this afternoon, they can afford to be made miserable for a day or two. They are sound asleep now, unmindful of coming consequences. The fine record we made when here before has gone all to pieces and that is really the worst thing about it.

September 26, 1862.
Friday.

Camp Millington again. A sort of trial called a court-martial has been held and the boys who celebrated yesterday, are meditating upon it in the guard-house, which by the way is a mule stable on the end of the sutler's shop. Our old tents were taken down and our new ones are up. Each one is trying to outdo the other in making them look homelike. Boards are in great demand for flooring, and already complaints are coming in from the natives, that every loose board or one that could be loosened from their fences or outbuildings is missing, and they have reason to think they came this way. We are delighted with our new tents. Each holds four men. Walter Loucks, George and Jim Story and myself make up our family. We have to lay straight, and at that there is no room to spare. But we are protected from rain, and the heavy dews that are almost as bad, and best of all, we can shut up tight and keep out the mosquitoes. Those that do get in we can smoke out in short order.

A rumour is afloat that another regiment has been raised in Dutchess County and is to come here. We think ourselves soldiers now and are planning how we will entertain the green-horns when they come.

September 27, 1862.
Saturday.

We are looking for the Dutchess County regiment as if their coming was an assured fact, yet it is only a rumour, and even that cannot be traced very far. Aside from our daily drill, which is not much fun, we manage to get some amusement out of everything that comes along. We visit each other and play all sorts of games. Fiddling and dancing take the lead just now. The company streets, now that the ground has been smoothed off, make a good ballroom. A partner has just been swung clear off the floor into a tent, onto a man who was writing a letter, and from the sound is going to end up in a fight. "Taps" are sounded at 9 p. m., which is a signal for lights out and quiet in the camp.

September 28, 1862.
Sunday night.

Meeting today. Chaplain Parker preached. He asked those who would stop swearing to hold up their hands, and so far as I could see every hand went up. After inspection in the morning we had nothing to do except to go to meeting and dress parade, which I believe we are to have regularly. We march to the parade ground, which is just back of our camp quarters, and form in line. The colonel, with the major and adjutant on his right and left, station themselves in front, the colonel opposite the colours, which are in the centre, between Companies C and H. The fifer and drummer pass along in front and back again when the colonel puts us through the manual of arms. A great many civilians come out and it must be a pretty sight, provided the orders are well executed. If we do well, nothing is said, but if not, we are cautioned to do better next time.

How I wish I could peep in on the old folks at home tonight! I imagine just how they are sitting around, talking, perhaps of me, or better yet, writing me a letter.

There is no use denying that I am homesick. I have been such a home-body, and my home life has been so pleasant.

The comforts of my home, though humble, have been many, and I have never missed them as I do tonight. I have only been away a short time, but it seems longer to me than all my life before. It has been crowded so full of strange and stirring events that it seems as if I would go crazy unless I can see and talk with our folks about it. Mr. Parker says confession is good for the soul, and I believe it, for after confessing to my diary as I have I feel better already. I will crawl in now and perhaps dream of home, which I often do, and which while it lasts, is just as good as being there.

September 29, 1862.
Camp Millington, Baltimore.
On account of the heat we were not taken out for drill today. We have cleaned up our quarters, for since getting our new and comfortable tents we are quite particular about appearances. There is a friendly rivalry as to which of the ten companies shall have the neatest quarters. All being exactly alike to start with, it depends upon us to keep them neat and shipshape. The cooks have tents as well as we, and altogether we are quite another sort from what we were a week ago. It has been a regular clean up day with us. The brook below us has carried off dirt enough from our clothing and bodies to make a garden. While we were there close beside the railroad, a train loaded with soldiers halted, and while we were joking with the men, someone fired a pistol from another passing train, and a sergeant on the standing train was killed—whether it was by accident or purposely done, no one knows; or whether the guilty one will be found out and punished, no one of us can tell. But I wonder so few accidents do happen. There are hundreds of revolvers in camp and many of them in the hands of those who know no better how to use them than a child.

September 30, 1862.
Battalion-drill today. It was just as hot as yesterday, and some say hotter. The lieutenant colonel, James Smith, came last night, and has taken charge of our military education. He has been in the service, and was in the Battle of Antietam. Some say he is a West Pointer. At any rate we have a drill-master who understands his business. One thing that has already made him dear to us is that he makes the officers come to time just as well as the men. He told them, in so many words, that they had as much to learn as we. If he holds out as he has started off, he will stand well with the rank and file, however he may stand with the officers. Hurrah for Colonel Smith!

October 1, 1862.
Wednesday.

Another hot day. How hot I don't know, but it wilted me. I tumbled down, completely used up while at drill. Several others did the same. We seem to be getting over it tonight, as the air cools off. The nights are cool, and that is all that keeps us from melting. Not cool enough, however, to stop the mosquitoes. The heat, together with our changed condition of living, is beginning to get in its work. Several are in the hospital.

Later. There is great excitement in Company B tonight. Orderly Sergeant Lewis Holmes, the one we voted to be our orderly, is to be set back and a corporal named Gilbert Kniffen is to be put in his place. As soon as the companies were organized at Hudson, we were allowed to vote which of the five sergeants of Company B should be orderly sergeant. We did not know then, but have since learned that the orderly sergeant stands next in the line of promotion to the commissioned officers. Kniffen is only a corporal, but he has friends at home who have influence, and this influence has been brought to bear so heavy that this move has been decided upon.

9 p. m. It is all over, and Lew Holmes is still orderly sergeant of Co. B, 128th N.Y.Vols. We, the enlisted men of the company, talked the thing over and decided we would not put up with it. We did not know if we would be able to prevent it, but we finally decided we would stand by Holmes, and fight the thing to a finish, whatever the outcome might be. When we spoke to Captain Bostwick he acted as if he was ashamed of himself, but he said the change had already been made and could not be unmade. We told him we could unmake it, and would, or die in the company street. So the matter rested until time for roll-call, when Kniffin came out with the book and called the name of William H. Appleby, the first name on the list. To his honour be it said, he remained silent, and was immediately put in the mule-stable, which was our guard-house. The next man's name was called, and he went to join Appleby.

This went on until the guard-house was full, when a council of the company officers was held, after which the captain gave us a lecture, telling us what insubordination meant, and that the whole regiment, if necessary, would be used to enforce obedience. We had agreed not to talk back, but to simply refuse to answer to our names when called by Corporal Kniffin, or in any way acknowledge him as orderly sergeant, so we said nothing. The men were brought back from the guard-house, and Kniffin again called William H. Appleby. He did not answer and was again put in the guard-house.

After a few more had been sent to keep him company another halt was made, the prisoners were again brought out, and the captain called the roll, when every man responded promptly. We were then ordered to break ranks and so the matter stands. But we have won our first battle, we feel sure of that, although we are warned that a company, and if necessary the whole regiment, will be called upon to shoot any who do not answer roll-call in the morning. My name is so near the bottom of the list it was not reached, and so I had nothing to do but look on and listen, but I am as determined as any, and I flap my wings and crow just as loudly as William H. Appleby does.

October 2, 1862.
Thursday.
Holmes called the roll this morning and we hear no more about being shot for mutiny. It may possibly come later, but from all I can see and hear the trouble was entirely a company affair and did not reach beyond it. If Colonel Smith, who is said to be very strict on discipline, had taken a hand in it, we might have fared worse, but I doubt if he would allow such a cowardly trick to be played on so good a soldier as Holmes is, and has been, to say nothing of jumping a corporal over the heads of five sergeants, who have all been prompt and faithful in the discharge of their duties. Our first real sick man was sent to the hospital tonight, one of Company B, from Dover.

October 4, 1862.
Friday.
Battalion-drill again today. That and talking about the new orderly is all I have to record today. The whole thing has blown over, evidently. If the cause had been just, I suppose there would have been some way to bring us to terms, but as it now appears, I think the company officers are ashamed of their part, and Kniffin, if he ever gets to be orderly sergeant, will have to come up by the regular route.

October 4, 1862.
Saturday.
Battalion-drill again. Learning to be a soldier is hard work. There has been no rain lately and the sun has dried up everything. There are no green fields here as we have at home. The ground is sandy, and where there is grass, it is only a single stem in a place, with bare ground all round it. So many feet tread it all to dust, which the wind

blows all over us, but mostly in our faces and eyes. The road past our camp is a mire of the finest dust, and as hard to travel through as so much mud. We eat it with our rations, and breathe it all the day long. It covers everything, in our tents as well as outside.

Our clean new tents are already taking on the universal muddy, red colour of everything in sight. The only good thing about it is, it serves every one alike, piling upon the officers just as it does on the men. We are getting to feel quite proud of ourselves as soldiers. We learn fast under the teaching of Colonel Smith. The 135th N.Y. and a Mass, regiment are with us on battalion-drill and sometimes several other regiments, so that we about cover the large plain out near the bay. We get tougher and harder every day. The fodder we so often find fault with, and the hard work we are doing, is making us hard, like the work and the fare is.

October 5, 1862.
Sunday.

On picket again today. We are at a new place, on the road to Frederick, but not as far out as Catonsville. It is plain to see it is only for practice, for we are only a little way from camp, and the other posts are far beyond us. Cavalry pickets are said to be farther out still. May be it is to give us a rest, for that it certainly does. We are out of the dust, our duties are light and the day after picket is also a day of rest. We also get fresh vegetables, which are a treat for us nowadays.

Night. We have had a day of rest. Two hours on post and the next four at liberty to loaf in the shade, is not hard work. We are in a lonely place, no houses near us, but we have had what we needed, a real rest-up.

October 6, 1862.
Monday.

Back in Camp Millington, and the rest of the day is ours. A letter from Miss Hull, in answer to one written her mother. It was full of home news, and I feel as if I had been there. My homesick fit has left me, but it was a terror while it lasted. I believe it is more common than we think. I see many faces yet that look just as mine felt. Like me they keep it to themselves, or possibly tell it to their diaries, as I did to mine. I am not the only one who keeps a diary. There are plenty of others who do, and others still who say they can remember enough of it without writing it down. In the afternoon Lieutenant Dutcher invited me to go for a walk. We followed the Baltimore & Ohio R.

R. for about a mile and came to abandoned camp grounds nearly all the way. We. found some housekeeping necessities which we brought back with us. After dress parade, we visited about until roll-call, and are going to bed early, for tomorrow the grind begins again. Good-night.

October 7, 1862.
Tuesday.
On duty at a place called "Monitor Mills." Have three men with me. It is only a little way out of camp, and all we have to do is to stay here for twenty-four hours, and change the guard every two hours. I have no idea why it is, but it is fun compared to drilling, and I am glad to be here.

A soldier has just gone from here who was in the battle of Anti-etam. He filled us full of tall stories, some of them so tall they would hardly go down. But if the half he said is true, we know little of real soldiering. Life in camp, he says, is a picnic compared with field duty. If he was as good at fighting as he is at talking about it, the Rebellion should have been squelched long ago. He made me think of some men I know, who can hardly wait to get at the Rebs, and yet who have managed to shirk everything they can in the way of duty or danger,

October 8, 1862.
Wednesday.
Have loafed about camp all day. Have not been out for drill since Saturday. But I am finding no fault. The weather keeps hot and dry, and the boys were a sight to behold when they came in from drill. Hot, dirty, tired and hungry. What would we do without the brook running past us? I wonder it doesn't choke up with the dirt it washes from us.

Today has been election day in Baltimore, and tonight the city seems to be on fire. We have a fine view of the city by day, and of the lights by night. Tonight everything seems to be ablaze, and we are wondering what it can mean. We will know in the morning when the papers come.

October 9, 1862.
Thursday.
Bonfires in honour of the election of Mr. Chapin, for Mayor of Baltimore, was what so mystified us last night. The latest reports said there were riots in the city and it was being burned by the rioters. It was quite a relief to find out the truth, although we knew the city was

there as soon as daylight appeared. The first death in our regiment occurred today in the hospital at Baltimore; it was that of John H. Smith, Hudson, N.Y. He was sick when we came here and was taken to the hospital at once. There are a few sick in our camp hospital, but nothing very serious as yet. At dress parade, a notice was read that we had been placed in General Emory's Brigade. I am sorry I cannot remember what other regiments make up the brigade, but I know the 150th N.Y. was not one. The Dutchess County regiment, lately organized, is the one hundred and fiftieth that New York has sent out, and we are greatly in hopes they may be with us all through the war,

October 10, 1862.
Friday.

The air is full of rumours today that we are to go somewhere, and that very soon, yet no one seems to be able to trace them. Experience has taught us that we won't know for certain when we go until we start, nor where we go until we get there. Train-loads of soldiers keep going past, and have been going past nearly every day since we came here. Seems to me I never saw such a dry place. Everything is so coated with dust it is impossible to tell its original colour. From appearances, the country all about us is dried up and dead. A wounded soldier has been here from the hospital. He was at Antietam—was shot through the arm, which is still in a sling. But the most wonderful thing was that as he was going off the field another ball hit him, or rather hit a pocket Testament in his breast pocket, and was stopped against the back cover, after going through the front cover and the rest of the book. He had both the ball and the Testament to show. What a sermon could be preached with that book and bullet for a text!

October 11, 1862.
Saturday.

Before daylight. We have been turned out, for some purpose, and are standing in line with our guns and accoutrements on.

Later. Are back in quarters, waiting to see what comes next. It has at last begun to rain and has every appearance of keeping it up. I don't suppose it will interfere with our movements, though it can make it unpleasant for us.

8 a. m. The papers have come, and say Stuart's Cavalry have invaded Pennsylvania, and are taking all the horses they can lay hands on.

Later. We have orders to pack up two days' rations, and have just been given forty rounds of ammunition. Begins to look like business now. We are in line waiting for further orders, and I am improving the time by keeping my diary right plump up to the minute. One man is missing, absent without leave. Not a soul of us knows which way we are to go or what for. If we were mounted I would think we were going to stop Stuart's horse-stealing, but as we are on foot that can hardly be.

Noon. At the foot of Biddle Street, Baltimore, waiting for transportation. From all I can learn, our movements depend on dispatches from some higher authority, yet to be received. Major Foster's horse fell and hurt the major's leg, but he has caught up with us, though he has quite a limp.

Night. Here we sit, or stand, just as we choose, still waiting for a train. It has rained nearly all day, and we are wet and cold, and everyone is cross, even to the officers. Just then our regimental postmaster caught up with us, and gave me a letter from Mrs. Loucks, also one from uncle Daniel. My sister says a box of good things is on the way for us. Too bad it didn't come before we left. No telling whether we get it now or not. Well, such is war.

October 12, 1862.
Sunday.
Relay House Station, on the Northern Central R. R.

Just where that is I haven't yet found out. We stood up or laid down in the street from noon yesterday until 3 a. m. this morning, when cars came and we went on board. They are box cars, no seats, but they have a roof, and that is what we most needed. We shivered and shook so our teeth chattered when we first got on board, and it was 5 a. m. before the train started. We were no longer curious to know where we were going. We were wet, cold, hungry and thirsty, and from lying on the pavements were so stiff we could hardly get on our feet. The major had to give it up—his leg was hurt worse than he thought. We are sorry not to have him along, for next to Colonel Smith, he is the most soldierly soldier in the regiment. Our two days' rations are gone and we are wondering when we will get another feed.

Noon. We are at Hanover Junction, Pa. We now feel sure we are after the rebel horse thieves, but unless we get a faster move on than this, they will get away with all the horses in the country before we get there. We are waiting for further orders from General Wool. The 144th N. Y. just stopped here, on their way to Baltimore. They are just out, and to hear them complain about being kept on the cars a whole day and night made us laugh.

5 p. m. We are full once more. Doesn't seem as if we could ever get hungry again after the feed we have just had. We are at Hanover, Pa. As the train stopped it seemed as if the whole population were standing beside the track, and nearly everyone had a basket of eatables or a pail of coffee. Men, women and children were there and they seemed to enjoy seeing us eat, even urging us to eat more, after we had stuffed ourselves, and then told us to put the rest in our haversacks. But they are terribly scared at the near approach of the rebel cavalry. We told them to fear no more. We were there, and the memory of the feast we had had would make us their special defenders. They distributed tracts among us, some of them printed sermons, and wound up by asking us to join them in singing the long-meter doxology. We not only sang it, we shouted it; each one took his own key and time, and some,—I for one,—got through in time to hear the last line from the others. We left them with cheers and blessings that drowned the noise of the train, and I prayed that if I ever got stranded it might be in Hanover.

Gettysburg, Pa. Night. The train has stopped outside the village, and a citizen says the Rebs are just out of the village on the opposite side. It is pitch dark and the orders are to show no lights and to keep very still. I have a candle and am squatted in the corner of the car trying to keep my diary going.

The officers are parading up and down along the train trying to enforce the order to be quiet. I am hovering over my candle so it won't be seen, for I must write, for fear I won't get a better chance.

October 13, 1862.
Monday.

Orders got too strict for my candle and I had to put it out. We made so much noise that the doors were shut on us finally and we were in pitch darkness in a closed car, with only room to lay down in. As the noise could be traced to no one in particular we kept it up until tired out and then slept as well as the circumstances would allow. Company B has a new name, "Bostwick's Tigers." It seems the colonel sent to find out who was making such a noise and was told it was Bostwick's tigers.[1] However, morning finally came, and the people of Gettysburg came down with a good breakfast, which in spite of our Hanover stuffing we began to need. They say the Rebs have gone on about five miles beyond the place. Lew Holmes and I got permission

---

1. The name stuck to us ever after, and came from this silly circumstance.

to go into the village, and I took the opportunity to write a letter home and to catch up with my diary.

Night. Just as I had written the above a horseman dashed into town and said the Rebels were on the way back to attack us. We ran for it and got back in time to fall in place, and had marched back into the village when another order stopped us and we remained all day long in the streets, not daring to leave for fear of an order to fall in. About 5 o'clock we were marched out of the village into open fields, to the north, I think, but as the sun has not shown himself all day, it may be in any other direction. Here we were broken into companies and guards posted. Not being on the detail for guard, Walt. Loucks, Len Loucks, Bill Snyder and myself have hauled up a lot of cornstalks beside a fence and I have written up my diary while they have made up the beds. Goodnight.

October 14, 1862.
Tuesday.

Well, I have had a good sleep, if I did have a hard time getting it. Our cornstalk bed which promised so well, did not prove so. The stalks were like bean poles, and the ears big in proportion. After turning and twisting every way, Walt and I left the others and started on an exploring expedition. It was pitch dark, and we had to feel our way, but finally came to a building. We felt along until we came to a door and went in. It appeared to be an empty barn, but soon after we spread our blankets and got into bed we found we were in a hen roost. We got outside much quicker than we got into the building and soon after came against another building. This we felt our way around, and on the opposite side found it to be a house, and the people not yet gone to bed.

We urged them to let us sleep on the floor by the fire, but while the man seemed willing, the wife objected, and there was nothing to do but try elsewhere. Finally we decided to try and find the cornfield again, and by taking the back track we succeeded in getting back where we started from. We made a bed under the fence and at last got asleep, being too tired to be very particular. We were not going to say anything about our adventure, but the others woke up first and in some way found out about it. We had breakfast, the stragglers were called in, and were soon in line waiting for the order to march.[2]

---

2. I was in Gettysburg in 1909 and was told by people who remembered our visit in 1862, that there were no Rebels anywhere near Gettysburg except in the imagination of the people, who were scared out of their senses.

2 p. m. In Hanover, Pa,, again. About 8 o'clock we marched through Gettysburg and tumbled into the cars. We soon reached Hanover, where we have since been. Along towards noon, we began to wonder if we would get another such feed as they gave us on Sunday. Somehow the people didn't seem as glad to see us as they did then. In fact they seemed rather to avoid us. Not all, for some were handing out everything eatable they had. Rather than ride these free horses to death, Snyder and I decided on another plan and it worked beautifully. We saw a house where the people were ready to sit down to the table—a man and a woman were already at the table—when we set our guns by the door and walking in, took seats at the table without as much as saying "by your leave." I passed my plate to the man, who all at once seemed to see a funny side to our impudence and burst out laughing. We had a good dinner and a jolly good time, and felt as if we had gotten even with one of them at any rate.

Night. Have stopped, and the report is that a bridge is broken down somewhere ahead of us and that we must stay here all night; a lonesome dismal spot, not a house in sight and only the remains of our army rations for supper.

October 15, 1862.
Have laid on the ground alongside the track resting and sleeping, waiting for the bridge to be repaired so we can go home.

October 16, 1862.
Thursday, 5 a. m.
The cars shrink, or the men swell, for certainly everybody had less room last night than before. Cross and crabbed, sore in every joint, and mad at everything and everybody, we crawled out of our beds (?) and shook ourselves together. In spite of strict orders to the contrary, some, fresh pork and some poultry found its way past the guards during the night. The owners needn't come looking for it, they would find only bristles and feathers if they did. I suppose the partaker is as bad as the thief, but I didn't feel guilty at all for accepting a slice of pork. I soon found a canteen with no owner, melted it apart over a fire and fried my pork and divided with my chums. There was no question about its being fresh, for we had no salt to make it otherwise.

About 9 o'clock we tumbled into the cars and with no more adventures reached Camp Millington late in the afternoon. Can anyone imagine our surprise and our great delight at finding the 150th N.Y. in camp right across the road from our camp? In a twinkling we were together. Discipline went to the winds. The officers tried to make a show of authority, but might as well have ordered the wind not to blow. All being from the same neighbourhood, we were one great happy family, reunited after a long separation. I doubt if there is a man in either regiment who has not a friend, if not a brother, in the other. They have passed through about the same experiences in the recruiting camp and passed over the same route to this place. They knew the same people we knew and could give us late information about them.

My own brother, John Van Alstyne, the same John who scolded me for enlisting, who called me a "fool" and lots of other bad names, had made the same sort of a fool of himself and was here with Uncle Sam's uniform on. Dozens of others I knew almost as well, and the same was the case all through, officers and men alike. As soon as the first round of handshaking was over and our volleys of questions about home and home people were answered, we took our turn at answering as to where we had been and what we had done, and how we liked it, etc., etc. Then we couldn't help standing up a little straighter, and showing as best we could the superiority of old bronzed soldiers like us over raw recruits like them. We had just returned from a sally against the enemy. The enemy had run off and given us no chance to show what we might have done, but that was no fault of ours.

But soon the pangs of hunger, which had been forgotten for the time, came back, and as soon as the 150th took in the situation, over the fences and into their deserted camp they went, and soon everything eatable that their camp contained was transferred to ours, and soon afterwards to our stomachs. And how much good it did them to see us eat! They bought out the sutler and fed us until we could eat no more. And then we smoked and talked and chatted until late into the night. Surely I have never seen so much supreme satisfaction crammed into so small a space of time. But we finally separated and have quieted down, and now that I have written up my diary I will crawl in with my snoring comrades.

October 28, 1862.
Camp Millington, Baltimore.
Tuesday.
From the time of our homecoming and the royal welcome given us by the 150th, I have only made notes which I will try now to write out. Nothing out of the ordinary routine of a soldier's life in camp has

transpired. I am getting more and more used to this, and the trifling occurrences that at first made such deep impressions are soon forgotten now. Still, as someone may read this who will never know of the details of a soldier's life in any other way, I shall try and keep to my promise to tell the whole story.

The box of good things that was mentioned in the letter I received while we lay in the street at Baltimore, waiting for a train to take us to Gettysburg, came a few days after our return to camp. In it was a great big package for me. I opened it and there lay the roasted body of our old Shanghai rooster. He was minus head, feet and feathers, but I knew him the minute I laid eyes on him.

I at once began to figure how many stomachs like ours he would fill, and then gave out that many invitations. All came, and brought their plates. With mouths watering, they stood about as I prepared to carve.

At the first cut I thought I smelled something, and at the next was sure I did. The old fellow, tough as he was, was not able to stand close confinement in such hot weather, and had taken on an odour that took away all appetite for roast chicken. Terribly disappointed, we wrapped him up again, and taking him out of camp, gave him as near a military funeral as we knew how. He was a brave old bird. I have seen him whip Cuff, mother's little guardian of the garden patch. "*He sleeps his last sleep. He has fought his last battle. No sound shall awake him to glory again.*"

Requests for passes to visit the camp of the 150th are the pests of the commanding officers of our regiment, and the same can be said of the 150th, As soon as guard-mount is over, and the other details for camp duty made, the old guard (those who were on duty the day before, and who are excused from all duty except dress parade for the next twenty-four hours) try for a pass to visit the city or the 150th, the two attractions now. John Van Alstyne often visits me, as well as others with him with whom I am well acquainted. These visits I return as often as I can get away. Our camp ground has been laid out in regular order and the company streets graded and made to look very respectable. There is a broad street, along one side of which are the officers' tents, the colonel's in the centre.

Back of these are the quartermaster's and the commissary's stores, the sutler's tent and the mules and horses. In front of the colonel's tent is the flag-staff, and running out from the street are ten shorter streets, one for each company, with cook-houses or tents at the bottom. Men are detailed every day to clean up and keep in order all these and are called supernumeraries. When it rains we that are not on duty lie in our tents and amuse ourselves in any way we can, or visit from tent to tent as the fancy takes us. In fair weather we have either company-drill or battalion-drill, and every now and then the regiments are put together for brigade-drill. Any of it is hard work, but it is what we are here for, and we find little fault. The weather is chilly. I notice but little difference in the weather here and as we usually have it at home. There we expect it, while here we do not and that I suppose makes it seem harder to put up with.

One of our company, Elmer Anderson, deserted and enlisted in an artillery regiment a few days ago. He came into camp showing his papers and was arrested and put in the guard-house. What the outcome will be I don't know, but it seems as if there should be some way of preventing such things. Sunday mornings we have what we call knapsack-drill. Why they save this for Sunday I don't know, but I suppose there is some reason for it. We pack our knapsacks, brush up our guns, clothes, shoes, etc., and march to the drill ground and form in columns by companies. Company A on the right and B on the left. This brings Company A in front and the first company to be inspected, after which they march back to camp and are through for the day. Company B being the last, it is something like an hour we stand there with our knapsacks open before us on the ground, everything in them exposed to view of the passer-by, who is the inspection officer and the captain whose company he is inspecting.

With his sword tip he pokes over our belongings, and if any dirty socks or handkerchief or any other article a soldier ought not to have is found, a lesson is read to him on the spot and repeated in plainer terms by the captain afterwards. As we must take everything we own or have it stolen while we are away, we take a great many chances. I shall never forget the first inspection. We knew nothing of what was coming, and such an outfit as that inspection officer saw I don't think any other one ever did. Little by little we learn the lesson, learn to put the best on top, for not all knapsacks have their contents stirred up. A great deal of allowance was made for us at first, but as we go along the screws of discipline are slowly but surely turned on, and finally I suppose it will be easy to obey. That one word, "obey," seems to be all that is required of us. No matter how unreasonable an order seems to us, we have only to obey it or get in trouble for not doing it.

November 1, 1862.

Have sent home my diary and am beginning another. I must be more brief, for the great mass just sent off covers but little ground and will tire the patience of any who read it. A cold I took the night we lay in Baltimore seems determined to make me sick. I have quite a sore throat and some days feel as if I must give up. Dr. Cook of the 150th has seen me and thinks I should be reported to our doctor. There is talk of our going farther south and I hope we may, for the ground is getting pretty cold here.

November 2, 1862.

Feel slim today, but am still able to do duty. There is so little to write about, as long as we make no change. I am going to wait for something to turn up worth noting.

November 5, 1862.

Something has happened. Last night, just as we were settling down for the night, orders came for a move. Dr. Andrus came round looking us over and ordered me to the hospital, as well as several others. Where the regiment is going is a secret from us yet. While the tents were coming down and packing up was going on, an ambulance drove in and with others I did not know, I was carted to what I understand is called "Stewart's Mansion Hospital." It is in the city, and I think near the place of our first night's stay in Baltimore. I was assigned a bed and for the first time since leaving home took off my clothes for the night. It seemed so strange I was a long time getting sleepy.

I am in a large room full of clean cots, each one with a man in it more or less sick. Not being as bad off as many others, I have written some letters for myself and some for others who washed me to do so. The room is warmed by two big stoves and if I knew where the regiment was, I would be willing to put in the winter right here. Nurses, men detailed for that purpose, are here just to wait on us and ladies are coming and going nearly all the time. They bring us flowers and are just as kind as they can be. I am up and dressed and have been out seeing the grounds about the place.

One building is called the dead house, and in it were two men who died during the night. As none were missing from the room I was in, I judge there are other rooms, and that the one I was in is for those who are not really sick, but sickish. John Wooden of our company is probably the sickest man in the ward. John Van Alstyne came in just at night to see how I came on. Snow is falling and the natives call it very unusual weather for the time of year.

November 8, 1862.

Snow going fast. A day more like May than November. Hear the regiment is on a vessel off shore waiting for something, I don't know what.

November 9, 1862.
Sunday.

Four men died last night. A major from one of the regiments came to see some of his men here. He doesn't enthuse much over the conditions on board ship.

Night. Hear the vessel with the 128th has sailed. I am left behind, but I am getting along so nicely I will surely be able to go soon. Am a little weak and have a troublesome cough, but upon the whole am much better.

November 10, 1862.

Two more deaths last night. As I have nothing better to do I will describe what I saw of a military funeral. It was an artilleryman in a plain pine box over which the U. S. flag was thrown. His comrades with guns reversed went first. Then came the gun-carriage with the coffin strapped on and six horses hitched to it. After a prayer by the chaplain the procession started in order as follows: First, the fife and drum, playing the dead march. Then an escort of guards, after which the body, followed by the horse the man had ridden, led by a soldier. He was saddled and bridled and his dead master's boots were strapped in the stirrups heels foremost, with his sword hanging from the pommel of the saddle. A corporal was in charge of the whole. At the grave, three volleys were fired across the open grave after the body was lowered, and then the procession marched back in reverse order, the fife and drum playing a lively march. The soldiers' graves are as close to each other as possible and a pine board giving the man's name and that of the command to which he belonged is placed at the head of each.

November 11, 1862.

John Van has been over again and says his regiment is going into winter quarters in the city outskirts. I hear the 128th has sailed for Fortress Monroe. The papers are all headed, "Removal of McClellan," and everyone is giving his opinion of the change. I say nothing because I know too little about it to venture an opinion. I went out and treated myself to a good square meal today and begin to think I was more hungry than sick, for I feel fit and ready for anything. Chaplain Parker has been here to see his boys, as he calls them. Says he left the regiment oft Fortress Monroe on board the *Arago*. He reports them well and in fine spirits.

November 11, 1862.

Yesterday and today I have been fixing to get away from here and join the regiment. Captain Wooden's mother from Pine Plains came in today and I am full of home news. I kept her answering questions as long as she staid. Dr. Andrus says I must not think of going yet, but if I get a chance I'll show him. Doctors don't know it all. I have had such good care and such nice warm quarters I am really myself again, only not quite as strong as I was once. My clothes don't fit very close yet, and if the looking-glass in the wardroom is correct I have had something that has made me look rather slim.

November 14, 1862.

Friday. Dr. Andrus is going today. He says I ought not to think of leaving here yet. But he does not forbid it, so if I get a chance I shall try it. I have burned my big pile of letters and discarded everything my knapsack was stuffed with except what belongs to Uncle Sam.

5 p. m. Mail in and a five-dollar bill came in a letter from home. I went right out and bought a pair of boots with it, which beat the low shoes I have so far worn.

7 p. m. On board the steamer *Louisiana*. I had a hard time getting here, making two miles in twenty minutes with my gun and accoutrements all on. Dr. Andrus went and as soon as the chance came I sneaked out and started. I was just in time, as the gang-plank was being pulled aboard when I came to it. Dr. Andrus was on deck and saw me and had them wait until I was on board. Then he scolded some and made me get into a berth where he covered me up in blankets and made me drink a cup of hot stuff which he prepared. I was nearly roasted by this treatment, but I am away from the hospital and on the way to be with the boys again and so did not complain.

CHAPTER 4

On Board the "Arago"

November 15 1862.

We are nearly out of sight of land. Wild ducks and geese cover the water. The sun is just coming up, and seems to me I never saw such a lovely morning. Besides the ducks and geese on the water, the air is full of them, some alighting on the water and others rising from it. They are so tame they only get out of the way of the boat, and if shooting was allowed, hundreds could be shot from where I stand.

I am sore and stiff from my run to catch the boat, but I am thankful to be here and take in these new sights on this glorious morning. Chaplain Parker is on board and is pointing out places and vessels, and helping us to enjoy it all.

11 a. m. We are sailing over the spot where the *Monitor* and *Merrimac* fought. An eyewitness who is on board has been giving a vivid description of it, to which I listened with the deepest interest.

Noon. We have landed at Newport News; so they call it, but there are only a few shanties in sight, and beside each one is a huge pile of oyster shells. The boys are here, having been brought off from the *Arago*, which lies off shore. Oysters are plenty and cheap, and I am full of them, the best I ever tasted, fresh from the water, and so large many of them make two good mouthfuls.

The *Monitor*, which saved the day when the *Merrimac* same out of the James River, lies nearby, and the wrecks of the *Cumberland* and *Congress* which were sunk, show above the water. The *Arago* lies just outside and at 2 p. m. we go on board. The only white men I have seen are soldiers. The negroes and their shanties are all I can see of Newport News.

November 16, 1862.

Sunday night.

The day has been cold and blustery. We have spent it in reading tracts the chaplain gave out, writing letters and swapping yarns. I am new to it all, and the boys have shown me all over the *Arago* where they are allowed to go. Our sleeping quarters are between decks, and are very similar to those on Hudson camp ground. That is, long tiers of bunks, one above the other from the floor to the ceiling above, just high enough for a man to sit up in and not hit his head. They are wide enough for four, but a board through the middle separates each into berths for two men each. They are the whole length of the room, with just enough space to walk between them.

Along the sides is a row through which are small round windows which can be opened, and which give the only light the room has. For ventilation, a huge bag hangs down from above deck which ends up in a big tin or iron funnel which is kept away from the wind and so is supposed to draw up the air from our bedroom when it becomes heated. Where fresh air comes from I have not yet found out, but suppose it drops down through several openings in the deck above. A swap was made with one who bunked with Walter Loucks so my crony and I could again be together. It is on the side, and has a window in it. Walt has kindly given me the light side so I can keep up my scribbling. What we are here for, or where we go from here, is not yet told us. In fact I don't know as it is yet determined.

November 17, 1862.

Monday.

On shore again. The well ones are drilling and the sick are enjoying themselves any way they can. Mail came today and I have a long letter from home. Every mail out takes one from me and often more. I have so many correspondents, I seldom fail to get one or more letters by each mail. On the bank or shore, up and down as far as I have seen, are negro shanties which look as if put up for a few days only. They dig oysters and find a ready sale to the thousands upon thousands of soldiers that are encamped on the plains as far as the eye can reach. This gathering means something, but just what, we none of us know. A case of black measles is reported on board ship and if true we may be in for a siege of it. I hope I may get entirely well before it hits me. Jaundice is quite common too, and many men I see are as yellow as can be and look much worse than they appear to feel.

November 18, 1862.

Orderly Holmes and myself have been on shore again. We went up the beach and found a soldiers' graveyard. We got breakfast at a darky hut, mutton chops and onions, hot biscuit and coffee, all for twenty-five cents. The boat that takes us to and from the *Arago* is a small affair that used to run up and down the James River. The Rebs have left their mark upon it in the shape of bullet holes most everywhere, but most often on the pilot-house.

November 19, 1862.

Have been paid off; $24.70 I got, and we all went ashore and washed up. The bunks on the *Arago* have been used so long by so many that they are lousy and most everyone has them. I, however, have found none as yet. We are kept on shore as much as possible, as a guard against disease, which would surely come when so many are crowded in so small a space. As there is no way to spend money here except for oysters, a great many gamble it away, then borrow again from those that win and pay any interest asked for. There is more and more sickness every day. Many are taken to a hospital at Fortress Monroe, which I am told is not far away.

November 21, 1862.

A death on board last night. The guns are being taken off the *Cumberland* and *Congress* by divers. Lieutenant Colonel Smith let himself out today, and says if there isn't land enough in the South for his men, he thinks they should be disbanded and sent home. Hurrah for Colonel Smith! He is a soldier all over and knows what is fair treatment better than the new officers, and acts as if he meant to have it. We have been on board all day and have put in the time trading watches and anything else. Everything goes here. Richmond is taken, so we hear, and hope it may be so.

November 22, 1862.

The sun rose clear this morning, and the air is just right. Our lower regions are hot and stuffy, but on deck it is delightful. Great birds, seagulls I hear them called, are all about and pick up, or pick at, everything that floats on the water.

We went ashore and while there saw General Corcoran and staff. If he amounts to much he is, like a "singed cat," better than he looks. My throat troubles me yet and tonight is about as bad as ever. Goodnight, diary.

November 23, 1862.
Off Fortress Monroe.

We left Newport News about six this morning, and came here where lie many other vessels loaded with soldiers. There's a big move going on, which I will know about when it comes off. Coal and hard-tack are coming aboard by the boat load. The colonel's horse died last night and went overboard. Poor things. They have more air than we, but have no chance to move. They do not lie down at all.

November 24, 1862.
Monday.

All night the coal kept rattling down, and it would seem this old craft would sink. There are about 1300 men on board.

November 25, 1862.
Tuesday.

If I have kept track right, this is Thanksgiving day up north. My mouth waters as I think of the good things they will eat today. I suppose we should feel thankful for the fare we have, but it is hard to do it, and is harder yet to eat it. Still I know how impossible it is to do much better by us than they do. The family is so big, the individual member of it must not expect pie and cake with every meal. Some drilling in the manual of arms is done on the quarter deck. It makes something to do, and anything is better than nothing. A gun feels pretty heavy to me these days. It is curious to see how we divide up into families.

Men who were friends and neighbours at home are even more than that here. Our duties may separate us, but when they are over we hunt each other up again. We know and talk with others, but confidences are all saved for the few. Our beds are next to each other, but with the fellows next to us on the other side we have little to do.

The waves run high today, higher than any I ever saw, and yet the sailors say this is almost a dead calm. Still the vessel pitches and dives, so we run against someone or something every move we make.

November 26, 1862.
Wednesday.

Rainy today. This keeps us below and such a racket as we make! I begun to wonder if I didn't make a mistake in leaving Stewart's Mansion. Dr. Andrus is dosing me and when it clears off I hope to feel better.

November 27, 1862.
Thursday.

This is really Thanksgiving day. So by my mistaking Tuesday for it I really have two holidays. The men are ashore for a Thanksgiving sermon. I am taking mine in my bunk. Have less fever but more sore throat.

November 28, 1862.

Lots of sick men today. I am better and was on duty again. Had only to attend sick-call and take the men to the doctor. There were only six from Company B, while some companies had twenty. Sergeants Noble and Kniffin were sent ashore to the Chesapeake hospital today.

Night. John Thompson and Isaiah Dibble, fresh from the North, came on board tonight. Gave us all the home news and many loving messages from those we love so well. But the way they spoke of our quarters was scandalous. Said hogs would die if confined in such a pen as this,

November 29, 1862.

Hurrah for camp once more! Our tents are being sent ashore and a detail from each company goes to put them up. This began just at night and lasted all night. Nobody slept, for some were working and the rest were thinking of living outdoors again.

November 30, 1862.
Sunday.
Camp Hamilton, right in sight of Fortress Monroe.

The last day of fall and as perfect a day as ever was. We are on the ground again and it feels cold after the heated quarters on the boat. God help us if it rains, for this bare ground would soon be like a mortar bed. But we are not to cross any bridges until we come to them. Still I think we had better pray for a dry spell.

December 1, 1862.
Monday. Winter.

Just think of it, and yet but for the almanac I should call it Indian summer.

December 2, 1862.
Tuesday.

On board the *Arago* again. That is, most of us are. Some were sent to the hospital instead, Leonard Loucks among them. Orders came in the night, we were routed out, tents struck and tied up. We waited until morning and then till 9 a. m., when we were put on a boat and taken back here, just what for nobody knows that will tell. I declare this "hog-pen," as Thompson called it, seems like home. There is a familiar smell to it, and the beds are dry too.

December3s, 1862.
Wednesday.
Rainy day. Many have taken cold from our stay in camp and coughing and sneezing is going on all over the boat. I manage to keep up at this, and for coughing I think I take the lead. I am lucky in one thing though. Dr. Andrus once knew a Van Alstyne who he says was a very decent sort of a man, and often stops to talk of those of the name he knows, and to ask me about those I know. In that way he is able to keep track of my condition and give me more of his attention than he otherwise would.

December 4, 1862.
Judging from appearances we are to move again. The anchor is coming up and there is hustling and bustling about all over the boat. Anything by way of excitement is good and I am glad something is going to happen. I miss a great many boats that were lying about us yesterday and every now and then one goes past us towards the open sea.

Later. We're off, heading in the only direction where no land is in sight.

Later still. Have learned this much. The Baltic is the flag ship, with General Banks and staff on board. She has stopped and all the other vessels are forming in lines. Each vessel has orders which are only to be opened in case of separation from the flag-ship. It is too dark to see or to write and the ship pitches and dives terribly. Water dashes on deck sometimes, and this was almost thirty feet above water before we loaded up with coal.

December 6, 1862.
Saturday.
Wind and waves both much higher. Nearly everyone except myself is seasick. Before it reaches me I am going to try and describe what is going on about me.

To begin with, our cabin quarters. I have told how the bunks are arranged, so just imagine the men hanging over the edge and throwing whatever is in them out on the floor or on the heads of those below them. The smell is awful. I was afraid to stir for fear my turn would come, but after a while did get out on deck. Here everyone seemed trying to turn themselves wrong side out. The officers bowed as low as the privates, and except for the sailors, there was no one in sight but seemed to be determined to gaze upon what they had eaten since the war began.

No one could stand without hanging fast to something, and fast to a rope that came from above to a ring in the deck were four men, swinging round in a circle, each one every now and then casting up his accounts on the back of the man in front. The deck was slippery and not being sailor enough to get about I climbed down again and after some narrow escapes reached my bunk to tell my diary the sights I had seen. I cannot tell of the smells. There is nothing I can think of to compare it with.

December 7, 1862.
Sunday night.

My turn came, but did not last long. I was able to see the others at their worst, and came out of it before the others were able to take much notice. Some are as sick as ever, but most of them are getting over it, and cleaning house is the order of the day. The sea is very rough, though not as bad as in the night. It seemed sometimes as if the *Arago* was rolling over. Lieutenant Sterling of Company D died a few hours ago. He had some sort of fever. We have a variety of diseases abroad if reports are true. I am getting careful about putting down what I cannot see for myself. It takes but little to start a story and by the time it has gone around the original teller would not believe it himself. For myself, I am all the better for my seasickness, and think those that are over it feel the same way. Rockets are going up from the different vessels in sight. I suppose someone knows what for, but I do not.

December 8, 1862.
Monday.

The storm is over and it is warm and pleasant. Lieutenant Sterling's funeral sermon was preached this morning on the quarter-deck. On account of lack of room only his company and the commissioned officers attended. His body will be sent home when we land.

December 9, 1862.
Tuesday.

Land ho! I was on deck by the crack of dawn, saw the sun come up from the water; a beautiful sight. Saw two vessels going towards home and wished I was on board. Wm. Haight of our company is very sick. He is a general favourite and we all feel badly at the possibility of losing him.

December 10, 1862.
Off the coast of Florida.
We must be going to New Orleans as has been reported. I did not believe it at first, as there was a report that Charleston was our destination.

Haight died about sunrise, and his death has cast a gloom over Company B. He was one of the best fellows I have met with in the army. He was a little wild at first but later seemed to change. Talked of the trouble his habits had caused his parents and seemed determined to atone for it by a right about face change. We shall miss his cheery voice. Such is war. It is over thirty-six days since the 128th and two companies of the 114th New York came aboard this vessel. It is a wonder so many are alive today. We get on deck now and the nights are so warm some of us sleep there. We suffer for good water to drink. What we have may be good, but it is distilled water, and there are so many of us we use it before it has time to get cold. On the quarter-deck, where we are not allowed to go, are barrels which contain *real water*, for officers' use only. I was let into a secret last night, how to get some of it, and I drank all I could hold. With a long rubber tube I crawled up behind a barrel and let the end down the bunghole, which is left open for ventilation, and sucked away as long as I could swallow. This will go on until someone is caught at it, and then the game will be up.

December 11, 1862.
In the Gulf of Mexico.
Flying fish and porpoises are in sight. The sailors say the porpoises are after the flying fish, and they skip out of the water and go as far as they can and then drop in again. It is a beautiful morning, and the water is smooth as glass on top. Under it, however, there seems to be a commotion, for the surface is up and down like hills and hollows on land. Ground swells, the sailors call it. In spite of the nice weather a great many are yet seasick. Three cases of measles are reported this morning. Everyone who has never had them seems to be having them now. Only a few new cases of fever were reported. A big shark is following the vessel, after anything that is thrown overboard. It keeps up easily and as far as I can discover makes very little effort to do so.

December 12, 1862.
At daylight Company B was called on deck and made to form in

a three-sided square, the open side towards the rail. Poor Haight was then brought up in a rough box, which was set across the rail, the most of it projecting over the water, the end towards us being fastened down by a rope fastened to an iron on the deck. The chaplain made a prayer, and just as the sun rose out of the water the rope was slipped off, and the box plunged down into the water. I should have said that the engines were stopped and except for the chaplain's words the utmost silence prevailed. I shall never forget this, my first sight of a burial at sea. It has all been so sudden, and so unexpected. He was only sick a few days. Never complained no matter what came, but always was foremost in any fun that can be got out of a life like this. It was at his father's house I took tea when home on my five day furlough, and I am glad I could give his mother such a good account of him. It is hard for us to understand why Lieutenant Sterling's body can be kept for shipment home, while that of Haight could not.

December 13, 1862.
Yet in the Gulf of Mexico.

Company C lost a man last night. Company G has been turned out of their quarters and a hospital made of it. That crowds the others still more, but at the rate we go on the whole ship will soon be a hospital.

10 a. m. We have stopped at a sandy island, which they say is Ship Island. The man who died last night has been taken off and they are digging a hole in the sand to put him in.

Ship Island so far as I can discover is only a sand bar with a small fort on it, and with some soldiers about it the only live thing in sight. We weighed anchor about 4 p. m. and the next morning, Dec. 14th, stopped off the mouth of the Mississippi for a pilot. I am told this is called the South West Pass, being one of several outlets to the great Mississippi River. It looks like a mud flat that had been pushed out into the Gulf farther in some places than others. As far as the eye can reach the land is covered with a low down growth of grass or weeds that are but little above the water. We passed a little village of huts near the outlet, where the pilots with their families live and which is called "Pilot Town." What they live on I did not learn. The huts are perched on piles driven in the mud, with board walks from one to the other and water under and about the whole.

December 15, 1862.

Went on up the river until hard ground appeared. Passed two forts.

Fort Jackson and Fort St. Philip they call them, and say Butler's men had hard fighting to get past them when they came up. The secret is out. Banks is to relieve Butler in the Department of the Gulf. I wonder what harm it would have done had we been told this long ago. Chaplain Parker went ashore and brought off some oranges. A small limb had twenty-four nice oranges on it and this the Dominie said he would send home to show our friends what sumptuous fare we have. Someone suggested his putting in a few wormy hard-tack with the oranges.

We have anchored opposite a large brick building with a few small wood buildings near it.

December 16, 1862.

The U. S. surgeon from the Marine Hospital has been on board looking us over. Found only four diseases, measles, scurvy, typhoid fever and jaundice. He did not put down the graybacks that keep us scratching all the time. For a long time after they appeared they left me alone, but one morning as I lay on my back in bed writing in my diary one came crawling up over my knee and looked me straight in the face; from that on they have seemed to like me as well as anyone.

CHAPTER 5

Quarantine Station, La.

Towards night the *Arago* swung up to the bank near the big brick building and we went ashore and piled into it. It was built for storing cotton, and is fireproof. The lower floor is of brick and the upper one of iron and so cannot well burn. The bricks seem hard and cold and are water-soaked. Still we spread our blankets and got some sleep and woke up hungry. The cooks have established themselves between us and the river so as to be near water. We have room to stir about at any rate and some went in bathing, but the water is cold. The only good quality the body lice possess is a habit of letting go of us when we move and grabbing hold of our clothes. Taking advantage of this we took the camp kettles as soon as breakfast was cooked and boiled our clothes. Those that had no change—and that was the most of us—ran about to keep warm until our garments were cooked and then after a wring out put them on and let them dry as fast as the wind and sun would do it.

By night we were dry and slept without a scratch, and strange to say none of us took cold. But not all would try this heroic remedy and consequently we expect to have to repeat the operation. A negro came across the river with his boat loaded with oranges. We bought the whole of them as fast as he could count them out, fifty cents for 100, and the doctor says eat all you want. The sick are in the wooden buildings outside, except in one, which the officers have taken. We acted like colts just turned loose and already are forgetting the close quarters we were in so long. Along the river is a narrow strip of hard ground and beyond that is a swamp which so far as I can see has no end. Sluggish streams flow with the tide back and forth from the river to the gulf, and between these the ground is covered with what is here called wild rice. Birds of all sorts are plenty; ducks and geese all feed upon the seeds that abound everywhere.

December 17, 1862.

Have explored the country up and down and back from the river today. Found much that is strange to me but met with no startling adventures,

December 18, 1862.

The officers gave a dance in the upper part of the store-house last night and the iron floor was fine for dancing. All hands were invited to join in and all that felt able did. Two men died yesterday, and last night another, all fever patients. Two were from Company A, and the other from Company I. They were buried just back of the quarters on hard ground, for this place, A catfish was caught by one of Company A's men today, that looked just like our bullheads, only bigger. As he was pulling him in over the mud the line broke, and I got the head for hitting him with an axe before he got to the water. The head weighed 14½ lbs, and the whole fish 52 lbs, A native that saw him said he was a big one, but not as big as they sometimes grow. My family had a meal from the head and Company A had fish for all their sick and part of the well ones.

December 19, 1862.

Fifteen cases of fever reported this morning, A dead man was taken out very early and buried in a hurry. This has given rise to the story that smallpox has come, too. It looks as if it might be so, for it's about the only thing we haven't got. Those that seemed strongest are as likely to be taken now as the weakest, I have been half sick through it all and yet I hold my own, and only for my sore throat and this racking cough would enjoy every minute.

December 20, 1862.

One day is so much like another that the history of one will do for several. I think about everything that can be done for our comfort is being done. There must be some reason for our being kept here and it is probably because of so much sickness. It would not do to take us where others would catch our diseases and yet it is tough lines we are having. Chaplain Parker does everything he can to keep up our spirits, even to playing boy with us. A new doctor has come to take the place of one that died while we lay off Newport News.

December 21, 1862.

Inspection of arms today and a sermon by the chaplain. We are thinking and talking of the letters we will get when we have a mail. Uncle Sam keeps track of us someway and sooner or later finds us. We have a regimental postmaster, who is expected every day from the city with a bag full. We have enough to fill him up on his return trip. The *Arago* is unloading all our belongings, which looks as if we were to stay here. Goodbye, *Arago!* I wish there was a kettle big enough to boil you and your bugs in before you take on another load. So many are sick the well ones are worked the harder for it. I still rank among the well ones and am busy at something all the time.

Just now I have been put in place of fifth sergeant, who among other duties sees that the company has its fair share of rations, and anything else that is going. I also attend sick call every morning, which amounts to this. The sick call sounds and the sick of Company B fall in line and I march them to the doctor's office, where they are examined. Some get a dose of whiskey and quinine, some are ordered to the hospital and some are told to report for duty again. Dr. Andrus and I play checkers every chance we get. We neither play a scientific game, but are well matched and make some games last a long time. He is helping my throat and my cough is not so bad lately. Our quarters were turned into a smoke house today. An old stove without a pipe is going and some stinking stuff is burning that nothing short of a grayback can stand. It is expected to help our condition, and there is lots of chance for it.

Christmas, 1862.

Nothing much out of the ordinary has happened since I wrote last. A man went out hunting and got lost in the tall weeds. He shouted until some others found him and then had great stories to tell of narrow escapes, etc. Harrison Leroy died this morning. He was half sick all the way here and did not rally after coming ashore. Dr. Andrus poked a swab down my throat with something on it that burned and strangled me terribly. But I am much the better for it. We have all been vaccinated, and there is a marked improvement in the condition of those not in the hospital.

The chaplain preached a sermon and Colonel Cowles made a speech. He thanked us for being such good soldiers under what he called the most trying circumstances war can bring. Loads of soldiers go up the river nearly every day. As the doctor allows them to pass the quarantine, I take it they are not in the fix we are.

December 26, 1862.

Leroy was buried early this morning. My part in it was to form the company and march it by the left flank to the grave. For fear this may not be plain I will add, that the captain and orderly are always at the right of the line when the company is in line for any purpose and that end of the line is the right flank. The tallest men are on the right also and so on down to the shortest, which is Will Hamilton and Charles Tweedy, who are on the left, or the left flank as it is called. This arrangement brings the officers in the rear going to the grave, but when all is over the captain takes command and marches the company back by the right. I got through without a break and feel as if I was an old soldier instead of a new one. But it is a solemn affair. Leroy was a favourite with us and his death and this, our first military funeral, has had a quieting effect on all.

Last night the chaplain and some officers, good singers all, came in and we almost raised the roof singing patriotic songs. Speeches were made and we ended up with three cheers that must have waked the alligators out in the swamp. Sweet potatoes and other things are beginning to come in and as they sell for most nothing we are living high. But we are in bad shape as a whole. Mumps have appeared and twenty-four new cases were found today. Colonel Smith, our lieutenant-colonel, has been up the river to try and find out if better quarters could not be had and has not succeeded. He is mad clear through, and when asked where we were to go, said to hell, for all he could find out.

December 28, 1862.

We have had a rain and the hard ground made the softest kind of mud. It sticks to our feet and clothes, and everybody is cross and crabbed. The sun came out, however, and our spirits began to rise as the mud dried up. There was preaching and prayer meeting both today.

Our chaplain's courage is something wonderful and many of us attend the services out of respect to him when we had much rather lie and rest our aching bones. The captain of the *Arago* sent word he will be along tonight on his way to New York and would stop for letters. He will find some, judging from the writing that has been going on.

December 29, 1862.

John Van Hoovenburg, another Company B boy, is about gone. The men are getting discouraged and to keep their minds from themselves it is said drilling is to begin tomorrow. The seed sown on the *Arago* is bearing fruit now. Something to do is no doubt the best medicine for us. I know I should die if I laid around and talked and thought of nothing but my own miserable self.

January 1, 1863.

The *Arago* did call for our mail and the body of Lieutenant Sterling was put on board to go to his family in Poughkeepsie. We gave the old ship three cheers, and then someone sang out three cheers for the lice you gave us. John Van Hoovenburg died last night. We made a box for him out of such boards as we could find. Though we did our best, his bare feet showed through the cracks. But that made no difference to poor Johnnie. The chaplain was with him to the end, says he was happy and ready to go. This is how we spend our New Year's day. We wish each other a happy New Year though just as if we were home and had a good prospect of one. After the funeral Walter Loucks and I went up the river quite a distance, so far it seemed as if our legs would not carry us back.

Negro huts are scattered along. I suppose white people cannot live here and so the darkeys have it all. Some cultivate patches of ground and in one garden we saw peas in bloom. We bought a loaf of bread and a bottle of molasses of an old woman, and though the bread was not what it might have been, it tasted good. There are some orange trees, but no oranges. The darkies say they will blossom in about a month. A man in Company E, a sort of poet, who was always writing songs for the boys to sing, was cutting wood today and the axe flew off the handle and cut the whole four fingers from the right hand. There were no witnesses and some there are who say he did it so as to get a discharge. The doctor has dressed the hand and he is going about in great pain just now.

January 2, 1863.
Friday.

Peter Carlo, the one who went through the medical examination at Hudson with me. died last night. He was found dead this morning and appeared to have suffered terribly. His eyes and mouth were staring wide open and his face looked as if he had been tortured to death. Companies A and B keep in advance on the sick list.

January 3, 1863.

Two more men died last night, but not from Company B. We sent off another mail today. I wish we might get some letters. We ought to have a lot of them when they do come.

CHAPTER 6

Camp Chalmette, La.

January 4, 1863.
Sunday.

Hip, Hip, Hurrah! The *Laurel Hill,* a steamer, has stopped at our camp and we have orders to pack up for a move. All that are able are to be taken to Chalmette, the old battle ground below New Orleans. Anywhere but this God-forsaken spot, say I. Chaplain Parker preached hot stuff at us today. Says we don't take proper care of ourselves, that we eat too often and too much. That made me laugh. *Dominie,* if you lived with us a while, ate at the same table and had the same bill of fare to choose from, I think you would tell another story. Poor man, it is getting on his nerves sure. But it sets me to wondering if our officers all think that way. If they blame us for the condition we are in, who brought these conditions about? Did we from choice herd in between decks like pigs, while the officers, chaplain and all had staterooms and a bed and good food to eat, well cooked and at regular hours? If they blame us for our condition today, I can only hope that at some time they may get just such treatment and fare and that I may be there to remind them it is their own fault. Chaplain Parker must do some tall preaching to make good what he has lost by that tongue lashing. It was uncalled for and a sad mistake.

January 5, 1863.
Chalmette. Monday.

Said to be just below the city of New Orleans. We left quarantine about 11 p. m. and reached here about 8 this morning. Many were left behind, too sick to be moved. We have put up our tents, and have been looking about. It is a large camp ground and from all signs was lately occupied and was left in a hurry. Odds and ends of camp furniture are scattered about, and there are many signs of a hasty leave-taking. A few of us went back across the country to a large woods, where we found many trees covered with long gray moss, hanging down in great bunches from the branches. We took all we could carry to make a bed of, for it is soft as feathers.

Later. The doctor won't allow us to use our bed of moss. Says it would make us sick to sleep on it, and much worse than the ground. This is said to be the very ground where General Jackson fought the Battle of New Orleans and a large tree is pointed out as the one under which General Packenham was killed. Ancient-looking breastworks are in sight and a building near our tents has a big ragged hole in the gable which has been patched over on the inside so as to leave the mark as it was made, which a native tells me was made by a cannon ball during the battle of New Orleans. The ground is level and for this country is dry. The high bank, or breastworks, cuts off the view on one side and a board fence cuts off a view of the river. Towards the city are enough trees to cut off an extended view in that direction, so we have only the swamp back of us to look at. But this beats quarantine and I wish the poor fellows left there were well enough to get here.

There are several buildings on the ground, which the officers are settling themselves in, while a long shed-like building is being cleared out for a hospital. It has been used for that, I judge, and is far better than the one at quarantine. We brought along all that were not desperately sick and have enough to fill up a good part of the new hospital. Walter Loucks has rheumatism in his arms and suffers all the time. He and James Story are my tent mates. We have confiscated some pieces of board to keep us off the ground. Company B has been hard hit. We left seven men at Baltimore, seven at Fortress Munroe and seven at our last stopping-place. It seems to go by sevens, as I find we have seven here in our new hospital. This with the four that have died makes thirty-two short at this time.

January 8, 1863.

Today is the anniversary of the Battle of New Orleans and is celebrated here like the Fourth of July at home. Drill has been attempted, but only about 200 men were fit for it and our camp duties are about all we are able to do.

January 9, 1863.

Were paid off today and the peddlers that hang out just across the guard line have done a thriving business. Walter gets worse every day.

His courage seems to be giving out and it is pitiful to see him suffer.

January 11, 1863.

Meeting today. Some way they have lost their force. We attend because we have to. The sermon at the quarantine is remembered. We seem to have lost faith, not in God, but in ministers. Colonel Smith with all his cursing has done more for our care and comfort than those that profess so much and do so little.

January 17, 1863.
Saturday.

On account of my cough, which is worse when I lie down, I have walked about evenings or sat and chatted with others about the camp fire until tired enough to sleep, and last night crawled in near midnight where my two bed-fellows were asleep. Soon after I got into a drowse from which I was awakened by a coughing spell and saw Walt standing by the help of the tent pole and groaning in agony. Soon I heard him say "I'll end it all right now," and with that he pitched over towards his knapsack and by the noise I thought he was after his revolver. I jumped across Jim, who lay asleep in the middle, and snatched the gun out of his hand before he had it out of the case. Out in the company street I threw the three revolvers and then grabbed for a sheath knife which I knew was there, getting hold of the handle just as he grabbed the sheath. By this time Story was in the game and we both had our hands full getting him down and quiet.

I went for Dr. Andrus, who after lighting a candle and looking in Walt's eyes, told us to take him over to the hospital. The struggle had put him in agony and it was pitiful to see how he suffered. We staid with him the rest of the night and by morning he was helpless. Every joint seemed as stiff as if no joint was there. For the next five days I did little but watch him and help in any way I could to make him more comfortable. Then he and others were taken to the general hospital in the city, where they will at least be warm.

We have had a cold rain and the camp is a bed of mud. The wind sifts through the cracks in this old shed and although a stove was kept running, it was too cold for comfort. I have slept but little in the last five nights, but the doctor has kept dosing me and I feel better than when this time with Walter began. Letters from home have made the world seem brighter and the men in it better.

January 18, 1863.
Sunday.

Yesterday the chaplain's tent for public worship came and this morning we were all gathered there and the chaplain was praying, when snap went something in the top and down came the tent upon us. He didn't have time to say "Amen," to say nothing of the benediction. In the after noon Isaac T. Winans, Jim Story and I went to see Walter and found him in a good bed and in a warm room. He is much better, but his wrists are swollen yet and look as if the joints had been pulled apart.

January 19, 1863.

It rained hard last night and before the tents got soaked up enough water sifted through to wet our blankets and we hardly slept at all for the cold. Not being called on for anything I lay all day and dosed, trying to make up for the miserable night. Isaac Brownell, of Company B, who has done more to keep up the spirits of the men than anything else, is down and very sick. He is a mimic and could mimic anyone or anything. His antics have made us laugh when we felt more like crying, and we are all anxious about him. A case of smallpox was discovered yesterday and the man put in an outbuilding, where he died this morning. Dr. Andrus so far has been alone, and he looks like death.

Later. He has given out and another doctor from the hospital is coming to take his place. The sick list grows all the time.

January 27, 1863.

Two doctors came to take the place of Dr. Andrus and they have had plenty to do. For several days the weather has been hot, which opens the pores in our tents so the first rain sifts right through. Last night it rained and we had another night of twisting and turning and trying to sleep and with very poor success. I cough so when I lie down that I keep up and going all I can, for then I seem to feel the best. Dr. Andrus still looks after us. He is getting better and we are glad, for he is the mainstay in the family. Brownell died this forenoon and I shall never forget the scene. He was conscious and able to talk and the last he said was for us to stick and hang. "But boys," said he, "if I had the power, I would start north with all who wanted to go and as soon as we passed over four feet of ground I would sink it."

January 28, 1863.

Cold day. Ice formed on puddles last night. I am staying in my tent, keeping as warm as I can, I begin to feel I am going to give out. I have kept out of the hospital so far and hope to die right here in my tent if die I must. But tomorrow may be warmer and my cough better, and under such conditions my spunk will rise as it always has. So goodbye, diary. I am going to try for a nap.

January 29, 1863.

For excitement today a man in the tent next ours tried to shoot himself. He is crazy. He rolled himself up in his blanket and then fired his revolver, on purpose maybe, and it may be by accident. At any rate he put a ball in the calf of his leg which stopped under the skin near his heel, and the doctor cut it out with a jack-knife. He has acted half crazy for some time and should be taken care of before he kills himself or someone else.

January 30, 1863.

The 28th Maine Regiment has encamped close beside us. They are well advanced in the art of taking care of themselves, for they stole everything loose in a short time after their arrival. Have been vaccinated again. This makes the third time since we left Hampton Roads.

January 31, 1863.

One of the Maine men put a bayonet through Charlie Tweedy's arm as he came from the river with a pail of water. Charlie crossed his beat, which he had no right to do. But it made bad blood and quite a quantity flew from the noses of the Maine men and some Company B blood flew too. Tweedy is the smallest man in the regiment, and has been plagued by all hands until he is very saucy and on account of his size is allowed to do about as he pleases. But it didn't work on the Maine men and may teach the Bantam a lesson.

February 6, 1862.
Friday.

The days are so much alike I have given up noting the doings of each as it comes. Since February 1st our meeting-house tent has been repaired and raised again. Rumour of a move came early in the week and has kept us guessing ever since. I think it means something, for the sick in camp hospital have been sent to the general hospital in New Orleans. The weather has been of all sorts. Cold and windy and then a thunder and lightning storm that shook the very earth. The hospital is filling up again, too. Twenty men from Company K were reported today, and five from Company B. I fear my turn is coming, for in spite of all Dr. Andrus does, my cough does not let up.

CHAPTER 7

Camp Parapet, La.

February 11, 1863.

Just at night, as I had finished the above, the *Laurel Hill*, the boat that brought us from quarantine to Chalmette, tied up in front of camp and down came our tents and on board we went. We came up the river past New Orleans and between that city and Algiers, which is quite a large place on the left hand shore. New Orleans seems a big city, but lies as low as the river. A high dock all along its front is built up with timber and is so high only the upper parts of the buildings show from the river. No streets are seen at all. We also passed a place called Carrolton and very soon after landed at what is said to be Camp Parapet. There are no tents near the river but there are thousands a short distance back. The outskirts of Carrolton come close up on the down river side, while the up river side has a high bank reaching from the river back as far as I can see.

Beyond that is an unexplored country (to me), and away in the distance appears to be just such a forest as was in sight back of Camp Chalmette. A good-looking dwelling house and a few small buildings are nearby and the ground is tramped bare of all vegetation, as if soldiers had just moved away. We came down the Levee and put up our tents and crawled in, for it was night by that time. We have had some rain and some sunshine, but the weather is warm and altogether I like our present place of abode the best of any we have yet had since we left Camp Millington. Another case of smallpox has developed, but he was hustled to a tent way back of camp and I suppose our arms will have to be pricked again. Mine looks as if a setting hen had picked it now. Miss Kate Douglass, from Amenia Union, came to camp yesterday and Captain Bostwick and several officers have gone to the city with her. Report says the captain and she are to be married tonight.

Six months in the service and I have so far been only an expense to Uncle Sam. But I have seen something of the big farm the Rebs hope to rob him of and I hope I may yet do something to put him in full possession of it again. Letters from home, also one from Walter Loucks, who is in the hospital at New Orleans.

February 16, 1863.

In the hospital after all. Dr. Andrus came last night to our tent and ordered me into the house I spoke of. I had a warm, dry bed and a good night's rest and feel much better today. The doctor has his office downstairs and the upstairs part is crammed full of sick men. A big tent is being put up and cot beds put in to put the fever patients in. Captain Bostwick was married last night, so it is said. Corporal Knox died in a fit this afternoon. It tires me to write so I must stop. Goodnight.

February 20, 1863.

Captain Bostwick came to see me today. Two men died last night, one in the hospital and the other in his tent. I don't feel as well today.

February 21, 1863.

Think I am really better today. If I keep on I'll soon be out of this and with the boys again. But they all come in to see the sick as often as they can and so we keep track of each other.

March 4, 1863.
Wednesday.

I have been very sick. This is the first time I have felt able to make a mark with a pencil. I was taken in the night, after the day I thought myself so much better. Was taken out in the tent, from which I judge I have had fever.

March 5, 1863.

Am very weak yet. A little tires me out. A letter from Herman just a month old. Coon died last night, but we none of us knew it till we saw him carried out.

March 6, 1863.

Getting better fast, but can't write much yet.

March 7, 1863.

Was carried back into the house today and put among the convalescents. I must be getting well, but it is slow. Most all the time I was worst off Dr. Andrus let me have anything I wanted to eat, but then I couldn't eat it. Now I can eat, he has cut me down to nothing. What he allows me only makes me crazy for more.

March 8, 1863.
Had a wash and a shave and am tired out. The regiment has marching orders. Wish I was out of this to go with them.

March 9, 1863.
Gunboats are said to be going up the river every day. I wonder what's up.

March 10, 1863.
Don't feel quite so smart as I did. This getting well is slow business.

March 11, 1863.
The boys say they are ready to march, but don't get any further orders. Letters from home. Have written to father—wish I could see him.

March 14, 1863.
Not feeling so good these last few days.

March 15, 1863.
Sunday.
Have my pants on and have made up my bed. If this keeps on I'll soon be able to hunt for something to eat,

March 16, 1863.
Ben Crowther is awful sick. He is a fine fellow and we hate to lose him. He is of better stuff than the average of us. I wish I could kill his nurse, for he has him tied down to the bed and stands laughing at his efforts to get loose. But it is the only way to keep him in one place, for he is out of his head. Talks to his wife as if she was right by his side.

March 17, 1863.
Last night I got a little box from home. That I may never forget a single thing in it I'll put them right down now. On top was a *New York Sun*, next a dear little letter from Jane. A little package of tea, a bottle of Arnold's Balsam, a pipe, a comb (wish it had been a fine tooth comb), a little hand looking-glass, a spool of thread, a lot of buttons, a good lead pencil, a pair of scissors, a ball of soap, half a paper of pins, a darning needle and a small needle, a steel pen and way down in the

bottom a little gold locket which made the tears come. God bless the dear ones at home. How thoughtful and how kind of them to think of so many things, and all useful, too.

March 18, 1863.

Too much excitement yesterday and I feel like two weeks ago. The doctor says I will have these setbacks though and it is only a part of the process of getting well. A man named Kipp died today. I don't know how many die out in the tent.

March 19, 1863.

Poor Crowthers died very peacefully about noon today. His cot is next mine and he seemed like one of the family to me. The company has undertaken to raise money to send his body home.

March 20, 1863.

Orderly Holmes is very sick. His discharge is under his pillow (or knapsack). He lies in a room next to this and I can hear him talk, giving orders to the company as if he were well.

March 21, 1863.
Saturday.

This is a hard spot to get well in. Two poor fellows are near their end to all appearances, and it is trying to hear then rave about home and their families. I am glad their friends cannot see and hear them. And yet the hardened wretches called nurses find something in it to laugh at. I wish I could change places between them and the sick ones. Wrote three letters today and don't feel so very tired. Begin to think Dr. Andrus was right. If he would only let me eat about four times as much, what a jewel he would be.

March 26, 1863.
Thursday.

The finest morning yet. The air is just right. The birds are singing, the sun shining bright and everything seems just right for getting well. A man named Barker died last night about midnight. He has seemed to be dying for a week and we have watched to see him breathe his last any minute. Orderly Holmes is better and may get well after all. Some of the boys killed an alligator today and cooked and ate his tail. They say it is just as good as fish and looked like fish.

March 27, 1863.

Have been downstairs. My legs just made out to get me there and back. Will they ever get strong again? But I am getting there, slow but sure, as I can see by looking back only a short time.

March 28, 1863.

Another fine day, and another trip downstairs. My legs behaved better this time. Am not near so tired. Now that I can write without getting tired I must put down some things I remember, but which I could not write at the time. I shall always remember them of course, but I want to see how near I can describe them on paper. First I want to say how very kind my comrades have been all through. I can think of many acts of kindness now that I paid little attention to then, but they kept coming along just the same. Whatever else I think of, the thought of their care for me and how they got passes and tramped miles to get me something to eat, always taking it to Dr. Andrus first to see if it would do for me—these thoughts keep coming up and my load of gratitude keeps getting heavier. Can I ever repay them? God has been good to me, better than I deserve. I was first taken to the room where I am now writing. I remember but little of what happened before I was taken out and put in the big hospital tent. It is a large affair, made up of several tents joined together endwise and wide enough for two rows of cots along the side, with an alley through the middle, towards which our feet all pointed.

I remember the head medical man coming through every day or so and the doctors would take him to certain cots, where they would look on the fellows lying there and put down something in a book. I soon noticed that most always such a one died in a short time, and I watched for their coming to my cot. One day they did, and I remember how it made me feel. Dr. Andrus was so worked down that a strange doctor was in charge, but under Dr. Andrus, who had charge over all. When he came through I motioned to him and he came and sat on the next cot, when I told him I would get well if I could get something good to eat. "All right," said he, "what will you have?" I told him a small piece of beefsteak.

He sent one of the nurses to his mess cook and he soon came back with a plate and on it a little piece of steak which he prepared to feed me. But the smell was enough and I could not even taste it. The doctor then proceeded to eat it, asking if I could think of anything else. I thought a bottle of beer would surely taste good and so he sent to the sutler's for it. But he had to drink that too, for I could not. He laughed at me and though I was disappointed, it cheered me up more than anything else had done for a long time. When I got so I could eat, I surely thought he would starve me to death.

A poor fellow across the tent opposite me got crazy and it took several men to hold him on his cot. The doctor came and injected something in his breast which quieted him for the night, but when it wore off he was just as bad and he finally died in one of them. On my right lay a man sick unto death, while on my left lay another whose appetite had come and who was begging everybody for something to eat. His company boys brought him some bread and milk which he ate as if famished. The next morning when I awoke and looked about to see how many faces were covered up I found both my right and left hand neighbours had died in the night and their blankets were drawn up over their faces. The sights I saw while I was able to realize what was going on were not calculated to cheer me up and how I acted when I was out of my head I don't know. At any rate I got better and was brought back to this room, where I have since been.

March 29, 1863.
Sunday.
Had a thunder shower in the night and some sharp lightning. Was not allowed to go out today on account of the ground being wet. We hear of hard fighting up the river, but reports get so twisted I put little stock in them. Still I hope they are true, for they are most all favourable to our side.

April 1, 1863.
Nothing worth writing for a few days. Today those we left at quarantine came up looking hale and hearty. Most of them have had smallpox or varioloid. The weather is warm and the boys who have been out of camp report alligators are plenty in the swamp back of us, and snakes of many kinds also. I am rambling about camp nowadays, but am not discharged from the hospital yet. General Neal Dow found a place next door to camp today where liquor is sold. He took every bottle he could find and smashed them across the porch rail after first locking up the landlord. Camp is being cleared and every precaution taken to keep away yellow fever. There is none of it yet, but it is expected this summer on account of so many soldiers that are new to the climate. Lew Holmes has been worse for some days and we fear we shall lose him yet.

Midnight. I am sitting up to let a tired out nurse get a nap. Holmes died a few minutes ago. He tried to tell me something, but his tongue was so swelled I could not understand what he said. He pulled me clear down to his face and his breath was awful. I pretended to understand, and he settled back as if satisfied and only breathed a few times more. His troubles are over, and those of his old father and mother and his wife and child will begin when the news reaches them. I am glad they did not see the end.

April 2, 1863.

Company B chipped in for a metallic coffin and Holmes will go home. A hearse from the city has just been here and taken him away. He was one of the best of fellows, and very popular with the men. I wonder now if Kniffin will be tried on us again. There is some reason for it now, but it should go to Riley Burdick, who is next in line.

April 3, 1863.

Two funerals today. We have quite a graveyard started. From all I can hear, by talking with soldiers of other regiments, none of them have been hit as hard as the 128th New York. And it all comes from our being stuffed into the hold of the *Arago* a month before we sailed. A big responsibility rests somewhere.

April 4, 1863.
Saturday.

Cleaning house day in the hospital. I have been helping so one of the nurses can get off for a walk outside. We found a burying ground where I counted fifty from the 12th Connecticut Volunteers. Nearly all died in August and September last. So we have not had all the sickness and death. I will try and not complain as much as I have. There were only eight from our regiment besides two we have sent home. From there we followed the parapet to the Jackson & Mississippi R. R., which runs not far back from camp. Saw a regiment of negro soldiers, who seemed to feel fine, were having all sorts of games and were in first-rate spirits. Their camp was clean and at the head of each company street were flower beds. Just outside they had planted a garden and onions and other things were growing. The commissioned officers were white. Everything else was black. But for get-up and style they beat any white regiment I have yet seen. It made me ashamed to go home. When I get out of the hospital I mean to try and get the boys to be more like them.

April 5, 1863.
Sunday.

Some time while I was sick Chaplain Parker left us. I hear he had some differences of opinion with the officers, but don't know what. Major Foster was in it in some shape, for his name and the chaplain's are the most common in the yarns that are told about camp. I used to believe all I heard, but I have learned to wait for the truth, and that doesn't always come out. Lieutenant-Colonel Smith is a rough and ready customer and stands in no more awe of the officers than of the men. So long as we behave half way decent he is kindness itself, but disobey orders and he is a raging lion. But he is our best friend, and is the only real soldier in the whole outfit. He is a regular army officer and his chief concern seems to be the welfare of the enlisted men. Now that I am able to be about camp and have no duties to perform, I enjoy seeing the captains and lieutenants put through their paces as well as the rank and file. For meeting today Major Foster read a chapter from the Bible, read a hymn and then sang it, after which he pronounced the benediction.

April 6, 1863.

One of Company A's men died today. His name was Burch. A boat-load of negroes landed here today and were taken down towards the city, what for I did not learn. Many of the men in camp are having diarrhoea, and some have to go to the hospital, where the diet can be regulated. Some corn and contraband goods were seized today a short distance up the river. A man has been suspected for a long time and today was seized upon with all his goods. We are expecting letters every day now. We watch the papers for the mail steamers, and if we get no letters are much disappointed.

April 7, 1863.

Two steamers due and yet no letters. Been loafing about camp so long I feel as if I was an unprofitable servant. But as there is nothing doing I am about as profitable as the rest.

April 8, 1863.

A little excitement today. An attempt was made to spike some guns near the negro troops headquarters. A few shots were fired but no one hit, hurt or captured. A letter from my sister, Mrs. Rowley. All well at home. For a change I have a troublesome boil on my leg. The weather is beautiful. Everything is growing—I never saw leaves and flowers come so fast.

April 10, 1863.

Yesterday I took the place of a nurse who was ailing, and today have been with several others to explore the country roundabouts. We came to an orange orchard and found and cut some sprouts for canes. General Dow and his staff were riding past, and seeing us, rode full tilt towards us, as if to run over us. The general was so busy watching us he never saw a ditch, and into it he went. The horse went down and the general went on his head, landing in the tall grass on all fours. He was not hurt, and after his staff had caught up and helped him on his horse, he came up and said, "To what regiment do you men belong?" Being told, he snapped out, "Report to your quarters at once and don't be seen cutting orange trees again." It is said he roams about like this, driving in any he finds outside, and in other ways making himself unpopular with the boys. However, he didn't take our canes and we have some nice ones to show for the trip.

Two letters today, and although they were a month old, they were full of news to me.

April 11-12, 1863.

About camp and hospital yesterday, getting well every minute. Except that I am skin poor and tire out easily, I am well. My little looking-glass first told me what a change my sickness made in my looks, but I can see my old self coming back every day now. A short meeting today, the only thing besides my diary to remind me it is Sunday, God's day. He only asks one day in seven, and it seems as if more attention should be paid it.

April 13, 1863.

Wrote and mailed some letters this morning. Wm. Partington died in this room this morning. He and I came here the same time and lay side by side. I was taken to the big tent and he left here. We were both hard sick and when I came back Bill was in just about the same condition I was. We both got round together and began to go out at the same time. A day or two ago diarrhoea hit him and now he is taken and I left. So it goes. We plan for tomorrow and tomorrow we are wrapped in a blanket and out we go.

April 14, 1863.

A letter from John Van, with one in it from George Willson and one from T. Templeton of the 150th. They are feeling fine and the regiment has little or no sickness to report.

April 15, 1863.

Reported for duty with the company this morning, but have to report to the doctor every day until I get my discharge from there. Have been appointed commissary sergeant. See to drawing the rations for Company B, and shall look out that they get their share. This relieves me from guard duty and from everything that interferes with my duties as commissary. It relieves me from duty in the ranks, adds another stripe to my arm, and two dollars per month to my pay. I am glad to have something to do. At night a citizen tried to go through camp and when halted by the guards started to run and was shot. What he was, or why he acted as he did I don't know, and he can't tell.

April 16, 1863.
Thursday.
A letter from Walt Loucks asking me to come and see him. Shall surely go if I can get a pass.

April 17, 1863.
Friday.
Went to see Walt. I had a first-rate visit. He is about well. I did little but answer questions about what has been going on since we parted at Camp Chalmette, who is living and who have died and what sort of a place we are in. Found three letters for me when I came back.

Later. Marching orders with two days' cooked rations and 100 rounds of ammunition, blankets and overcoats. I am going too, unless Dr. Andrus stops me. Must stop and write a letter before taps.

April 18, 1863.
Saturday.
The regiment has gone and I am left. When will I get clear from the hospital? One of the hospital cooks, E. Furguson, died today. There are hardly enough men in camp to bury him, only the sick and convalescent being left.

April 19, 1863.
Sunday.
We buried Furguson today. The grave was full of water and we had to punch the box down with sticks until the earth held it. Hear nothing from the regiment.

April 20, 1863.
No real news yet. Lots of rumours though, one of which is that they are all cut up and the rest captured. We don't believe it.

April 21, 1863.

Drew ten days' rations today, so I guess there is some of Company B left and that they will be back to eat it.

April 22, 1863.
Wednesday.

The regiment came back today. Have been gone four days. Had some hard marching and lived high on pigs and chickens found by the way. They went up the Pearl River, and captured a small steamer loaded with tar and rosin. They feel fine and to hear them talk one would think this matter of putting down the Rebellion is nothing if only the 128th is given a good whack at it.

April 23, 1863.

The officers have drawn new tents and the captains have given the cooks their old ones for cook houses. We tore down the old shanty, and put up the new house in short order.

April 24, 1863.

The morning paper gives a glowing account of the great expedition of the 128th. Speaks well of the behaviour of both officers and men and their great respect for private property. But Colonel Cowles has been lecturing them and his account differs from the newspaper reports on nearly all points.

We were paid off today and the money flies. We have floors in our tents now. An order has gone forth for camp inspection once each day. The tents, the cook houses and cooking utensils and everything will be inspected, and must be as clean as possible or trouble will come. Taking it all in all we have good times. One of the boys has a fiddle, and some are good singers. We have only enough to do to make us hungry when meal time comes.

April 30, 1863.

Walter Loucks has returned to camp and looks well. He feels some sore from sleeping on a board, after his stay in the hospital, but that will wear off. General Dow has cleared the peddlers out of camp and torn down some shanties near, where pies, etc., were sold. My throat has got sore again and I must get Dr. Andrus to fix it up. We have had marching orders a couple of times, but each time they were countermanded.

May 6, 1863.

Nothing unusual has happened since my last entry. I have written and have received several letters; have been on duty all the time, although I am supposed to be in the hospital yet. Have seen the doctor every day and he keeps tinkering at me. We hear all sorts of rumours of big battles and big victories and believe what we are a mind to. My office, commissary of Company B, is not very exacting while in camp. It keeps me out of the ranks though and until I get round again I am glad of it.

May 10, 1863.
Sunday.
Yesterday this regiment and many others were reviewed by General Banks. Evidently something is going to happen soon. The health of our regiment is fairly good now. I begin to find out that some had rather be sick than to be on duty, and they play it till Dr. Andrus sends them back to camp. We have some very hot weather, and then again some not so hot. Mosquitoes are the pest of our lives. They hide in our tents, ready to pounce upon us the minute we enter, and the only place we are free from them is in the hot sun outside. At night and on cloudy days they give us no peace. Their name is legion.

May 11, 1863.
Monday.
Charles Wardwell, and a fellow named Hamlin made me a call today. I was as much surprised as if they had risen right out of the ground before us. I did not know Charlie had enlisted. He is in the 23rd Connecticut, which is doing guard duty along the railroad between Algiers and Brashear City, which they say is not very far from here. It in a nine months' regiment and their time is out in August. Though the news they could tell was rather old, I was very glad to see someone from God's country again, and we had much to tell each other of our experiences. They had only about a week on the transport and came through in good shape. They swallowed hard and tried to take down what I told them of our experience on board the *Arago* and in camp and hospital since, but I don't feel like blaming them if they did think I was lying. But in the short time we were together the half could not be told.

Night. Marching orders. Three days' cooked rations and ten days' raw, to be packed for an early start tomorrow. Wardwell and his friend stay with us tonight.

May 12, 1863.
"Pass Man Shak," or South Pass, La.
Tuesday.
We left camp in charge of an officer and the convalescents and

marched out on the plain about a mile, where a train stood waiting early this morning, and after a short ride stopped here, the most God-forsaken looking place I have yet seen. It is a sort of connecting link between Lake Ponchetrain and Lake Marapaugh.[1] Our regiment and the 6th Michigan came. We soon came to the woods we had so often looked at from camp, and from that on it was one unbroken forest of the biggest and tallest trees I have yet seen. There was water in pools all along and on every hand as far as can be seen.

The railroad is built on piles driven in the mud, sawed off on a line and huge hewn timbers laid on them to support the ties and track. Not a foot of dry ground anywhere and not a ray of sunshine could get through. But mosquitoes, I thought we had them in camp, but we did not.

It was only the skirmish line; the main body is here. I am writing this with one hand while the other is waving a bush to keep them from eating me alive. The men were ferried across on a small steamer and they went on out of sight, scrambling over the ties as best they could, for in places the woodwork has been burned out and then they had to climb down and wallow through the mud and then up on the ties again until the last of them were out of sight.

I have really no business to be here as the captain objected, fearing I would be more bother than I was worth. Dr. Andrus was not even consulted. When the train started I could not resist the temptation to go and I swung on and here I am with the quartermaster and the commissary stores, which are to go up the pass to where the men have gone. There is a large space planked over, and we are in the dry and waiting for the boat to come for us. Men are busy rebuilding the burned out places in the trestlework and bridging the river, which is narrow here. Everyone calls it a "pass," but it has quite a current and is a river just the same.

May 13, 1863.

We heard firing this morning and think the boys may be at work. A man came back about midnight last night. How he ever did it I don't see, but he said two soldiers fell through the trestlework and were hurt and had to be left behind.

10 a. m. The men who got hurt have crawled back and are here, just bruised up a little. I guess they didn't try very hard or they might have gone on.

---

1. Spelled as they sound.

2 p. m. Another straggler has come back and says the boys captured fourteen Indians after a short skirmish. They are being sent back under guard and will soon be here. Here they come, and a tough-looking lot they are; fourteen of them are said to be Indians, but they look more like plain niggers to me. There are three white men. Rebels I suppose, but they don't act like very ferocious ones.

May 14, 1863.

We slept in a drizzling rain, but the mosquitoes kept us so busy we took no cold. A boat came in the morning and we loaded the stores and started up the river, reaching a small lake called Lake Marapaugh (don't know how these names are spelled, so put them down according to sound), which is rather a widening of the river than a lake. The river is narrow and very crooked. The boat would run up to a bank, send a rowboat across with a line, which was made fast to a tree and the boat turned around a corner. This was done many times on the way up. Alligators lay on fallen trees and on the bank and many were swimming in the river. One came close to the bow of a barge which was lashed to the steamboat, and I hit him a whack on the snout with a piece of coal. From his actions he didn't like it. The water and the land seem to be on the same level. The tall cypress trees grow thick all the way and no opening appeared of any size. Some trees hang over the water so it was all we could do to get past and one did sweep the commissary's scales overboard.

We finally came to hard ground and the live oaks and other trees took the place of the cypress, which only seems to grow in wet ground. A curious thing about the cypress is the way the roots grow up out of the ground. Cypress knees, they call them. They grow straight up, sometimes as high as ten feet and all the way down from that. No branches or shoots grow from them and they vary in size as much as in height. We finally tied up at a place called Wadensburgh, a small village which proved to be the end of our journey by water. Sergeant Drake and a couple of men went back in a boat and were fortunate enough to hook onto the scales that were lost and bring them up. In getting ashore I landed right beside a cotton-mouth moccasin snake, said to be as poisonous as a rattlesnake. He lay in some weeds and raised up as if to strike at me. I still had hold of a pole I had used to jump off with, and with it I hit him and broke his back.

A man standing by told me what it was. Quartermaster Mace, who came up with the regiment, soon appeared with some teams and as soon as loaded we started for Ponchatoula, where the regiment is. It was dark when we started. It was said to be three and a half miles, but they were long ones. We got stuck in the mud, the wagon broke down, and we were wet to the skin with rain before we reached our destination. We had no lights and only knew we were in the road because we were not in the bushes which grow thick along it. We reached Ponchatoula about ten o'clock, wet, tired and hungry, but not cold, for the weather is quite warm. Our coming alarmed the guards and the entire force turned out to receive the enemy. We lay down on the floor of an empty building, and wet as we were, slept sound until morning.

The sun shone bright the next morning, May 15th, and as soon as our joints began to limber up, hunted for and found Company B. They are in good spirits and have enjoyed the outing from camp very much. But they were glad when the cook called them up for coffee and hard-tack. The ground is high and dry for this country. A pine forest of immense trees is close by on one side and in sight everywhere. The Jackson & Mississippi R. R. goes through here, and is the one that the troops came on, A picket line is somewhere outside and cavalry videttes outside of that. Fresh beef is plenty and there is now and then a chicken. The people are as civil and respectful as can be expected, when we remember what a lot of uninvited guests they are called upon to entertain.

May 16, 1863.

A cavalryman came in for a horse this morning, his having been killed in the night. We heard firing in the night, but it seemed a long way off. Company B went on the picket line this morning and I find being commissary in camp and being commissary in the field are two different things. The company must be fed no matter where they are. I got hold of a horse and cart and with it made the rounds. A couple of cavalrymen who were wounded during the night have been brought in. At night a report came that a rebel detachment had got past the vidette guard and would most likely be heard from before morning. Orders are being given out and ours is to stand fast in case of an attack. That sounds easy at any rate.

May 17, 1863.

No attack came. The only enemies that found us were the mosquitoes and how they did punish us! My hands, face and ankles are swollen full, and this when I was awake all night and fighting them off in every way I could think of. Seventeen prisoners have just been brought in and after a feed started on toward Pass Man Shak.

May 18, 1863.

There has been much shifting about today. Orderlies riding here and there, and a move of some sort is the next thing to look for. Have orders to be ready with coffee and a day's cooked rations. That doesn't mean a long journey.

Later. The quartermaster's stores have gone towards Wadensburgh.

May 19, 1863.
Night. Camp Parapet again.

We started from Ponchatoula about 4 a. m. and at 11 reached Pass Man Shak, by way of the railroad. The trestlework is burned in places and across these we passed the best we could. One man dropped a frying pan he had stolen, and in getting it stirred up an alligator, and decided he didn't want the frying pan after all. Several fell and were more or less hurt, but we all came through and were nearly the rest of the day being taken across in small boats. Then without mishap we came on to a point opposite camp and were soon here. The trip has done me a world of good. I don't ask any odds of any now that I am well again. I guess I only needed parboiling, and that I got sleeping in clothes soaking wet. The men are all feeling fine and the stories they are telling such as did not go are wonderful to hear.

May 20, 1863.
Camp Parapet, La.

We settled down early last night and on account of the little sleep we had had were not called this morning. I slept right through the night and until after twelve today, then found orders for another move. Must get two days' rations ready right away. I wonder where we go this time.

Chapter 8

Port Hudson, La.

May 21, 1863.

We left Camp Parapet about eight last night and marched to Carrolton, only a mile or two below camp, where we stopped in the street. Getting no further orders we, one after another, sat down and finally lay down on the cobblestone pavements and slept till morning. We then went on board a steamer, the United States, lying at the dock and found it crammed full of soldiers. We soon cut loose and started up stream, and as we passed Camp Parapet, I wondered if it would ever be our home again. Lieutenant Pierce is in command, and says Captain B. has left us to become major for a negro regiment. Some are glad and some are sorry, but all are indignant at his way of going off. Never as much as said goodbye. Sneaked off in the night, it is said, and it looks like it. Maybe he feared we would remind him of his many voluntary promises that he would never leave Company B as long as a man was left in it.

At noon I asked one of the boat crew if it was possible to buy or beg a cup of coffee and he took me to the forecastle and gave me a full dinner. Up the river we went until night and then began to look for a spot big enough to lie down on.

May 22, 1863.
Friday morning.

We awoke from the little sleep we were able to get and found ourselves at anchor opposite Baton Rouge. The dropping of the anchor nearly scared the life out of me. I slept under a built up portion of the deck where the anchor chain lay coiled and when it went out it made a terrible racket. I wonder none of us were hit by it, for every space around it was occupied by a sleeping soldier. The city lies on high ground, which gave us a pretty good view of it. There seems to be a few fine buildings, but the most are small and not over two or three stories high.

About 9 a. m. we went alongside the steamer *Creole* and got some rations, which we needed badly. We soon started, still going upstream and felt certain Port Hudson would be our next stopping-place. We stopped finally and landed in the woods. Not a foot of cleared land in sight. There are four regiments here with ours. The Sixth Michigan, Fifteenth New Hampshire and a negro regiment. Boats kept coming and unloading all the afternoon. The Indiana Mule Battery is here and it appeared to be a gathering-place for all sorts of troops. It rained most of the afternoon, but it rained warm water, so we didn't mind it. The troops all moved forward during the night, leaving only a guard for the commissary and quartermaster's stores.

May 23, 1863.

In the morning Isaac Mitchell and I set out to find the 128th. We followed the road, which was now a quagmire, but were met by an ambulance with wounded men and a cavalry guard, who told us that only an armed force could get through and that it was eight miles to where our brigade was then. We decided to wait. The wounded were put on the *Sallie Robinson,* to be taken to some hospital. About midnight the mortar fleet, which is farther upstream, began firing and made a noise worse than several Fourths of July. We could follow the shells by the burning fuse, which looks like a shooting star. This we see first, then hear the boom of the mortar, then the hiss of the shell through the air and last the explosion when it strikes the ground.

Sunday night. A team for the quartermaster's stores came early and we were all day getting through to the regiment. Soldiers covered the ground. I have no idea how many there were. We were near the breastworks, but a belt of timber hid our view of them. We were in a clearing maybe one-half mile square, with woods on all sides. There was a house near us, the only building in sight.

May 25, 1863.
Monday morning.

We had orders to advance last night and our brigade formed in column, where we remained all night, and where we are yet. One by one we dropped down and went to sleep on the grass, where the dew soon soaked one side while the wet ground soaked the other. A man lying near me jumped up and raved around like a crazy man; he kept pawing at his ear as if in great pain. A doctor sleeping near was soon at him and found a bug had crawled into his ear. After the sun had dried us off we began to look for rations. The mail soon after came, and I had two letters. One of them contained a photograph of my dear old father and mother. I won't try to tell how rejoiced I am to have this with me. I don't think either of them ever had one taken before. Dear old couple, how glad I am they cannot see their boy and his surrounding's just now!

Night. Lots of powder has been burned today, but Port Hudson is still there. Our brigade has been skirmishing and one of the Sixth Michigan is wounded. Roads are being cut through the woods, and everything looks and acts as if business would soon begin. It does no good to ask questions, no one seems to know any more than I do, and I only know what goes on right close by me. Generals with their staffs are racing about, and everything is in a whirl. Evidently something is going to happen. All sorts of rumours are in the air. Human nature shows even here. Some news gatherers seem to know all about it, but I notice that what happens rarely agrees with their predictions. One of Company B, I won't write his name, is nearly scared to death. The doctor says he will die of fright if kept in the ranks. Another is nearly as badly off, and he has been the biggest brag of all; has hungered and thirsted for a chance to fight and now that he has it, has wilted. I hope he will be kept at it. I have often envied him his courage, but I shall never do it again. I don't deny that I am a coward, but I have so far succeeded in keeping it to myself.

The 128th is nearest the point where the road enters the woods in the direction of the biggest noise. The skirmishers that have been down this road say it soon reaches the corner of another open field; that a house and outbuildings are on the side next the fortifications and only a short distance from them; that rebel sharpshooters are in those buildings and it is they who are picking off every man that sticks his nose out of the woods on that side. From one of the Sixth Michigan who was on the skirmish line I have such a vivid description I have mapped out what he says is about the thing.

Every now and then a shell comes tearing through the woods, and so far, in the direction of the 128th. None of them have yet burst, but from an examination I made of one, they are intended to. This one was perfectly round and painted black. A big screw head shows on one side, and is turned off smooth with the shell. It is about six inches in diameter. It hit the ground beyond us and rolled up against the foundation of the house I have mentioned and stopped. It was then I examined it.

Later. Just as I had written the above, one did burst right over Company B. The pieces, however, kept on in the same direction the shell was going and no one was hit or hurt. Such dodging though I never saw, and I didn't see all of it at that. Myself and two others were filling our canteens from a kettle of coffee which sat on the ground near a big tree. When we heard the shell coming through the tree tops we expected it would go past as all the others had done. But it burst when right over us. We all jumped for the tree, and our heads came together with a bang. The first thing I saw was stars, and the next was men all over the field dodging in every direction. This was our first experience under fire. One could not laugh at another, for so far as I could see all acted alike.

Later. They keep coming, and we dodge less and less. If they keep at it long enough I suppose we shall get used to it, as we have to a great many other things. A cavalryman went down the road marked with an arrow, and his horse has just come back without him.

Night. About 5 p. m. a detachment from another regiment and Companies A, C, H and I from ours, went down this same road, and soon the most infernal racket began. They drove the rebels out of the "Slaughter House," and set fire to every building there. (The man who owned the house is named Slaughter). Only one man was wounded, but Captain Gifford of Company A has not returned, and we fear the Rebs got him. The house near us has been taken for a hospital. From appearances we will need it. Our brigade remains where first halted, but troops of all kinds are constantly on the move about us, some going one way and some another. It is plain that a general movement is soon going to be made. It seems to me as if all of Uncle Sam's army must be here, there are so many. The 128th is only a small affair just now. We have thought our brigade was about all there was of it, and that that was largely composed of the 128th New York. I will put up my diary, and get what sleep I can with all this confusion about me.

May 27, 1863.

Was awake early. In fact was often awake all night long. No news of Captain Gifford yet. His men have searched everywhere it is possible to go, and we think he must have been captured, just how, none of his company can imagine, for he was with them all through the squabble at the Slaughter house, and himself gave the order to fall back. Heavy firing is heard to the right and left of us. This must keep the Rebs in our front busy, for no shot or shell have yet come our way. Commissary sergeants have orders to be ready with rations all the time. It looks as if the fight would be over and the 128th have no hand in the taking of Port Hudson.

Later. The noise grows louder all the time. A general assault on Port Hudson must be what is going on, and Dow's Brigade seems to be forgotten. On the right and left, as far as sound can be heard, there is heavy artillery firing, and now and then the rattle of musket firing gets through the noise of the bigger guns.

May 28, 1863.

There was too much going on yesterday for me to write any more. Dow's Brigade was not forgotten. Soon after noon it went through the woods to the open space beyond, and was soon in the thickest of the fight. The guns in our front, that had sent us no message all the forenoon, soon began to send them rattling through the tree tops again. We non-combatants were in a terrible suspense. Finally my curiosity got the better of my fears and I started after them, for I wanted to see what a real battle was like. When I got to the cleared space I saw very little but smoke. I met a wagon with a wounded man on the seat with the driver, his face covered with blood, which ran over it from a wound on his head. He was mad clear through, and swore vengeance on the Rebs, when he got at them again. In the wagon, lying on his back, was another who was groaning terribly, but so far as I could see was not likely to die from his wounds, for only a little finger was gone from one hand, which he tenderly held up with the other. I was glad to note he did not belong to the 128th.

I ventured on and came upon Sergeant Bell of Company G standing beside the dead body of Colonel Cowles. Bell said the colonel was killed when the Rebs first opened on them, his uniform making him a marked man. Bell said he was near him when he fell and helped him to a sitting position, turning him about, as he said he wanted to die facing the enemy. Captain Keese of Company C was also near when the colonel was hit and was directed to take command. Several others lay around where they had fallen. Venturing on I came to the magnolia grove in which the Slaughter mansion stood. Company B was here, in support of a section of the Indiana Mule Battery. Having nothing to do but defend the battery, if an attempt was made to capture it, they were lying close to the ground behind the big trees. The battery was shelling the Rebs, and the Rebs were shelling the battery, and the shot or shells had furrowed the ground.

The boys said Philip Allen and Sergeant Kniffin were both badly wounded, and had been taken off the field. Riley Burdick, our orderly sergeant, was missing, as were several others. I could see nothing of the rebel works for the smoke, but the noise was deafening. As it might be an all-night job, I decided to go back and try and get something for them to eat. I got back as fast as I could and with the cooks started with a big kettle of coffee and some hard-tack. We kept in the edge of the woods to a point nearest the company and at right angles to the line of fire and then I scuttled across with the coffee. After passing it around I returned for the hard-tack, and was giving them out when a shell came through, hitting the ground and throwing dirt all over us. Soon another one came, hitting a big tree a glancing blow, and went on into the woods beyond. The sergeant of the battery said he could see the flash and would sing out, which would give me time to fall before the shell got there, and I legged it for all I was worth.

About halfway across he yelled, and I tried to fall, but before I hit the ground the thing was beyond me. In fact it didn't come very near me. I was going at right angles to the line of fire, and might have known they couldn't see me for the smoke, and would not waste a big shell on one man. The musket firing was on lower ground and nearer the breastworks, but I only knew by the popping of the rifles and what the boys told me, for the smoke hid everything. We got back just in time to see the doctors fix up a shattered shin bone for General Sherman. He lay on a stretcher and was talking constantly, though the doctors said he knew nothing and felt nothing. From the hole in his leg, something bigger than a bullet had gone through it. They pulled out the loose pieces of bone with pincers, taking hold and yanking at every end that showed. Then they ran their fingers in and felt for more. Finally they stuffed it full of cotton to stop the blood and then bound it up with long strips of muslin. The firing grew less and less, but the wounded came faster and faster.

Colonel Cowles's body was sent under a guard to the landing, on its way to New Orleans, where it will be made ready to send home. Sergeant Bell went with it, taking his sword, watch, and other personal effects, also his dying message, "Tell my mother I died with my face to the enemy." General Dow, our brigadier, was shot in the foot and taken to the house right by us. George Story is detailed for his bodyguard. One of the boys said the Rebs began at the wrong end of the general. The dead soldiers were left where they fell. After we got settled down and the excitement began to wear off the question of something to eat came up. The boys on duty at the front would be hungry by morning, and we wondered if we couldn't find something more filling than hard-tack. John Pitcher had found out that not far away some Irish potatoes were growing and big enough to eat; also that directly behind the house where General Dow was nursing his foot was a yard with a high board fence around it, with two blood-hounds on guard inside, and that along one side of it was a bench upon which were several hives of bees, and that a gate or door in the fence opened out, and only a little way from the end of the bench. We got a rope from the quartermaster sergeant and set out.

The potatoes were easy—simply had to crawl into the patch and dig with our fingers until our haversacks were full. The bees, however, were not so easy on account of the dogs. As they had barked pretty much all the time since we landed in the neighbourhood, no one came from the house to see about it. We found they would follow on their side of the fence wherever we went on ours. John then went along the fence, and the dogs followed, leaving me at the gate. When they were at the farthest side, I opened the gate and having made a slip-noose in the rope, I had just time to slip it over the nearest bee-hive and get out before they were there. I kept still and soon John had them on his side of the yard again, when by quick work I yanked the hive through the gate and closed it before they got to me.

The hive had landed on its top, and the bees and honey, were all smashed together. But enough of them could crawl to make it lively for us before we got the mixture into a mess pan. We were stung several times before we got home, but we got there and all hands had a feast of hard-tack and honey. We had no way to strain the bees out, so we spread bees and honey on the hard-tack and then picked the bees off as well as we could. As it was, I got a stinger in my tongue, which soon began to swell. It kept on until I was afraid I would need a doctor and in that way give the whole thing away. But it finally stopped and by morning I was all right again. This brings us up to this morning, May 29th.

May 29, 1863.
The big guns' firing began early. The detail from Company B was relieved and all evidences of honey and potatoes were soon out of sight. General Dow sent out to know who had stolen the honey, but

no one knew anything about it. Philip Allen died during the night. The wounded were carted off on their way to some hospital. Sergeant Kniffin was badly wounded in the head, and it is doubtful if he lives.

About 8 a. m. an agreement was made to stop fighting until 2 p. m., so the dead can be picked up and buried.

Orderly Burdick's body was found and some others who had been reported missing. The Rebs say Captain Gifford is a prisoner in Port Hudson. We were glad to know he is alive and well, for we will get him when we get the place. Lieutenant-Colonel Smith came up from the city and took command. He called the regiment together in the woods and made a little speech, some of which was good and some of which seemed uncalled for. He said he had been told that some of the men hid behind trees and stumps, and, turning to the officers said, "If you catch any of them doing that again, shoot them down." Then he added, "I have also been told that some of the officers hid themselves in that same way," and, turning to the men, said, "If you catch them doing that again, shoot them down." That evened up matters, so we gave him a good hearty "hurrah." Then he said, "Heretofore guards have been posted to keep you from running off, but that won't happen while I command. You can go where you want to, but God help you if you are not here when I want you."

The 128th was stationed in the edge of the woods facing" the rebel works, to support the Indiana Battery, which had been scattered along in the bushes. There being no smoke I was able to get a better understanding of the lay of land than yesterday. The grove that stood about the Slaughter house is directly in our front, where the ground begins to slope towards the rebel breastwork, and that accounts for the shells hitting the ground where we were yesterday, and then going high over our sleeping-quarters. The breastwork looks like a big pile of dirt. In shape it is most like the letter U, with the curved end towards us and running up hill each way from us, so that the ground inside is plainly in sight for some distance. There is great activity there as well as on our side, and I suppose both are taking advantage of the lull in firing to get in the best position when it begins again.

By asking questions, and by keeping my eyes open I have learned that for miles in front of the fortifications the Rebels were scattered before we came. They had rifle pits, which are nothing but ditches, deep enough so that the ditch and the dirt thrown from it will hide a man when standing up. They also had mud forts, which are like the rifle pits, only wider, and had big guns in them, intending to whip us before we got near the main works. Our advance had some sharp fighting to drive them out of these and into the main fortification, where they were before I saw the place. That accounts for the wounded men that were sent back before we left Springfield Landing,

May 30, 1863.

The Rebs shelled our quarters at night and we were ordered back to our old sleeping ground. Bill Snyder and I had such a good place behind a big tree that we staid there and slept sound all night, although a big chunk of bark was knocked off the tree in the night, and our gunners kept up a steady fire all night long. This shows that my reputation as a sound sleeper has not suffered. About 8 o'clock our guns dismounted the rebel gun that has been our greatest pest, and have twice since that knocked it down just as they had it almost in position. We have nothing to do but lay here and swap yarns with the battery men. From all I can learn, someone has made a big blunder, and a great many lives and a great deal of expense to Uncle Sam is directly chargeable to it. It appears a general assault all along the line was planned to come off early on the morning of the 27th. General Weitzel on the right began the charge on time, and the Rebels massed all their forces against him. When they had nicely disposed of him, the left under General Augur went in and they, too, were cut up and driven back.

The centre, under General Sherman, about the middle of the afternoon went in and took their medicine. This plan of attack allowed the Rebs to shift from one point to another, and whip us by detail. What would have happened if we had all charged at the same time none of us know for sure, but we all think Port Hudson would now be ours. Reports say the 128th lost two officers and twenty men killed, and the whole army about 300 killed and 1500 wounded. It doesn't seem possible that so much lead and iron could have been fired at us and so few men killed and wounded. The mules and horses killed were left where they fell. The stench is awful, and seems to be getting worse all the time. Great birds, as big as hen turkeys, are tearing them to pieces; turkey buzzards, they call them, and in fact they look just like turkeys at a little distance. They are not afraid of us, but keep coming and going, quarrelling among themselves over the choice bits. General Dwight now commands Sherman's division, and Colonel Clark, of the Sixth Michigan, takes General Dow's place in our brigade. The Sixth Michigan and the 128th New York have been so much together that we have come to be like one big family and are fast friends.

May 31, 1863.
Sunday, p. m.

This morning a foraging party, made up of a squad from each company, went outside, on Port Hudson Plains, a beautiful country, to try for some fresh meat. I managed to get on the detail from Company B, We had the quartermaster's wagon to bring in what we might find. We soon got separated, and each detail going its own way, that from Company B were lucky enough to come upon and shoot down a two-year-old heifer. We dressed the animal and strung the hindquarters on a pole and started back, leaving a man to watch the rest until the wagon came around. We lugged the beef home and it was soon being cooked, some of it in the kettles and some on the ends of ramrods stack in the fire. After we were full we began to feel generous, and invited in our friends until only the bones were left. We sent some in to General Dow, and asked Colonel Smith and the other officers to have some. Nobody refused, not even General Dow, who is so dead set against foraging.

About noon the wagon came in and the whole regiment had a feast. I never tasted anything so good as that chunk of beef roasted in the fire. This does not reflect on your cooking, mother. You never let me get so hungry as Uncle Sam has. No doubt you would make it taste even better than it did. I did not know I was so hungry until I began to eat. It tasted so good I was actually sorry when I could eat no more. There are lots of things I have not written about, and now that my crop is full, and there is nothing else to do, I will try and catch up.

In the first place, I must say that this region is headquarters for snakes. I don't suppose there is a spot on earth where there are so many snakes to the acre as right here. We have cleared them off from our near neighbourhood, but go in any direction on ground that is not occupied and there they are. The most common is the moccasin; two kinds, one with a white mouth, called cottonmouth moccasins and said to be poisonous. The other looks just like our water snakes at home. Black snakes and king snakes come next, the latter the nearest to handsome of any snake I ever saw. They are of a pepper-and-salt colour, and grow large, those I have seen being between five and six feet long and large in proportion. They are said to be deadly enemies to all other snakes and that they kill and eat any of the other kinds.

Several rattlesnakes have been killed, but I have only seen one. That was lying across a path we had made through the weeds, and I came near stepping on it. Just as one foot was coming down I saw him, and managed someway to jump clear over him from the one foot that was on the ground. I have tried to make such a jump since, but cannot go half so high or so far as I did then. I hunted up a club and hit him across the back, when I first found out that some rascal had killed him, cut off his tail and then placed him across the path to scare some other fellow. I left him there to scare someone else. Then all over and everywhere are a sort of lizard that they call chameleons. They change colour, taking on the shade of anything they are on. They are as spry as squirrels, and seem to enjoy running over us when we lie down and then darting up a tree, or off through the bushes.

There are some mosquitoes, but they are not nearly so plenty or so bloodthirsty as in other places we have been. The meanest thing is a small black bug, just like what we call at home snapping bugs. Their delight is to crawl in someone's ear when asleep. We sleep with cotton in our ears every night. They make a man raving crazy. The doctors pour oil in first, and then syringe them out. Nearly every night there is a bug case. The woods are full of squirrels. I have seen black squirrels, gray squirrels and a fox squirrel, all in sight at one time. The blacks and grays are very common. The one fox squirrel I saw was about as big as a half-grown cat. The blacks are between our red squirrels and grays for size.

Blackberries, the high bush kind, are ripe here now and are plenty, but we have to go farther and farther to get them, on account of there being so many pickers. There are plenty of magnolia trees right here in the woods about us. They are in bloom now, though the blossoms are so high up we can get none. After a shower the scent is so strong as to be sickening. The trees are like our large forest trees. The leaves are long but not very wide, are a sort of brown on the underside, but the deepest dark green on top. We have some hard thunderstorms. The loudest thunder crashes and the sharpest lightning flashes I ever saw. Lying in the woods as we do, it is strange none of the trees are struck or that nobody is killed. We are soaked to the skin on an average once every day, sometimes several times in one day and night. We have only the clothes on our backs, so we make no changes.

If the sun shines we sometimes wring out and hang on a bush for awhile. But it is so warm we don't mind it. Some have blankets. Everyone is supposed to have one, but many got lost, mine among the number. I don't much care, for now I don't have to lug it about. Wet or dry we take no cold. We are tough as grain-fed horses and in fact we sometimes have to endure what a horse could not. God is good to us, otherwise we could not live and thrive as we do.

Night. A new style of a fighting machine has just gone from here, on its way to the right wing. There were two light carriages, upon each of which were mounted twenty-four rifle barrels, all made to be loaded and fired by one operation of a lever. Goodbye Johnnies when they get at you. It is too dark to write more.

June 1, 1863.

Monday. The artillery keeps up an irregular firing, and now and then the Rebs reply. Major Bostwick and the negro troops are busy every night digging rifle pits, and today there is what looks like a fort, which must have been built in the night, and from which there is firing today. We hear today General Sherman has died of his wounds.

One or two of Company B are on the sick list. I wish they would hurry up and do something, for the more there is going on, the better we all feel.

June 2, 1863.

Tuesday.

Another day of doing nothing. A man got up this morning and found a big king snake had crawled up close to his back for warmth, and was fast asleep yet when the man got up. Once this would have made a commotion in camp, but little was thought of it, and Mr. Snake was scared off into the bushes to look up and breakfast on some other snake.

June 3, 1863.

Wednesday.

The artillery kept firing all night, and the mortar fleet, which is said to be right opposite us, also sent shell after shell over into the works. The Rebs got real careless too, and fired right at our sleeping quarters. They seem to have a better range on us than ever before. I got behind my tree and went to sleep again. One of Company G was hit and badly hurt, and it is said a man farther down the line had both legs shot off.

June 4, 1863.

Thursday.

Last night we had another serenade. No one was hurt so far as I can find out. The regiment was routed out again and moved back to the other side of the woods, on account of the shot and shell which have a way of coming right at us lately. I stuck to my big tree, for although it has been hit two or three times, nothing can ever go through it. The day has passed like the others lately, with nothing to do but loaf about. Two deserters came out of the woods across the field in our front. They say there is but little in Port Hudson to eat, and a great many there to eat it, and that they will eat themselves out soon, even if not another gun is fired.

June 5, 1863.
Friday.
The mail went out today and I sent a letter, also my diary up to this time. The Rebs have done all the shooting today. Why our side don't answer I don't know. I expect something is going on, maybe getting up a surprise party. I hope it may surprise the enemy worse than the other did. Deserters came out again this morning. They sneak out during the night and hide in the bushes until daylight and then come in. They are first fed and then sent to the landing, and I suppose to some prison down the river. They all tell the same story, that Port Hudson must soon surrender on account of fodder giving out. The Rebs have been shooting a new kind of shot at us today. I got hold of one that held together and will describe it. There are six iron plates about a half inch thick, with a small hole in the middle and a row of larger holes about halfway from the centre to the outside.

In these larger holes are cast iron balls, held in place between the plates by the larger holes, and the whole thing held together by a rod through the centre holes. The plates are round and fit the bore of the gun. They make a different and much louder noise going through the air than anything else that has come our way. But like the others, they do little more than trim the trees about us. Colonel Smith thinks the cook fires show through the trees, and give them our range, so he has ordered them back out of sight.

June 6, 1863.
Saturday.
Nothing more than usual has happened today, but it is plain to see that preparations are being made for a move of some sort. Artillery, infantry and cavalry are constantly on the move. Officers are riding helter-skelter in every direction, and everything and everybody seems to be busy but ourselves. So long as the battery is not attacked we have

only to look on. If that should happen, my diary might read different, if it read at all. We lie here doing nothing but eat, sleep and guess what is going on. Whatever it is, is kept mighty secret, for we have ways of finding out most everything but what the next move will be. Some firing today, but not as much as for the past few days.

June 7, 1863.
Sunday.

Lieutenant Pierce has gone off sick. This leaves Sergeant Hummiston in command of Company B. He is a good fellow and no doubt will give a good account of himself. The day has been a busy one. Just as if the final preparations for some great move were being made. We all expect it tomorrow. Now while I have a chance I must tell how a snake scared me today. Some of the boys told of great big blackberries about a mile out, and we went for them. They were even bigger than we were told, and we ate all we could, and put some in our haversacks for the rest. An old rail fence ran into the bushes, which were thick for a rod or more on each side. We walked the fence, holding onto the bushes, and picking as we went. I happened to be the farthest in, and seeing some that looked even better than any we had yet found, I kept crawling along on the rickety old fence until I was out of sight from the rest. Just as I was going to quit, I saw such a big bunch that I could not resist getting them.

The bush was high above me and I could only reach a leaf by which I gently pulled it down until I got a better hold, and almost had the berries within reach when a great big black head and neck raised up and looked right at me. If my eyes did not magnify, the head was as big as my fist, and such part of the neck as I saw was as big as my wrist. I had only my bare hands to fight with, and was at a terrible disadvantage on the top of that shaky old fence, with no place to jump off for a long ways. I was scared nearly out of my senses. I let the bush go back in the same careful manner in which I had pulled it down, and then made my way out as fast as I could go, which by the way seemed awfully slow to me.

What the snake did, or what became of him, I don't know. I saw the last of him as the bush came between us. I made the mistake of telling how big the snake was. The boys were ready to believe I had seen one, for they said my looks showed I had seen something, but when I told its size they rolled on the ground and laughed. The idea of such a thing as I described lying on the top of a blackberry bush was too much for them. I don't know what he lay on nor do I care. All I know is that he was there. What held him up was of no consequence to me. He was the biggest snake I ever saw by all odds, and I don't yet think I stretched the story at all. But the boys added to it every time they told it. It is going about with all the variations they can think of. It is the first real good one they have had on me, so let them go it. If the expected battle comes off tomorrow it is time to go to bed, so here goes.

June 8, 1863.
Monday.
No more signs of a battle than there have been for a week back. I may as well finish up my snake story, for there is nothing else in the air. The wind-up was the most exciting part of it. I dreamed about it as soon as I was asleep. Many of us have bush houses to sleep in. Bill Snyder and I were partners in one. We had set up poles against our big tree, and covered them with weeds and bushes, leaving a hole on one side to crawl in. I crawled in first and was soon asleep. Just as Bill was crawling in, the snake, which I had seen coming for me for hours, it seemed to me, made a jump and landed on me. I jumped, and at the same time gave a yell that aroused the whole regiment, and the boys say was heard on the picket lines. I went clear over Snyder, who grabbed, and got hold of me just as I was diving into the bushes outside. The first I knew I was being shaken so my teeth rattled.

It was some time before we got settled down again. The snake let me alone after that. The boys say the snake did come, and it was to pay me for lying so about him. The Rebs made a move last night farther to the left, and came outside their works in quite a body. After a short but rather sharp skirmish they went back and staid there. The mail has come and I had six letters and three papers. Good news from home, or at least no bad news. Am glad enough to hear from them and to know they are well. One letter was from John, and from its tone he is well and feeling fine. The 150th is still in Baltimore.

June 9, 1862.
Tuesday.
All quiet yet. Now and then a shell comes out of the rebel works, I suppose to let us know they are still there. We are waiting for the signal to go at them. Things have settled down, as if the troops were all in position. I went down along the left wing today, but could see nothing but soldiers. There are enough here to take Port Hudson, if numbers

can do it, and why it isn't done none of us can imagine.

June 10, 1863.
Wednesday.

There has been considerable firing along the lines both to the right and left of us. From all I can find out, we, on the centre, are the nearest to the rebel works of any, and our batteries are able to keep them inside. Both to the right and left there seems to be a strip of disputed ground, occupied by both sides, who are entrenched in rifle pits, which each side keeps pushing forward, and it is the fighting over these that we hear most every night. Last night they fired on our position for awhile, and at one time they came so fast my bedfellow left me and went back with the regiment. But my old tree had not failed me yet, and I was not going back on it, so I staid and slept like a baby through what, by the looks of the trees and limbs, was quite a sharp cannonading.

June 11, 1863.
Thursday.

About three this morning one of the hardest showers we have had broke right over us, and we were nearly drowned. So much water ran down the tree that I thought I was going to be washed away. So I crawled out and found that by standing up I did not catch half as much water as when lying down. But a little more or less made no difference, for I was soaked as wet as water could make me. The lightning was something awful and the thunder beat even the bombardment on the day of the fight. The lightning lit up the woods in great shape, and between flashes it was blackness itself. As soon as it was over and daylight came, we stripped and wrung the water out of our clothes, after which we had some hot coffee, which made it all right again. The batteries kept up their five-minute firing just as if the sun shone, and about the usual number of replies were made by the Johnnies. A detail from Company B and another from Company H had a wrangle over a spring where the Rebs had been getting water in the night. One of Company H was badly wounded. Deserters come out every morning, and all tell the same story, that Port Hudson is ours just as soon as we are a mind to go and take it.

A Wisconsin regiment marched past our quarters today going towards the left. Next the colours was a man with a pole like a flagstaff, on the top of which was a board about three feet square. The board was set on a slant and the staff appeared to run through it for a foot or so, and ended up with a short crosspiece, upon which sat a live eagle. He looked like a hawk, only larger. He had a chain on one leg, the other end of which was fast to his perch. Sometimes he would rise as high as the chain would allow, and fly along, no faster than the man walked. I quizzed one of the men, who said the eagle was given the regiment before it left home and that they had kept it with them ever since. That a man was detailed to carry and care for it, who had nothing else to do. There is something mysterious going to happen soon. Loads and loads of cotton bales are being piled up to the left of our position, and hundreds of picks and shovels and axes are stacked up near the cotton. I guess they are going to bury it.

June 12, 1863.
Friday.

A detail from our regiment was called out during the night, and this morning the mystery about the cotton is solved. They met other details near the cotton bales, and they rolled them out to within about twenty rods of the breastworks, and piled them up in fort shape. Then with picks and shovels they piled the dirt against them, others filling bags with dirt and piling them up where directed, and as directed. A "bomb proof" they call it. It is large enough to hold two or three regiments. These were marched in and it is up to them to hold the fort until night comes again, when guns are to be planted there. The Rebels did not know a thing of it until this morning, and then they banged away at it for a while, until our guns from above and below took their attention. The men kept there are safe enough from the Rebs, but the sun will roast them. There isn't a particle of shade, and the sun is a hot one in the middle of the day. It is reported that another cotton fort was built up on the right, in the same way.

One of our men got hit on the arm by another fellow's pick, otherwise no one was hurt. Deserters who came out this morning say there is great activity in Port Hudson these days, though food for man and beast is very scarce. It has been an unlucky day for Company B. One man shot his finger off and another cut off his big toe cutting wood for the cooks. The toeless man went to the hospital, but his toe has been going around from one to another and turning up in the most unexpected places. Just before night we were called together, and an order from General Banks' headquarters read to us.

In effect it said that the 128th New York Volunteers had so far performed their duties in such a manner as to give great satisfaction to the commanding general. That in the immediate future their duties would be still more hard and dangerous. That any member of it whose conduct in the past and in the future entitled him to promotion should receive it. It then went on to say that any violation of orders would call down speedy vengeance on our heads. That looks as if something was going to be done, and the 128th would have a hand in it.

June 13 1863.
Saturday.

The cotton fort, as we call it, was finished during the night. We were left alone, for a wonder. When the big guns were being mounted the Rebs made quite a time about it, firing every gun they could bring to bear on it. Also at the right, as well as farther to our left, there was heavy firing. It seems as if we are pretty well fixed for it in case another try is made. Much better than before. Besides, they have lost a great many men by desertion since then. Have just learned that two men and a horse were killed on our front, and that on our right there was a real stubborn fight over the gun planting.

P. m. About 10 o'clock a terrific fire from our new and old batteries began and lasted for an hour. So far as I could see not a rebel gun was fired in reply. The 128th was then given a taste of the dangerous duty spoken of in the order last night. They were marched out in front of the enemy and went through several evolutions like a battalion drill, the object being to draw the enemy's fire so our gunners could get their range. But it didn't work, for not a gun was fired at them, and they came back with the fife and drum playing a quickstep.

Later. A white flag is waving over the cotton fort. What it can mean none of us know.

Later still. It is said General Banks by way of the white flag has notified the Rebs to get all their women and children and non-combatants out of the way, as he intends advancing on their works tomorrow.

June 14, 1863.
Sunday.

The noisiest kind of a sermon is being preached here today. It has been a busy day. We served rations at 3 o'clock this morning and have orders to be ready for a change in position at any minute. That has kept us picked up and waiting, but up to this time, 9 a. m., have had no other orders. The 128th and the Twenty-Sixth Connecticut went off in the direction of Springfield Landing. The firing seems to be all along the line. The Rebs must have more guns than we thought, for they are talking back at a great rate.

11 a. m. Walter Orr has just come in with a thumb shot off. He says they went but a little way towards the landing before they came to a road leading to the left, and they went into action as skirmishers about a mile from here, through bushes and over rough ground. The rebel skirmish line lay hid in the bushes until our line was almost on them, and then rose up and fired right in their faces. Walt is the only one hurt on our side, so far as he knows.

June 15, 1863.
Monday.

As I heard no more about a move, and as the regiment did not show up, I set out to look them up. I got the best direction I could from Orr and went and went, and kept going, inquiring all the time for the 128th New York. No one seemed to know. The troops were all strangers. I could not even find our brigade. Darkness came and I was completely lost. The firing had about stopped, and men lay everywhere, some dead and the rest sleeping. I don't know what time it was when I gave up the search, but all at once I found myself completely tired out. I was following a path, and not daring to lay down in it, I crawled under a bush near it and in a minute was sleeping as sound as the rest.

When I awoke this morning the sun was shining. I lay still trying to get my wits to working again, and the first I remember was a great buzzing of flies behind me. I mistrusted a dead soldier was close by and upon getting up found two, a captain and a lieutenant, that had been laid there to keep them from being run over in the night. There was only a little picket shooting going on, everything else was resting up after the hard work of the day before. About 10 a. m. I found the 128th way down towards the river, and within musket shot of the rebel works. Walt Orr's thumb was the only loss to Company B, but several were wounded in the other companies. As this was to be our permanent quarters I hurried back to get the commissary stores ready to move.

June 16, 1863.
Tuesday.

In our new quarters on the field, I had just got back yesterday, and had a drink of coffee, when the adjutant rode up with orders to pack up, as the wagons would soon be there. I was so near played out that I gave the order and then went to sleep. Everything was loaded and ready for a start before I woke up, and we reached here in time for supper. When I get rested and slept out I will tell what sort of a place we are in, and how we got here.

June 17, 1863.
Wednesday.

We were nearly drowned again last night. One of the showers, such as only this place can get up, came down on us just as we dozing off. Every hollow became a puddle before the fellows sleeping in it could get out. The best thing about these downpours is, we don't have to dread them. We are soaking wet before we know it. Then they only last a short time, and the weather being hot we are not chilled. We stand around and growl for awhile and then settle down and are soon asleep again.

I have been to the river and had a swim, also washed out my clothes. We are near neighbours with the enemy now. Directly opposite us is their water battery, so called because it is near the river. Just beyond us, to the right, the ground is about covered with rifle pits belonging to both sides, and near enough together to talk across. Both sides are resting up I guess, for there is next to no firing today. A strip of road just beyond us, and where we had to go over when we came here, is open to the enemy's fire and they made us scratch yesterday. They are bad marksmen, for so far they have hit no one. The men crossing this open space are the only ones they have tried to shoot.

Night. An order—they call everything an order here—has just been read, calling for 1,000 volunteers to go into Port Hudson, or die in the attempt. A "*Forlorn Hope*," it is called. I believe it must be a joke. If the whole 19th Army Corps together can't get in, how can a thousand men expect to do it? The order congratulates the troops on their good behaviour, and the steady advance they have made on the enemy's works. We are at all points upon the enemy's threshold. "One more advance and they are ours." Then it calls upon the bold men of the corps to organize a storming party of a thousand men, to vindicate the Flag of our Union, and the memory of the defenders who have already fallen. Officers who lead the column shall be promoted, and the men composing the storming party shall each have a medal, and have their names put on the roll of honour. That is the substance of the order, which has raised the greatest sort of a commotion among us.

Later. Although we have until morning to decide, Company B has made up its mind not to try for the medals. We don't believe one thousand men can hope to do what all the thousands of the 19th Army Corps have twice failed to do. I wish General Banks and his army of advisers could have been at our conference, for we spoke our minds no matter who it hit. From the best evidence possible to get, *viz.*, the deserters that daily come out.

General Banks has at least ten men to the enemy's one. We could swarm over the breastworks on some dark night and bring every man in Port Hudson back with us. We wouldn't send them word to get ready, and have their guns pointed at us before we started, neither would we allow the cannon to bellow the news of our coming for an hour or two beforehand. This was done on May 27, and of the last attempt word was sent in by a flag of truce the day before. Companies G and E are of the same mind as Company B, so if any go from the 128th it must be from the other companies.

June 18, 1863.
Thursday.

Another squad of deserters came in this morning. I suppose they come in on other parts of the line just the same. This must weaken the enemy faster than our fighting has done. They all tell of hard times and short rations. The weather is hot, and a horrible stench comes from the dead horses and mules, which the buzzards are tearing' to pieces. There is scarcely any firing between the sharpshooters. The lines here are so close the men talk with each other, and have agreed to warn each other when the officers come around. At other times it is more like visiting than anything else. It is terribly hot in the rifle pits. I made the rounds today, and had a chat with a middle-aged Johnnie. He said we were not at all like they had been told, and there were some who believed we had horns on our heads, and had feet like cattle. Now that they know better they don't want to fight us, and will only do so when obliged to. Three men were sun-struck while in the trenches today.

June 19, 1863.
Friday.

Three more men knocked out today. One sunstruck and two wounded. The Rebs have men posted way back inside the works, with rifles having telescope sights, and it is these that do the mischief, rather than those in the rifle pits. Now that we are warned of these fellows, we must look sharp, and maybe then get a clip. This explains how a couple of balls whistled past me yesterday when no sound of a gun was heard.

June 20, 1863.
Saturday.

One of Company B, while poking about yesterday, had the good luck to shoot a cow, and last night he came in dragging as much of it as he could. So we have had another fill up and the world seems well with us now. I went for another swim in the river, and gave my clothes another washing. My one shirt has shrunk so I can hardly get into it. Not a button is left on it. The wristbands only come a little below my elbows, and the bottom only just reaches to my trousers. I have no way to tell how I look, but the others are about as black as the negro troops, and I suppose I must be *ditto*. The rifle pits are being extended and the Rebs are shoving theirs just as fast, each keeping about the same distance from the other. No shooting is done, a sort of agreement having been made not to fire on each other until another assault is made along the whole line.

June 21, 1863,
Sunday.

My diary says today is Sunday. If I have kept my reckoning right it is, but nothing else hints at its being the day set apart for rest. Directly in front of our sleeping quarters is a high knob or hill, and directly back of that is the water battery on ground just as high and only separated from it by a V-shaped hollow between. There are men making a road up that knob, and I think it is going to be fortified. The storming party is said to be full, and are to report at General Banks' headquarters tonight. It is said thirty-five go from the 128th. If all the regiments send a like number there will be several thousand instead of one, as was called for. Nearly half from this regiment are from Company C. Company A is next, with nine, and the rest are from the other companies, except B, G, and E, which send none. They go way up to the right of the line, but where they will make the attempt is not told, if it is known.

Captain Keese goes in command of the squad from the 128th, and with sixteen from his own Company C, nine from Company A, three from Company D, one from Company F, two from Company H, three from Company I, and two from Company K, making thirty-six in all. making a big showing from our regiment. We bid them goodbye, for some of them, and perhaps all, have gone on their last march. There are men left who have proved themselves just as brave as these have ever done. We don't all see it alike, that's all. We feel as if we had had a big funeral in the family, and are a sober set tonight.

June 22, 1863.
Monday.

Another drenching shower last night made our night miserable, though the sun soon dried us off this morning. A foraging party was sent out for fresh beef today, and came in minus one man, who it is supposed was picked up by guerrillas. Parties of them are said to be hovering about outside of our lines. The Rebs asked our pickets today when that thousand men was to come and get them. They would not tell how they knew of it, but perhaps General Banks has sent them word, as he has done of every move yet. No doubt the exact time and place will be told them by someone. I am more glad than ever now, that none of Company B went. The general opinion is now that the boys that have volunteered have been sacrificed, and that if the thing was to be tried over again, few, if any, would stir a step.

All quiet today except now and then a gun just to keep up appearances.

June 23, 1863.
Tuesday.

Another detail for foragers today. I made out to get on this time. The quartermaster's team goes to bring in the beef or mutton or whatever it is we may get.

June 24, 1863
Wednesday.

It is only by pure good luck that I am in my usual place of abode today, and able to write in my diary of yesterday's foraging expedition. A detail of three from each company set out with a four-mule team. We went until about opposite our old quarters, on the centre, and then turned towards Port Hudson Plain. We divided up into squads, Smith Darling, the drummer boy, and myself of Company B making one, and each hunting on our own hook. If firing was heard, it would indicate a kill, and the wagon was to come for the game. We found cattle, but they were wild, and very soon the Company B squad found itself alone and out of sight or hearing of the others.

Along in the afternoon we started to find our way back to camp and soon after came upon and shot a two-year-old steer. We fired our guns several times and then went to work and dressed the animal as well as we could with only our knives. We got the backbone apart and strung the hindquarters on a stake. Giving the drummer the liver and tongue, we started, hoping the wagon would pick us up on its way back. The country seemed new to us and we soon made up our minds we were lost, as likely to be going away from Port Hudson as towards it. Just about sundown we came in sight of a house, and before we got to it saw General Dow and George Story ride up. They dismounted, and the general went into the house, leaving George to put up the horses. George had pulled the saddle from his horse when we came up and hailed him. He was as glad to see us as we were to see him. He said the general was stopping there and his foot was getting well fast. He told us to take a path through the bushes and we would soon come to a negro shanty, where he thought we could trade some beef for an old mule the darkey had and so get the rest of the meat into camp.

Just then we heard the clank of sabres coming, and fearing it might be some hungry cavalry squad who would want us to divide, we got into the bushes as fast as we could. We were just nicely hidden when they dashed up. We heard them talking with Story and soon after heard them ride on down the road in the direction from which we had come. Why the general left the good quarters inside the lines for this out-of-the-way place is a query we don't understand. We soon reached a clearing and were able to trade a chunk of beef for an old gray mule. It was then dark, but with directions from the darkey we were able to strike the road to camp. Smith rode the mule with the beef strung across in front, and the drummer and I followed on with the liver and tongue.

When we were within a couple of miles of home a shower came upon us and soon soaked us through. The thunder and lightning was something awful, but except for the lightning I don't know how we would have kept the road. We reached camp at 10 o'clock, wet, tired and hungry enough to eat raw beef. The team with the rest of the foraging party had got in about dark, and until we came in, it was supposed some wandering squad of rebel cavalry had bagged us. Altogether we had a sufficient supply of beef to last us for some days.

June 25, 1863.
Thursday.
We have been listening and expecting to hear the beginning of the third attempt to take Port Hudson by storm. But the day has passed without any great excitement. Five deserters came in this morning, and said there was others that would come if they were sure of good, fair treatment. They had agreed upon a signal, which was to be a green

bush fastened upon the end of an old building close by. If the bush was put up it would mean they were well treated, otherwise they were to say nothing about the signal, and it would be a warning to their comrades to stay where they are.

A letter from Jane today. They have just heard where we are, and are very anxious. The newspapers have Banks' army all cut to pieces.

June 26, 1863.
Friday.

Lieutenant Pierce is half sick yet, and ought not to be here. He wished this morning he had some blackberries, so three of us got permission to go for some. So many pickers have cleaned them up, so we found only a few here and there. We went a long way out, and made a thorough search. A shower overtook us and gave us a fine washing. Just after noon we heard the ball open again. It seemed to be all along the line from right to left. One said it was General Banks' notice to the Rebs to get ready to whip him again. We hurried back with what berries we had. The shot and shells were flying both ways. Company B was out on the skirmish line, and did not get in until morning. The firing stopped about dark, and so far as I can find out no one has been killed or wounded.

June 27, 1863.
Saturday.

Too many blackberries yesterday have made me sick today. I certainly feel slim. I don't care who has Port Hudson; I don't want it. I wouldn't turn my hand over for the whole Confederacy.

Later. Am feeling better, but don't hanker after blackberries yet. Company B turned up four men short but they came in later. They got so close they had to crawl on their bellies for a long ways before they dare stand up.

June 28, 1863.
Sunday.

Am all right again. Today has been a busy one. A big gun, the biggest I ever saw, "Old Abe" it is called, was dragged here last night and got up on the point opposite the Rebels' water battery. Today the gun has been got into position. Being so near, and having so little to do. I put in the day with them, helping in any way I could. The fort is made of cotton bales, backed up by bags of earth too thick to be shot through. When all was ready it was most sundown. A limb with thick leaves hung over one side, and under this I got to see what happened.

When "Old Abe" finally did speak, the shell went into the ground way under the rebel gun, and after what seemed a long time exploded. The whole thing went up in the air, and when the dust settled, the muzzle of the gun lay sticking over the bank, pointed up toward the moon. So ended the famous "water battery" that we have heard so much about.

"Billy Wilson's" Zouave regiment, our left-hand neighbour, then came up the ravine dragging a long rope they had got from the gunboats, and slipped it over the muzzle of the gun, intending to drag it over. But they couldn't budge it, and finally gave it up. Next they came back with hand grenades which they fired and tossed over. They had cut the fuses too long and they had no more than landed on the other side when the Rebs threw them back. That made the red legs skedaddle, and all that saved them was the fact that in coming up they had come on a slant, while the grenades rolled directly down.

As it was, a piece hit a drummer boy, and he lies here on the ground apparently breathing his last. The top of his head has a large piece chipped off. There has been a good deal of powder burned today. What has been done besides tearing up the water battery I don't know. Tonight the mortar boats have been throwing shells into the works. They pass directly over us. We are so near, the report is almost stunning. The fuse is cut long enough to last until they drop. I hope none of them may go off while over our quarters.

June 29, 1863.
Monday.
The Rebs shelled our quarters last night, and kept us huddled in the ravine until some were asleep. The weather grows hotter every day. Many give out in the rifle pits, though they contrive every way to get in the shade of something.

June 30, 1863.
Tuesday.
Last night the Zouaves made another try to get the guns from the water battery. Two of them came back on stretchers, and the guns are still there. A man was killed today while lying on the ground right among us. Pie was resting his head on one hand, when a shell burst and a piece as large as my hand came down and passed through his shoulder and so on through his body, coming out near his hip. He merely sank down and did not stir. An order has just come from General Dwight for every man to sleep with his accoutrements on, ready to move at a minute's notice.

July 1, 1863.
Wednesday.

Nothing happened at our house last night, although we were ready for visitors or to go visiting at the shortest possible notice. It is reported that a part of the Sixth Michigan got into the water battery last night and brought out a rebel captain with them, and without loss on their part. The enemy are reported gathering in our rear. They captured General Dow and George Story yesterday. We are sorry about George, but no one feels very sorry about the general. A man from the right says General Banks made a speech to the storming party last night, and promised them that Port Hudson would be taken inside of the next three days.

July 2, 1863.
Thursday.

Last night the shot and shells flew thicker than at any time. The Rebs seem to be getting madder all the time. I got my closest call, too. I was sitting on a plank; laid across the ravine when a shell burst in front of me. I don't know how I knew, but I did know a hunk of it was coming straight for me, and I dove off into the weeds just as it struck and tore up the ground behind me. It must have gone within an inch or less of the plank, and right where I sat. It is reported that General Dow and Story were recaptured last night by our cavalry. We hope for Story's sake it is true. An orderly rode in a few minutes ago with an order for troops, saying the Rebels had attacked Springfield Landing. The Zouaves and the 162nd New York have started, and probably others from farther up the line. All our stores of supplies are there. The *Essex* has up with her anchor and gone down there and if there is any fighting we shall hear it soon. If our supplies are captured we will have to fight on empty stomachs or be captured ourselves. How the Rebs would laugh at us if such a thing should happen, and who could blame them!

July 3, 1863.
Friday.

It was only a scare. The troops came back before midnight. A guerrilla squad attacked a wagon train and were fought off by the guards. But it gave us something new to think and to talk about at any rate. If General Banks hoists the stars and stripes in Port Hudson tomorrow, he will probably begin getting ready today. No doubt for some of us it will be our last celebration. Who will be taken and who will be left none of us know, and what a blessed thing it is we don't! Now we can each think it will be the other fellow. We have never had any great love for our head surgeon, Dr. Cole, and tonight we hate him more than ever. Yesterday Corporal Blunt of Company K went to him for an excuse from duty, as he was sick. He told him he was able for duty and he went back into the rifle pit and died. How we wish it had been the doctor instead.

Just at night a pair of oxen were discovered in the bushes nearby and Smith Darling and I were sent out to capture them. We got near enough for a shot without being discovered, and each got his ox at the first shot. The mules came and dragged them out where they are handy and tomorrow we expect a beef stew. The officers will have beefsteak, of course, but we are not particular about the part so long as we get some. Three of the Zouaves, who were captured during the fight on May 27, made their escape and came in tonight. They had got into the river and swam down, coming in as naked as they were born, and almost starved.

July 4, 1863.
Saturday.
Company K lost another man by sickness today. There are a good many sick. The health of the 128th has, up to a very recent time, been good. We have had hard usage but seemed to thrive under it until this terrible hot weather came on. Two of Company B go to the hospital today, and several others are grunting. Out of the eleven hundred we set out with we have only three hundred and fifty now, and the other regiments can tell the same sort of a story, and some of them even a worse one.

Being a sort of jack-at-all-trades, I help out in any way I can, for so many being laid off, makes double duty for some others. I have been filling out the last two months' pay and muster rolls today and that gives me a chance to know about my own company and regiment. So far as we know, General Banks did not take Port Hudson today. If I were he I wouldn't set any more dates. It has been a very quiet Fourth of July. Have heard a bigger noise at the "City" many a time.

July 5, 1863.
Sunday.
Something wrong with the pay rolls, and I have been all day trying to find out what it is.

Captain Gifford, of Company A, who was captured when the

Slaughter buildings were burned, came in today. He escaped last night, swimming the river and getting here about naked. He says from all he was able to discover, the bulk of the enemy's forces are in front of us, here on the left. Where is that storming party? Somewhere on the right, I suppose, unwinding red tape. I'll bet, if every officer in Banks' army, and General Banks with them, was tied up in a bag and dumped in the river, the privates could take Port Hudson in the next twenty-four hours.

July 6, 1863.
Monday.

Another hitch in the pay rolls, though made out as they always have been since I had anything to do with them. The figures are right, but the form is not. This time they are according to the new form and I suppose will stay put. The Rebs are getting real saucy again. They have taken to shooting at the men who carry rations to the men in the rifle pits. Last night a darkey was carrying a kettle of coffee to Company E and a ball struck the rim of the kettle, knocking one side against the other, and also knocking down the darkey and spilling the coffee all over him. Narrow escapes are an every-day occurrence. Today a man took off his hat to scratch his head. That brought the hat up in sight and a rebel bullet went through his fingers, crippling his hand. Four men died from sunstroke today. The weather is very warm though we have no way to tell just how warm.

July 7, 1863.
Tuesday.

Hip, hip, hurrah! Vicksburg has surrendered. The news has just reached us, although the place surrendered on Saturday at 10 o'clock. The gunboats got the news some way. The first thing was three cheers from the men, and then three broadside salutes. Next, we have shouted ourselves hoarse, and the news is passing along up the line to the extreme right. The Rebs sent out a flag, to know what ailed us, and were told the joyful news. Someway they didn't seem as glad as we are.

Afternoon. Our regiment and the Sixth Michigan have got marching orders. I wonder what is up now.

Later. The Rebs have again threatened Springfield Landing and the 128th New York, the Sixth Michigan, and the Gray Horse Battery have gone off on the double quick. We hear that 27,000 men and over 200 guns were surrendered at Vicksburg. There is no doubt about it now. Details are coming in all the time, and a whole lot of powder has been burned celebrating. The Rebs on our front seem as glad as we, for they know Port Hudson must surrender or be smashed between the forces of Banks and Grant. The detail sent out towards Springfield Landing has come in and reports the trouble all got along with. They didn't fire a gun. We are happy tonight, about as happy as if Port Hudson was ours. In fact it is ours, for they must give up now or catch it from front and rear at the same time.

July 8, 1863.
Wednesday.

A flag of truce came out this morning, and after a short council went back. We don't know what it means, but can guess it is the beginning of the end of the siege of Port Hudson.

Later. The flag was to ask for twenty-four hours cessation of hostilities, looking to a surrender. A few hours were given them to think it over, and we put in the time comparing notes with the Johnnies on our front. They are hard up for tobacco, and for bread. They have plenty of corn meal and molasses, but very little else. I have given away and swapped off everything eatable I have, and am going to make a johnny-cake, for a change. The meal is as much of a treat for us as our hard-tack is for them.

Afternoon. Port Hudson has surrendered and possession is to be given at once. The story goes that only a few regiments will go in with the staff officers to receive the surrender. We are so in hopes our regiment will be one of that few. I am dying with curiosity to know what the ceremony of a surrender is like, and I also want to see what the inside of Port Hudson is like. The outside I know all I care to know of, but to go away and not see or know how the place looks after the banging it has had, is too bad. But there is no use thinking about it. Some higher power will decide, and we have only to put up with it.

July 9, 1863.
Thursday.

In Port Hudson. Just as I was wondering what regiments would be taken in to receive the surrender, and was worrying for fear ours would not be one, the order came to pack up and go. We marched up to General Auger's headquarters, and slept in the road last night. There was a drizzling rain most all night, but this morning was bright and we soon dried off.

We marched on towards the right until we came to a road that entered the fort, but which did not show signs of recent usage. Here we formed in the order we were to go in, the storming party at the head, then came the 116th and 75th New York, and then the 128th New York. After us were several regiments, about six I think, for I have seen members of that many regiments here today. At eight o'clock we marched in, and I should say went three-quarters of a mile, when we found the Rebs in line. We marched along their front and halted, faced to the left, and stood facing each other, some twenty feet apart. Both lines were at "order arms." The officers held a short confab, and then took their respective places, as if on parade.

Our regiment was directly opposite "Miles' Legion," or what is left of it. The commanding general then gave the order, "ground arms." This was repeated by the company commanders, and then for the first time I felt sorry for the brave fellows. If their cause is not just, they have been true to it, and it must be like death itself for a brave fighter to lay his arms down before his enemy. However, I did not see any signs of tears. A detail was made to collect and take care of the guns and ammunition, and the order came from both sides to break ranks. In a twinkling we were together. I met the man I had the corn meal from, and we put in some time together. The Rebs are mostly large, fine-looking men. They are about as hard up for clothes as we are. What clothing they have on is gray, while ours is what has been a sickly blue, but is now nearly the colour of the ground on which we have slept so long.

Some of them are glad the fight is over, and others are sorry, at least that is the way they talk. They are asking all sorts of questions about the thousand men who were to storm their works. They think it the biggest kind of a joke. They have known all along much more about what went on outside than we did about the inside. Their scouts have been right among us, wearing the clothes of those they captured on May 27. The officers, without an exception, appear like gentlemen, in spite of the ragged clothes they wear. They have treated the prisoners as well as they could, giving them the same sort of food they ate themselves. Provisions are very scarce, and the men say they have had no meat but mule beef for some time. A whole wagon-train loaded with provisions has come in and they eat as if famished. There are acres of fresh looking graves, showing that they have suffered as well as we. They say, however, that few have been killed, considering the many efforts made to kill them, but there has been a great deal of sickness, which has caused the greatest destruction among them.

There are about 500 in the hospital, sick and wounded together.

They have suffered for medicines. The wounded had to be operated on without chloroform, and many died while being operated on.

The rebel soldiers are to be paroled, but what will be done with the officers I have not learned. Some of the men say they will fight again as soon as they have a chance, and others say they have had enough. The majority of them that I have talked with feel that their cause will finally lose, and they are for ending it now. There is a large space covered with barrels of sugar and molasses and there is quite a quantity of corn left. They have a curious mill for grinding the corn. A locomotive stands on the track with the drivers jacked up clear from the track. On the driver is a belt which turns a small mill and it looks as if it would grind a grist as quick as any other mill. I have been hunting about the place all day, and have seen many curiosities, or at least things strange to me. The earth is honeycombed with cellars and tunnels where the men hid themselves from our shot and shells.

Along the bluff facing the river are several savage-looking guns, made of logs, smoothed off and painted so as to look exactly like cannon. The real guns were all needed for use against the besieging army. We are looking for a good night's sleep tonight. The guns that have made our nights so miserable are all under guard. Things are settling down for the night and I must stop writing. I have written every minute I could get and the half is not told yet. If all goes well I will try again tomorrow.

CHAPTER 9

Donaldsonville, La.

July 10, 1863.
Port Hudson, La. Friday.

The rebel troops are going off by the boat-load. Guards have been placed over the sugar and molasses, also the corn. As fast as the paroles can be made out the men are going to their homes. They each swear they will not fight again until regularly exchanged. One of the Rebs has showed me how to make johnny-cake. I have made several, and while they don't taste like mother's used to, they are really very good. One fellow, after filling up on it, said "What's the use of women anyway? We cook our own victuals, wash and mend our own clothes, make up our own beds—and what more could women do?" All the same there is one woman I would awfully like to see, and I flatter myself that same woman would like to see me.

We were surprised yesterday at the small number of small arms surrendered, and wondered how they were able to stand us off so long with them. Today the secret has come out. The best arms were buried in the ground and many of the newly-made graves in the graveyard contained rifles instead of dead Rebels. I don't know how they were discovered, but have been told that so many newly-made graves excited the suspicion of a Yankee officer and he began prodding into them and struck iron.

July 11, 1863.
Saturday.

We have marching orders. It is said we go to Baton Rouge as escort for the Vermont Gray Horse Battery. That means we will have to take a horse's gait, and it is said to be twenty-five miles. We have been swimming in the river and washing our clothes and are that much better off anyhow. We have filled up on corn bread, and are waiting for further orders. Our regiment seems to be the only one that is going, at least we are the only one getting ready. I hope my clothes will get dry before we start, for it is hard getting around in them now. I am almost ashamed to say it, but we are lousy with all the rest. There are always some who don't care for them and they always have them. When we get a change of clothing, I'll bury or burn my old ones. We hope we are on the way to Camp Parapet, where our tents and knapsacks are. Baton Rouge is in that direction and that is the only good thing we have in sight.

July 12, 1863.
Baton Rouge, La. Sunday.
Here at last and about tired out. We left Port Hudson about dark and were all night and until noon today getting here. Many of the men gave out and slept by the side of the road. I suppose they will be coming in all the afternoon. Some of them were skylarking around Port Hudson and did not get any supper. We were all hungry as bears when we got here, and my clean suit, that I felt so proud of, shows no signs of its recent washing. It had not got dry and the dust we picked up seemed to all settle on and stick to me. However, we have had a feed and I have shook out the most of the dirt I brought with me. We hear good news from down the river, that 5,000 Rebs were captured at Donaldsonville.

The boys that were wounded at Port Hudson May 27 are here, and except those in the general hospital at New Orleans, the company is together again. This is the capital of Louisiana, and like most all southern cities, is built up of low wooden buildings although there are houses of all patterns, sizes and shapes. The streets are narrow and dirty, and the citizens mostly speak French among themselves. Negroes are everywhere, little and big, some jet black and some almost white. As we may have to stay here, I won't run down the place or the people any more. We are already settling down for the night, and hope for an all-night's sleep.

July 13, 1863.
Monday.
Nothing has happened today worth writing about. We slept soundly all night, and late this morning. Some have gone at it again and act as if they would sleep all day. We have been strained up so long, it begins to tell on the toughest. I had my sick spell last winter and spring,

and since that I have been one of the toughest. Have not been off duty a minute since I left the hospital and I can't think of another man in the company that can say that. But then my duties have been light as compared with theirs. Upon looking over my diary I find I did not mention a talk we had with the prisoners at Port Hudson.

We were telling each other our adventures, when one of them asked what regiment it was that came out to draw their fire on June 13. When told it was the 128th New York, they allowed it was the "doggondest" piece of impudence they ever saw. They told how they begged to fire on us and were not allowed to do it. The rebel officers knew what it was done for and had rather let us go than expose their position. I can't help thinking it was a good thing for us they didn't shoot, but we told them they couldn't hit the side of a barn, say nothing of so small a mark as a man. The firing they did do comes pretty near proving that we told them the truth.

July 14, 1863.
Tuesday.
All kinds of stories are afloat concerning the fight at Donaldsonville. Some say our folks got the worst of it and some say the Rebs did. Between the two we are in the dark as to what was done. A great many of the men are on the sick list. There seems to be a sort of letting down all around, I begin to think active duty is the best for us after all. I got hold of some boards today and have put them up to sleep under, and to sit under. It is great, for it lets the breeze blow through and at the same time keeps off the dew at night and the sun by day. The boys are all getting fixed up, but they put their boards on the ground and make fun of my overhead shelter.

July 15, 1863.
Wednesday.
Marching orders again. Donaldsonville is our destination. They have undertaken a job down there without consulting the 128th New York and consequently have got into trouble, which we have got to go and fix up.

Dr. Andrus joined the regiment this morning and we cheered most as loud as when Port Hudson surrendered. Dr. Cole came soon after and was received in silence. We have not forgotten Corporal Blunt yet. He is a murderer, pure and simple. How he can hold his head as high as he does, I don't see. I hope he will get what he deserves some day, but such people seldom do. I saw a New York paper today. It was full of the fight at Gettysburg. From all I can make of it our forces got the worst of it in the first day's fight, but as it was still going on when the paper was printed the scale may have turned. I suppose the 150th was in it, and I shall want to see another paper to know how it ended, and if John was hurt.

4 p. m. On board the steamer *St. Charles.* We expect to make Donaldsonville by eight tonight. The sail down the river is glorious. Whatever comes when we reach our destination, we are having a regular picnic now. Going with the current, the boat cuts the water like a knife. There is too much to look at and to enjoy for me to waste the time writing, so goodbye till tomorrow.

July 16, 1863.
Donaldsonville, La. Thursday.

We landed here about midnight last night. A heavy shower overtook us on the way and wet us to the skin, consequently what sleep we had was on wet ground and in wet clothes. This has been a very pretty place. The levee hides it from view from the river, but the place and the country around it is beautiful. It has been fortified, and when the gunboats fought their way up the river a year ago they were obliged to mar its beauty somewhat. There is a sugar mill nearby with lots of sugar and molasses in it. The best thing is an immense cornfield right beside us, and the corn is just right to roast or boil. It is the southern variety, great big stalks, with great big ears on, and we can get a mouthful at every bite. There are a lot of troops here—I should think at least 10,000. Just what we are here for none of us have yet found out.

The coloured population is all I have yet seen. I visited the sugar mill and from an old darkey learned all about making sugar and molasses. There is a long shed, and under it is an endless chain arrangement upon which the sugar cane is laid as it comes in carts from the field. This carries the cane into the mill, where it passes between heavy iron rollers, which squeeze the cane so dry that it is used for fuel under the boilers that furnish steam to drive the rollers. The juice runs into a big copper kettle, where it is boiled awhile and then dipped into another and so on, until when it comes from the last it is run into what I should call a cellar under the sugar house. This is made tight in some way, probably with cement, and in it the sugar settles to the bottom. I was told that the bottom of this cellar slopes from the sides towards the centre, so that the sugar settles in the centre. Over this cellar is a floor that slopes from the sides to the centre just as the cellar bottom does.

The getting of the sugar into hogsheads is the next operation. Hogsheads are placed on the sloping floor, with one head open. Holes are bored in the lower head and into these sugar canes are stuck before any sugar is put in. They have immense great hoes, with long handles, and with these the men dig up the sugar and dump it into the open-ended hogshead. The molasses drains out through the holes in the bottom and runs back into the cellar, "vat," he called it. The men are all barefoot, and when I asked him if they washed their feet before beginning work, he said the molasses did that just as well as water. The hogsheads are left as long as any molasses drains out, when they are headed up and are ready for market. The molasses is scooped up with long-handled scoops and the barrels filled, any waste there may be running back into the vat.

It is said we are here to attract the attention of the Rebs until Grant can get in their rear, and so force them to a fair field fight. A New York paper has been going the rounds until it is worn out. When I got it I made out that General Lee got the worst of it at Gettysburg, and that he himself was wounded. Also that his line of retreat is cut off. Good enough, if true, and I hope it is. But General Lee ought to pattern after some officers I know and keep out of danger, when danger is near. After the danger is past then he can come out and shout as loud as any.

July 17, 1863.
Friday.

Nothing new today, unless it be a new pair of government pants which I was lucky enough to get, and which I very much needed. A good swim in the river, and the new pants have made me feel like new. The body of a man floating in the river was pulled out here and buried today. He had no clothing on and it is not known whether he was a native or a northern soldier. We are a lazy set here. We eat corn and sleep and that leaves very little to write about.

July 18, 1863.
Saturday.

The weather continues hot. What would we do if our old friend, the Mississippi, should dry up? We wash in it, swim in it, drink from it, and boil our dinners in it. Today I borrowed a washtub from a native and washed my clothes. I had soap and I gave them the first good one they ever had. My shirt is more like a necklace than a shirt. I hardly know myself tonight. We have been cutting each other's hair. One of the boys borrowed a pair of shears and I guess they will wear them out. The best thing though was a fine-tooth comb, which has been in constant use today. That too was borrowed. I am ashamed to tell it, but when I got the comb I pulled out five lice from my hair the first grab.

Strange as it may seem, I got no more, and now that my hair is cut close to my scalp the most careful search does not show any signs of others. I guess they must have been having a picnic in some favourite grove and all got caught at one haul. Body lice we don't care for. We just boil our clothes and that's the end of them. Their feeding time is when we are still for awhile, but at the first move they all let go and grab fast to our clothing. But the head lice are more difficult to deal with unless it be the kind that I had, which all attend one church and at the same time.

July 19, 1863.
Sunday.
Mail came today. We have dodged about so lately the mail could not find us. I got two. All well at home. I dread to hear, for fear I will hear father or mother are sick, and yet I am all the time hoping to get a letter. Some stamps too. If I only had some place to keep them. I must hurry up and write to everyone while they last. How different a letter from home makes the world seem. Dear ones, how good you are to me and what a debt I shall owe you when this is all over with! We are expecting our pay every day. Some of the troops have theirs, and our turn will come. We get all sorts of news from the North. First a victory, and then a defeat. We are sure of two places, Vicksburg and Port Hudson, and we have almost forgotten them. A great many are sick. I am sick myself of corn and have gone back to hard-tack. I wish we might go back to Camp Parapet, or else our things be sent us.

A letter from Walt Loucks says he expects a discharge. Several have been discharged on account of disability. From his letter though he is in good spirits and says he will come up and see me before he goes home. Poor Walt, he has seen the hard side of soldiering, and I hope he will be sent home.

July 22, 1863.
Wednesday.
Sunday, Monday and Tuesday all passed without a thing happening

worth recording. Except the regular detail for guard duty there has been little going on except sleeping and eating. It seems as if I would never get sleep enough, now that there is no excitement to keep me awake.

P. m. Have just received a Pine Plains paper which says John Van Alstyne was killed at the Gettysburg fight. Dear me, what will father and mother do now? George Wilson of the same company and regiment is reported wounded. I have seen another paper giving the list of killed and wounded in the regiment and John's name was not in the list. On this peg I hang my hopes of a contradiction of this sad piece of news, and shall feel very anxious until I know the truth. John Thorn, who deserted before we left Hudson, reached us today. He says he gave himself up, but more likely someone gave him up, as they ought to. He has missed some hard knocks, and some fun, but he will get his share of each from this on.

July 23, 1863
Tuesday.

Have written four letters today. At first I thought I was going to join the sick squad, but writing the letters has cured me. A great many are sick; quite a number from each company attend sick call every morning. Dr. Andrus and I play some desperate games of checkers these days. I shall try hard to keep out of his hands otherwise, for if I should get down now our folks would have me to worry about, and if the news about John be true, they have plenty of trouble now. The man Thorn has been transferred to Company F. I am glad of it. Company B. has no room for him.

New Orleans paper dated 18th says General Lee is not yet out of danger from General Meade. How I hope the next paper from the North will tell of the capture of his whole army.

I have got mixed up on time some way and find this is Saturday, July 26. I have let my diary go for some days. For one reason, there was only the usual routine of camp life to write of, and another reason is I have been too lazy. I just lay around and rest, or play checkers with the doctor. We have showers most every day, and are either getting wet, or getting dry again nearly all the time. We have a great deal of what farmers call catching weather. The sun shines clear and bright, and the next thing you know down comes the rain in torrents. The only good thing about it is that it is warm. Our old sutler, John Pulver, has come back and set up his tent. His stock is mostly gingerbread and plug tobacco, with some currant wane and live cheese for a change. He trusts everybody and his stock wall soon vanish. But payday will come, and his debtors will have to settle whether it takes all or only a part of their pay. Some of the troops have already been paid, but Major Vedder, who pays the New York troops, has not yet put in an appearance.

Major Bostwick came down from Port Hudson today to settle up his accounts with Company B. He stays in camp tonight and is then going to New Orleans. His regiment has remained at Port Hudson since the surrender, doing guard duty.

July 26, 1863.
Sunday.

Went to church today. It was a Catholic church and the sermon was in Latin, so I don't know whether he prayed for or against us. There were a great many Sisters of Charity there. In fact they are everywhere. Black and white people were all mixed up and so far as I could see were all treated alike. I was ashamed of my clothes, but they were my best, and none of them could say more than that.

We drew a ration of flour today and had quite a time making pancakes. Lieutenant Pierce took supper with us. I mixed up the stuff and Mitchel did the baking. I got some *saleratus* for I remembered mother used that, but I did not remember that she also used salt, so I didn't think of it. They didn't look much like mother's, and when we came to eat them they didn't taste much like them. But it was a change, and that is something we are always glad to get.

Our tents have just overtaken us, and we sleep under cover tonight for the first time since we left Camp Parapet.

July 27, 1863.
Monday.

We have been put in the Third Brigade, in the Fourth Division, under Emory. There seems to be a regular reorganisation going on. I suppose things are being arranged for another campaign. The darkeys had a dance in the road last night. I had gone to bed, but there was so much noise I got up and went to the ball. They had no music, but one of them patted his hands on his leg, at the same time stamping his foot, and it answered every purpose. Half the regiment was there looking on and there was lots of fun. They were in dead earnest too, and there are some right down good dancers among them. The dignity of it all, and their extreme politeness to the ladies, would shame some white dances I have attended.

A New Orleans paper says General Lee has got safely back into Virginia. We hoped for a different report from that. But there is no such thing as suiting both sides in this business. It also tells of a riot in New York City on account of the draft. Here comes the mail man, so goodbye.

Later. I have a letter from Jane and have read it. John is dead, killed at the first fire that came his way. The 150th marched thirty-six miles to get there, and were put right in as soon as they reached the field. Poor John! I'll bet he was in the front ranks, for he always was in anything he undertook. He was instantly killed. To know he did not suffer as some have to, is a great relief. I had hoped the Pine Plains *Herald* report was not true, but I can hope no longer. I feel so for father and mother. I must write them oftener now, for they will feel more than ever anxious to hear from me. Jane says they are brave, but I know that sort of bravery cuts like a knife. Colonel Ketcham wrote them a nice letter, telling what a good soldier John had been, and how he sympathized with them in losing him. I suppose his body can sometime be brought home, that is, if it can be identified. If many were killed they were probably tumbled into a long ditch together, for that is the way it is usually done.

Through rebel sources we hear General Dow is in Libby Prison. Also that Charleston is taken. Also that Lee, with his army, is safe in Virginia. How I wish I knew more about the Gettysburg fight. How it came about, and how it came out. How Lee and his army came to be in Pennsylvania. Why he was allowed to go so far north without a move being made to stop him. For all we know or can find out, he dropped right down from the clouds, and then our forces were gathered about him, some of them from long distances, and were just able to drive him back into Virginia.

July 30, 1863.
Thursday.
Tuesday and Wednesday I spent writing letters, that is all the time I could get. The heat is something awful. It is almost as bad in the shade as right out in the sun. The only comfortable place is in the river. Several have given out and if it continues many more will do so. We have signed the pay rolls for March and April, and hope to get the money today or tomorrow. If we do I am going to eat something off the top of a table, if it takes the whole two months' pay. The story is we are to go back to Baton Rouge, but what for, or when, has not

yet been told.

July 31, 1863.
Friday.

Pay day. As I was at the quartermaster's this morning, drawing rations, I was sent for to fall in for pay. If there is anything good to eat in this town I am going to fill up. Seems to me I never had such a dislike for army fare as has lately come upon me.

August 1, 1863.
Saturday.

A year ago today I cradled rye for Theron Wilson, and I remember we had chicken pie for dinner with home-made beer to wash it down. Today I have hard-tack, with coffee for a wash-down. Have I ever described a hard-tack to you? If not I will try, but I am doubtful of being able to make anyone who has not used them understand what they are. In size they are about like a common soda cracker, and in thickness about like two of them. Except for the thickness they look very much alike. But there the resemblance ends. The cracker eats easy, almost melts in the mouth, while the hard-tack is harder and tougher than so much wood. I don't know what the word "tack" means, but the "hard" I have long understood. We soak them in our coffee and in that way get off the outside. It takes a long time to soak one through, but repeated soakings and repeated gnawing finally uses them up.

Very often they are mouldy, and most always wormy. We knock them together and jar out the worms, and the mould we cut or scrape off. Sometimes we soak them until soft and then fry them in pork grease, but generally we smash them up in pieces and grind away until either the teeth or the hard-tack gives up. I know now why Dr. Cole examined our teeth so carefully when we passed through the medical mill at Hudson. I tried some of the southern cooking today and am better contented with army fare than I have been for some time. Marching orders. Must get the commissary stores ready right away. Goodbye till next time.

August 2, 1863.
Sunday.

My twenty-fourth birthday. We left Donaldsonville about nine last night and marched up the river until midnight. We slept in the road until four this morning, when we started and marched at quick time till 9 o'clock, when the men began to fall out with the heat, and we halted for the stragglers to come up. It is a very warm day, even for this country. The doctor is patching up those who gave out, and I see no signs of going any farther today.

P. m. We have pitched what few tents we have with us, which means a stay of some length. There is a large plantation here, said to be owned by a man who has remained loyal to Uncle Sam, and from what I can learn we are to protect him from his rebellious neighbour. Big thing that, for the crack regiment of Sherman's division. I have been thinking of my last birthday, and remember that John Loucks and I went fishing on Long Pond, above Sharon.

August 3, 1863.
Monday.
We killed an ox this morning, and are full. The hide, horns, head, legs and every other part of that ox that we didn't divide up among the companies was seized upon by the darkies and is as completely gone as if it had never existed. A swarm of flies over the place where the tragedy took place is all there is left to tell of it.

August 5, 1863.
Wednesday.
The sick we left at Donaldsonville have been brought on, and I suppose the rest of the stuff will come sometime. Landon P. Rider of our company died last night, and we buried him in a little graveyard here. It is the first man we have laid away in such a place since we came south. It is a pretty little plot, and for his parents' sake I am glad we happened here at this time. Curtis L. Porter, whom we left sick at Baton Rouge, died on July 23. So we go! These last two men were among our toughest and best men. We gave Landon a military funeral, and it went off without a hitch, even if I did have charge of it. That was my job before I was sick at Camp Parapet, and since that this is the only time we have done anything more than dig a hole and put them in.

August 6, 1863.
Thursday.
We drew five days' rations today, the first time in most three months that we have drawn rations in bulk. Company savings commence today. (Note. I don't remember what this statement refers to. L. V. A.). This will add to the duties of commissary sergeants. Their accounts must agree with the regimental commissary, his with the brigade commissary, and so on through each department up to the quartermaster general. If errors are found it is safe to say they will

come back to the company commissary, for he has no one below him to pass them along to.

Walter Loucks came back to the regiment this morning. His discharge was not granted and he is greatly disappointed. He looks as if he had lived in the shade, he is so white. Our faces are so black it don't seem as if we would ever be called white again. Poor Walt, he has had the best of it lately, but he suffered enough last winter and spring to make up for it. Now he will have to take it with the rest of us and it will be hard on him for awhile. The mail leaves today. I have four letters, and some money for father, to go.

August 7, 1863.
Friday.

We have moved our camp across the road to higher and dryer ground. We have the prettiest place for a camp we have yet had. We have a fine view of the river, up and down, for miles. The river falls every day, and grows narrow. I don't think the water is over three-quarters of a mile wide. The natives say it will not get much narrower, though it may get lower. It is about all channel now. It don't seem possible it could ever fill up to the levee. One gets some idea of the amount of water it sometimes carries by looking across it and imagining it full from levee to levee. As fast as the water falls, the mud dries up, and in a few days grass sprouts up, and so it is green almost to the water's edge. We have some glorious swims. The water is always muddy but it loosens up the dirt, which runs off with the water when we come out. The calluses on our hips show most as far as the man. They are a redder red than the rest of the body, and are about as wide as my hand and nearly twice as long. They show how hard have been the beds we have slept on.

August 10, 1863.
Monday.

Saturday was a wet one. A tremendous shower with thunder and lightning and high winds came up about noon, and swept everything before it. It blew over before night and left it cool and pleasant. It doesn't seem possible that dame Nature could change her face as she did in a few hours this afternoon.

Sunday, yesterday morning, a boat landed about a half mile below us, and unloaded our camp equipage. There were about forty loads of it, and it kept us busy most all day. The things were all mixed up and we pulled and hauled the piles over as fast as they came, looking for our individual belongings. We put up all the tents that were needed. We don't need as many as we did once.

Marching orders have come. Just as we have got settled down in the finest location we have yet had, we must pull up and leave for some other. It is too bad, but it is a part of the bargain and it does no good to complain. We are all torn up and ready to go when the word "march" is spoken. The quartermaster's teams have not returned from Donaldsonville, where they went for rations. The gunboat *Essex* has dropped anchor opposite us, also another gunboat which I cannot make out. A part of the regiment is on picket, and until they come in we shall probably remain as we are. Eph. Hammond and Will Haskins are quite sick in the hospital tent and quite a number are about half sick in the quarters.

August 11, 1863.
Hickory Landing, La. Tuesday.
No move yet. We stuck up some tents in the night and crawled in. Fresh orders this morning are to keep one day's rations cooked ahead, and be ready to go at a moment's notice. Eph. Hammond is dreadful sick today. He is our acting orderly and one of the best fellows that ever lived.

Later. Eph. is dead. Whatever it was that struck him it took him quick and nothing the doctor could do seemed to help him. Poor Eph., we shall miss him. He was a leading spirit in any deviltry that was going on, but was one of the sort that no one could find fault with. He was a general favourite. There are a dozen others that would not be missed as he will. John Pitcher, the same John who helped me get the honey at Port Hudson, was taken to the hospital today. We have just buried Hammond. I have marked some boards for his grave and Rider's, for it is possible they will be sent for. What hardened wretches we have become.

The word came, "Eph. Hammond is dead, hurry up and make a box for him." He was one of the best-liked men in the regiment. Yet not a tear was shed, and before his body was cold he was buried in the ground.

We will talk about him more or less for a day or two and then forget all about him. That is what less than a year has done to us. At that rate two years more and we will be murdering in cold blood. The day has been sultry hot, but for a wonder we have had no shower. Goodbye, before I get another chance to write we will be somewhere else.

August 12, 1863.
Wednesday.
What a poor prophet I am! We are here yet. So many are sick, the colonel has decided to wait for a transport to take us to Plaquemine, about twenty-five miles above here. The doctor says anything like a hard march would add greatly to the sick list. The plan just now is to wait until the heat of the day is over, and if no boat comes along to start and march by easy stages through the night, and then rest up tomorrow. Company B has but thirteen men now that are not sick or ailing.

August 13, 1863.
Plaquemine City, La. Thursday.
Twelve miles below Baton Rouge and on the opposite banks. Last night about five we were all packed up for a start on foot, and while in line waiting for the word to start, a boat came in sight and was hailed. She swung up against the bank and in less than an hour we were on board. The well ones took to the upper deck and had a delightful sail by moonlight. We reached here about 11 p. m. and had a good nap before our wagon train came in.

We have laid out our camp near the river, where we get the breezes if any there are. The officers' tents are up and every- thing we possess is given over to us again, which leads us to think we may stay here for some time to come. We are too lazy to do more than loaf today, but tomorrow I mean to look about and see what Plaquemine City looks like.

August 14, 1863.
Plaquemine, La. Friday.
Plaquemine is quite a place, in spite of its name. There are several stores with quite a decent assortment but the prices are way out of reach. I was going to buy a paper of tobacco, such as we used to buy at home for a shilling, but when I found it was $1.50 I decided to wait until our sutler got here and get it for half that. A fine large house which was furnished, but not occupied, has been taken for a hospital. Colonel Smith is acting brigadier general and quartermaster. Mace is acting brigade commissary. Several wrecks of steamers lie near the mouth of a bayou that enters the river here. I suppose they were destroyed by our folks last spring or else by the Rebs to keep them from being captured. The people are civil, but not real friendly. They do full as well as I could if the conditions were reversed.

140

August 15, 1863.
Saturday.

We have drawn five days' rations and are settling down for real living again. A general improvement in the sick shows already, probably on account of such good quarters. We hear today that Major Bostwick has been promoted and is now colonel of the Ninetieth United States Coloured Infantry. I did not suppose there was more than half a dozen coloured regiments in the field. Lieutenant Pierce has gone to Port Hudson to see him. All sorts of stories are afloat about it, and one is that Colonel B. will have the privilege of choosing his regimental staff from the 128th New York. The weather keeps hot and seems to get hotter.

August 16, 1863.
Sunday.

Whew, what a scorcher this has been! Not a breath of air stirring. The river is as smooth as glass. The reflection from it is almost blinding. Even the water in the river is hot. We have put in the day trying to keep cool. It's too hot to even write about it.

August 17, 1863.
Monday.

We got cooled off before the day was over, yesterday. A shower came up and a hard gale of wind with it. The rain soaked up the ground so the tent pins pulled out, and one after another our tents went down until only one was left that stuck and hung until a fellow crawled out and started one peg, and then that went. We had to lie on our tents to keep them from blowing away.

A darkey caught a catfish today that weighed twenty pounds and one he called a buffalo fish that weighed ten pounds. We have spent a lot of good money for hooks and lines, but so far have not had a bite. I got fast to a log or something, and broke my hook. The weather is cloudy today, and there is every sign of a real rain storm.

August 18, 1863.
Tuesday.

It doesn't rain yet, but it looks as if it would every minute. The mud here is as slippery as grease. There is hardly a man among us that has not wiped up one or more places with his clothes. Never mind, we have plenty of water and plenty of time to wash up. A box that was sent Major Bostwick last June has just reached camp. It had found the major finally, and after taking out what was for him, he sent it to the regiment, for several were remembered in it. I had four pairs of socks, a shirt, a watch cord, some dried peaches and some preserved cherries. Also some paper and envelopes. Bless their hearts, how good they are to bother so much about us! I looked long at my bundle, and thought of the dear hands that had so carefully wrapped it up. I wish they could know how much I appreciate the gift, and how much more I appreciate the givers.

9 p. m. Something is up. Companies C and H have been called out and the others have orders to be ready at a moment's notice, but to avoid all confusion and noise.

August 19, 1863.
Wednesday.
Nothing new. C and H have not reported yet and we are as much in the dark as ever about their errand. There has been some talk of a shift about among the non-coms, in the regiment and now it has come. I am still in the commissary department. The new order of things, "company savings," it is called, will give me more to do, and for this I am thankful.

August 20, 1863.
Thursday.
Ration day again. Heretofore we have drawn what was needed, whether it was full rations or half, and the quartermaster has credited back what was not taken. Now things have changed. We must draw a full ration for every man reported on the monthly roll. Some are in the hospital and some are dead, but we draw for them just the same. The extra rations we are expected to sell, and turn the money into the company savings account. I suppose if we should all stop eating we would soon be rich, that is, if the company savings ever do come back to the men, as they are supposed to do. It is a queer arrangement, and I may not understand the plan, but that is the way I now understand it.

August 21, 1863.
Friday.
The day has been hot. No hotter perhaps than some others, but it has made us more miserable. Everyone is crabbed and cross, and finding fault, not only with the weather, but with the way the war is conducted, and everything in general. There are plenty of men in Company B that believe they could have wound up the war before this time, had they only been at the head of affairs, or even been consulted. Time creeps along. The summer we dreaded will soon be gone,

and then the winter, which may be ten times more uncomfortable, will come. I suppose we shall keep right on finding fault just the same, and it will do us just as much good as it does now.

August 22, 1863.
Saturday.

A boat touched here this morning and we got some papers. The *Era* says General Franklin is to supersede General Banks and that General Banks is to supersede someone else, and that a regular cleaning-house time is about to come. The whole army of the Gulf Department is to be reorganised. Regiments that are cut down below a certain number are to be joined with some other, and the extra officers mustered out and sent home. We have learned not to swallow anything whole that we see in the papers, but there does seem to be some sense in such an argument. The 128th has only a third of its original number, and if three such regiments were put together there would be two sets of officers that could be disposed of. If this is the case all through the army, a tremendous saving could be made.

But what of the good record the 128th has gained. If we lose our name and number our record would soon be forgotten. Two regiments, one white and one black, have just gone down the river.

Night. We have marching orders. There is a rumour now that a great expedition is being made up at New Orleans to go and capture Mobile. Of course they can't do it without us, and it may be there is where we are to go.

August 23, 1863. Sunday.

The regiment was invited to attend church in a body and we went. That is the rank and file did, and a few of the officers. I knew there was a Catholic church here, but did not know of a Protestant church. The church was in a shady grove, and in spite of the heat of the day it was comfortably cool. The preacher was a middle-aged man, and he appeared to favour the Secesh cause. At any rate he prayed right out loud for it, but failed to get an Amen from us. He explained at great length which cause was right, and then prayed that the right might prevail. The congregation was mostly of the 128th, and for specially invited attendants we got mighty little attention from preacher or people.

August 24, 1863
Monday.

Through an interpreter I sold over ten dollars' worth of rations today, to a Frenchman. Everyone here is French though the most of them can talk United States. Sol. Drake, the regimental commissary clerk, sent for me today, and said a list of the names that Bostwick wants to make up his official staff had been sent in and that he had seen it. Also that his name and my own was among them. Just when we will be transferred he doesn't know, nor does he know yet for certain that the transfer will be made. I am to say nothing about it outside, nor will he, until further developments.

Something is going on about here. About noon forty men were mounted on confiscated horses and hastily left camp. They are probably on picket duty some ways out, and will give us warning before trouble can reach us. I presume it is some scattering guerrillas, such as gobbled General Dow and George Story at Port Hudson.

August 25, 1863.
Tuesday.
The mounted men came in and reported no enemy in the neighbourhood. They brought in some beefsteak and have divided up handsomely. They won't tell where they got it, but very likely they robbed some butcher shop. They showed good taste in the selection, at any rate.

August 26, 1863.
Wednesday.
Ration day again. As we drew five days' rations again it looks as if we might stay some time yet. Mail came late last night. No letters, but an old New York paper. No news good or bad. Everything seems to have come to a stop. A darkey, named Jack, who has been furnishing the cooks with wood, came in today with a log on his back bigger than himself. When he threw it down a cottonmouth moccasin crawled out of a hole in it. It made Jack almost turn white, he was so scared. The log was full of holes as if mice had eaten their way through it in every direction, and was most as light as cork. It is strange how the negroes fear a cottonmouth, and yet they go everywhere barefoot, and never seem to think of a snake until they see one. This is the first one I have seen since we left Port Hudson. I thought we had got out of the snake country.

August 28. 1863.
Wednesday.
Yesterday passed like any other day, trying to keep cool. Nothing happened worth telling of. Today a party has been mounted and sent

out to gather up the horses that are running loose all over the country. They came in with quite a drove. They went toward Donaldsonville. What the horses are for we do not know. Perhaps we are to be made over into mounted infantry.

A mail came in last night and I was skipped again. I hope they have not forgotten me. Ransom White is now our second lieutenant and Lieutenant Pierce is promoted to first lieutenant. Second Lieutenant John Langdon of Company K is now its captain. These are all good promotions. They are all deserving of them. I suppose Tom Dutcher will be our captain as he is in line for it. He is one of the very best of the whole lot, but has been on detached duty so much of the time, we have almost forgotten him. A change has come over the weather. It is cool and pleasant as it can be. For this we are truly grateful. Lieutenant Pierce hinted to me about a change in fortune for me, but would not let out what it was or when it would come. I expect it is what Drake spoke of a few days ago. I hate to think of leaving the 128th, and yet I would hate to miss a better job.

9 p. m. Colonel Smith, who has been in New Orleans, came up on the Thomas about 5 p. m. and soon after the *Arago* came up, having order to report to Colonel Smith. This means a move, sure. We went right at it and are all packed up and waiting. The *Arago* has anchored close to shore and seems to be waiting for us. (Something wrong with dates here for the next is Saturday and yet it appears to be a continuation of Wednesday, August 28.)

Saturday Morning.
(No date.)
Reveille aroused us from an uneasy sleep on the boards that had formed the floor to our tents, and before it was fairly daylight, two days' rations were distributed, and the finishing touches to our packing up had been made. At 9 a. m. we were once more on board the *Arago*, that old prison that held us for those dreary six weeks and killed off more of us than the Rebels have yet been able to. About noon we unloaded at Baton Rouge and went into camp just back of the Orphan Asylum. We are in a good place, in the city and yet out of it. We can get into the city in a few minutes if we want to. A great many seem to want to, for Lieutenant Pierce has been busy writing passes to go down town. I guess I will go too and see what the place looks like. When we were here before we were glad to lie and rest, and that is about all we did.

CHAPTER 10

At New Orleans, La.

August 31, 1863.
Monday

Was too busy yesterday to even write in my diary. A general order from department headquarters came and was read to us in the morning. Several enlisted men and some commissioned officers from the 128th are ordered to report to the general mustering officer in New Orleans, for muster into the *Corps de Afrique* for recruiting service, your humble servant being one of them. Just when we go I cannot say, but suppose as soon as we can get transportation. Reuben Reynolds and Henry C. Lay from Company A; Charles C. Bostwick, George S. Drake, George H. Gordon and L. Van Alstyne from Company B; Captain George Parker, Charles Wilson and Wm. Platto from Company D; Lieutenant Rufus J. Palon, Martin Smith and Charles M. Bell from Company G; Garret F. Dillon, John F. Keys and George A. Culver from Company H. Richard Enoch and Charles Heath from Company I; Jacob M. Ames from Company K, and several other names of people I never heard of before, and have no idea to what regiment they belong.

The most of us are sergeants, and as we are ordered to rip our stripes off and turn them into the quartermaster we are expecting to have shoulder straps instead. We were not discharged from the service, only from the regiment, but we are in honour bound to report for this new service, and then the shackles will be put on for three years more, if the war should last that long. Just what to think of this new move none of us seem to know. Some feel an inch or two taller already.

I have not fully come to my senses so as to know how I do feel. Things have happened so fast it has kept me busy to keep up with them. We seem to have no choice in the matter. Men are transferred from one company or regiment to another every little while, and now our turn has come, and that is all there is of it.

September 1, 1863.
Baton Rouge, La.

We are waiting for a boat to come along and take us to New Orleans. Our commissions came and were passed around last night. We each got one and I suppose will get pay accordingly. Bostwick is colonel; Captain Parker lieutenant colonel; Lieutenant Palon is major; Dick Enoch is a captain; Charlie Heath, Garret Dillon, Rube Reynolds, Charlie Bell, Mart Smith, Sol Drake and Henry Lay are first lieutenants; Jacob Ames, John Keys, George Culver, Charlie Wilson, Wm. Platto and Lawrence Van Alstyne are second lieutenants. I may wish myself back looking after the fodder of Company B, but so far my only regret is leaving the boys. We have seen good times together and times not so good, but we have hung together through it all like so many brothers. But every day brings something new to think of, and the day before is soon forgotten.

Sundown. On board a steamer called the *Exact.* She lies at the dock, and is taking on the First Vermont Battery. They are the fellows that we supported when posted in the woods on the centre at Port Hudson. They don't know any better than we do what is before them. With good luck loading, and no accident going down, we ought to see New Orleans by morning.

September 2, 1863.
Wednesday.

On board the steamer *Metropolitan* going to New Orleans. We remained on the *Exact* until midnight with no signs of a start. Just then the *Metropolitan* came along on its way from Vicksburg, and took us off. It is said General Grant and staff are on board. I am looking out for General Grant, for I have a great curiosity to see him. There are so many officers of all grades on board that I may have seen him already, but I have enquired out all those that make the biggest show and none of them were him. One is covered with badges and medals, but he proved to be a foreigner of some sort. At any rate, he has quite a brogue.

I finally gave it up and went up on the hurricane deck and smoked while watching the sights along the river. A solitary soldier, with nothing on him to tell of rank, had his feet cocked up on the rail and I joined him. He asked if I knew whose fine place it was we were passing, and just then an officer came after him and I had the whole deck to myself. I had a lot of thinking to do and I was glad to be alone. The news today is that Charleston is taken. So many are talking of it, I began to think it may be true.

New Orleans. Night. We landed about 1 p. m. I watched for General Grant but did not see him. If he was on the boat he must have kept in his stateroom, but I don't think he was on board, for I would surely have seen him go ashore. We, late of Company B, left the others and went to the French market and filled ourselves full. If I ever had so good a meal I have forgotten it. None of us being very well off for money, we began to consider a suitable place to stop at. We decided on the Murphy House on St. Charles Street for the night, and then to look for a place more in accord with our pocketbooks. We found Colonel Bostwick at the St. Charles, the principal hotel of New Orleans. He looks pale and thin, but says he is well. He had no orders for us and will have none until we are mustered. He hardly knows what we are to do, but supposes we will go with an expedition that is being fitted out here, under the direction of General Franklin. Its destination is said to be Texas, but by what route no one that knows has yet told.

September 3, 1863.
New Orleans, La. Thursday.
A mail steamer came in last night, and the mail will be distributed at eight this morning. We are going to head off the carrier and get our letters, if we have any.

Later. We did it, and I have a letter from Jane. God bless her, she writes for all the family. This time she sent me her photograph, so I won't forget how she looks. No danger of that, but I am glad enough to see her. The folks are all well. That's the best news I can get, and is what I am very thankful for. Sol and I set out to find cheaper board and lodging. We were directed to a place in Gravier Street and made a dicker at a very reasonable price.

After supper we went up to the St. Charles and found it crammed with army officers and city officials, and that General Grant was among them. He was sitting at a table covered with papers and was busy talking with those around him. I worked my way in, determined not to miss this chance, and imagine my astonishment when I saw it was the fellow I had sat beside on the upper deck of the *Metropolitan.* A couple of small stars on his shoulder was his only mark of rank. Of all the men I saw on the *Metropolitan* he was the last one I should have called General Grant. The troops in the Gulf Department are to be reviewed at Carrolton tomorrow and I suppose this was what they were planning for.

September 4, 1863.

We were up early and at the St. Charles to see General Grant and staff start for Carrolton. General Banks has his headquarters in Julia Street, and soon after we got to the St. Charles he and his staff rode up. A horse was led out for General Grant, which took two men to hold. He was in full uniform now and made a better appearance mounted than on foot. It was a fine sight to see them ride off up St. Charles Street, and I wished 1 could see the review. I had much rather see it than take part in it, for there is a lot of hard work about such affairs. Later we went to the mustering office and reported according to order received at Baton Rouge. We also got our fatigue uniforms and are now ready for business.

This is the first I have been off duty since I left the hospital at Camp Parapet last spring. We have had quite a rest up and upon the whole are anxious to tackle the unknown which now lies before us. The strangest thing to me has been to undress and go to bed. I have not, and I do not expect to sleep sound again, until I can drop down as I am and pulling a blanket over my face to keep off the mosquitoes, know that however sudden the call I can be ready inside of two minutes.

September 5, 1863.
Saturday.

Our boarding place at 184 Gravier Street has not proved to be all we hoped for, that is, the sleeping accommodations are not quite as desirable as we would like. In the first place the room is close and hot. The mosquito bars shut out what air there might be, but still have holes enough to let through the hungry varmints by the dozen. Then there were bed bugs that act as if they had been starving all summer, and could never get blood enough. The rooms were alive with cockroaches, but these we didn't mind so much, for they did nothing worse than make a noise running across the floor. But on the whole we concluded to move and are in much better quarters at a house on Carondalet Street. I told Sol, as we had nothing to do but scratch and as our play spell might end any day, we should not be so particular, but he was decided and we went.

September 6, 1863.
Sunday.

Sailing down the river on the steamer *A. G. Brown*, the very one our regiment and the Sixth Michigan captured on Pearl River last May. She has been repaired and chartered for the use of Colonel Bostwick and his "nigger stealers," as the Secesh call us. The colonel says we are going with Franklin's expedition, whose destination is said to be Texas. We had a busy time getting off, for we had no hint of our departure until afternoon. I attended church this morning, but it isn't much like going to church at "The City," where everyone knows everyone else. We were hunted up and told where the boat lay, and were none too soon in getting to her. We have formed an officers' club, "Officers' Mess," it is called here, each one putting in $5 towards the expense of grub. We have to board ourselves now. We are each allowed one government ration for a servant, and as none of us have servants we will live on that until pay day.

It is a beautiful night, too much so for me to waste time scribbling any longer.

September 7, 1863.
Monday.

In the Gulf of Mexico again. We passed the too familiar quarantine station where we landed from the *Arago*, and where we started quite a graveyard, and came on down past Forts Jackson and St. Philip, reaching the South West Pass early this morning. I don't know how many boats there are, but the water ahead of us seems covered. I did not suppose the river boats ever went out into the Gulf. We rock and roll like chips on the water. It is curious to watch the tall smokestacks. They slant in every direction at the same time. It is good weather, and the water is smooth. It is what the boatmen call ground swells that are tumbling us about so.

September 8, 1863.
Tuesday.

We are just over the bar inside of Sabine Bay. The light of campfires can be seen on the Louisiana side, but whether of friends or enemies we know not.

The captain of the boat told us today what he says is the object of this expedition. Through his scouts, General Banks has learned that the Rebels under (General Dick Taylor are at Vermillionville with 20,000 troops. That Banks had sent about as large a force up the Red

River to Marksville, from which place they were to march upon Vermillionville. Another force had been sent by rail to Brashear City, and then up the Bayou Teche (pronounced Tash) to get at Taylor from the other side, while Franklin with his expedition is to land and cut off the retreat. I don't know enough about the geography of the country to know whether any or all of this can be true, but that is the way it is given to us. We had a rough night of it. The horses and mules on the lower decks had hard work to keep their footing and could not have possibly stood up on the deck we are on. There were times when it seemed as if we were going over, but the sailors didn't seem scared and so I tried to act as if I was not. We came through all right, and that is the main thing.

September 9, 1863.
Wednesday.
I was mistaken last night. We only arrived off the bar this morning. The fires I saw and thought were camp-fires were dry grass on the prairie, and which is still burning. The fleet is lying outside the bar, and unable to cross, though these boats are said to run on a good big dew. General Franklin is on the *Suffolk*, and signals are being wig-wagged from vessel to vessel. The wind is getting stronger every minute, and what will become of Franklin's expedition if it really comes on to blow can be guessed to a certainty. It will fetch up on the bottom of the Gulf of Mexico.

Later. We are going back. What's the matter I don't know. We were signalled to go back and that it all we need to know. The water is rough, and if it were not for the danger, which is becoming apparent to all, the sight of the boats pitching and diving, this way and that, would be worth sitting up all night to see. We are going farther out from land than when we came, but that makes little difference, for at the nearest we are too far to swim ashore. The wind is dead ahead, and our progress is very slow.

September 11, 1863.
Friday. Pilot Town, in the mouth of the Mississippi.
Our boat is tied up here, repairing damages. We got in early this morning after the most exciting twenty-four hours of my life, and I think many others can say the same.

Yesterday the wind kept blowing harder and the water kept getting rougher. For sea-going vessels it was nothing, but for these cockleshell river boats it was anything but fun. Wednesday night the water was rough. I got into my berth for a nap and the next thing I knew I was sprawling on the floor, where a lurch of the vessel had thrown me. There was no more sleep that night. The boat not only rolled, but it pitched and dove. The wind and the waves seemed to get up more steam every minute and I for one was glad to see daylight. But except for the light there was no improvement. We could see several of the boats, but not a quarter as many as were in sight the night before. Whether they had gone to the bottom or were just out of sight none of us knew.

The *Laurel Hill* was nearby. Both her smokestacks were gone, shaken off even with the upper deck. Another boat tried to get hold of her, but did not make out. Another one, which we could just see behind us, had a signal of distress flying and the flagship signalled us to go back to her. When we turned broadside to the wind, I surely thought we were going over, but we got around and in a short time were close to the *Laundress*, whose flag was flying upside down, which was the reason of our being sent back. She was loaded with men and animals, and wanted a tow. We made two turns about her trying to get a line to or from her, and then gave it up. Both boats were rolling about like chips on a mill pond, the great high smokestacks swinging first towards each other and then far apart. It did not seem as if either boat could stand it much longer. The only thing that kept my spunk up was to hear the captain and mate swear. It didn't seem possible that men could swear like that if the danger was as great as it seemed.

We came on and what became of the *Laundress* I don't yet know. By noon the wind was at its highest. Life preservers were got out, but not distributed. There were islands, or sandbars, all along towards where the shore must have been. We could see these only a part of the time, on account of the waves. Colonel B., who went to the captain and first asked, and then ordered, him to run in between the sandbars and so get into smoother water, was told to "go to hell. I'll run this boat to the South West Pass or to the bottom of the gulf." After that no attempt was made by the landsmen to dictate to the boatmen.

About noon the upper cabin seemed to be tearing itself loose. The woodwork was splintered in several places, and the groaning of the timbers added to the alarm that was felt. I went below to find a place where I could keep still, but it was worse there than above. Everything was soaked. The engines and boilers were crusted white with salt water. The live stock was in a pitiable condition, scared to death and pulling every way on the hawser to which they were tied. The lower decks of these river boats are close to the water. On them is the machinery and fuel, and freight, when any is carried. Everything, living or dead, was soaking wet, including the boxes of hard-tack. On the next floor or deck is the dining room and sleeping berths, and above that the hurricane deck, on which is the pilot house.

How he made out I don't know, but the fact that we got here shows he stuck to his post. A few got drunk, so drunk they could just hang on to something and slam about with it. No one thought of eating or sleeping. Some were dreadfully seasick, and these were the only ones I envied. They just lay on the floor and didn't care whether we sank or swam. Towards night we could see the worst was over, though the pitching and diving kept up about the same. As night came on we settled down as best we could and got what rest we could. I did not think I slept any, but I must have, for the first I knew we were in smoother water and were soon tied up here. The day has been pretty warm, but we are not complaining about that.

Pilot Town is a curiosity to me. It is where the pilots live, that pilot vessels out and in the river. They go out in small boats as soon as they see a vessel, and the one that gets to her first gets the job of bringing her in over the bar, and sometimes way up the river to New Orleans. Then if they are lucky they get a boat to pilot down the river and out into deep water again. Some vessels have some particular pilot that they will take on, and so this racing out after a job amounts to nothing. Then again some captains know the river so well they only have use for a pilot while crossing the bar. It seems the bar, as they call it, shifts its position, and this the pilots keep track of, and so no vessel ventures in or out without their aid. They have a little house on poles from which someone is always looking by day, and from which a light is kept burning at night.

There is no dry ground. The houses, which are only little small one-room affairs, are built on piles, high above the water, and along in front of them is a wooden sidewalk about even with the floor. Here they live and raise families. They are as ignorant as can be on all subjects except that of their trade, piloting. There is a little store, where tea, coffee and tobacco are the main stock in trade. I saw what I took to be calico on one shelf. When the tide is in they are surrounded with water, and when it is out there is nothing but mud. When I told him of the time we had had, he said "yaas, it was a bit nasty." The boatmen are cleaning up, getting the salt off the machinery and making things shipshape.

The horses and mules are taking their rations and from all appearances have already forgotten the uncomfortable trip we have just had. Fish of many kinds are swimming about the boat, and with .some borrowed tackle the men are having great fun catching them. I saw one that looked as big around as a barrel. My friend, whom I have kept busy answering questions, says it must have been a porpoise, and that they often come in for whatever they can find to eat. From a boat that has just gone up we learn that two gunboats, the *Clifton* and the *Sachem*, were captured. That an unknown fort, just inside the Sabine River, had crippled one, and when the other went to her assistance, that was also crippled and both crews made prisoners. That the *Laurel Hill* threw overboard 240 mules. So far as I can find out no other boats were lost. What become of the *Laundress*, which we tried to help, no one seems to know. The most of them must have got in ahead of us, for very few have passed us today. Franklin's expedition seems to have been a failure.

Later. Another boat says a transport, name not known, was lost with 700 men. That may have been the *Laundress*. We may never know any more about it. Something else will come and take our attention, and this trip will soon be forgotten.

Night. New Orleans again. We got here about 3 o'clock, after a delightful ride up the river. Colonel Bostwick tells us he doesn't know what the next move will be, but we are to be ready for it at any time. In the meantime we may enjoy ourselves in any way we please. That will be eating at a cheap boarding place and picking our teeth at the St. Charles, I suppose. I wrote nearly all the time we were at Pilot Town and have just got caught up. Goodnight.

CHAPTER 11

Brashear City, La.

September 24, 1863.
Brashear City, La.

We remained in New Orleans until the 16th waiting for orders. Having just enough money to live on, we tramped about the city, which I find very interesting, especially the part below Canal Street which is here called the French part of town. Above Canal Street the people mostly speak English, and below Canal Street they mostly speak French. The houses in the French part are low squatty buildings as compared with those on the other side. Canal Street seems to divide everything. It is very wide, with a horse-car track in the middle and a regular street on each side of it. The cars are all drawn by mules. The car tickets each have a picture of a car drawn by a mule, and pass for five cents anywhere, just as money does. These cars runs as far out as Lake Ponchartrain I am told, but on account of the expense I have not been out there. I am told it is the summer resort of the people who have money to go there.

The "shell road" which I have read about is a continuation of Canal Street. It is wide and as smooth as a floor. After a shower it glistens like snow, for it slopes each way so the water runs off and leaves it as clean as you please. Way out along the shell road is a tremendous large cemetery, and this I must tell you about. The old lady where I boarded had a son on one of the river boats. He died last week and his body was brought home and buried from her house. The old lady invited me to attend the funeral and I am glad I went, for it was all so strange. The only thing that seemed real was the mother's grief. There were several carriages and I had one all to myself. Some others I found out went empty. The graves in the cemetery are all on top of the ground and are like little brick houses, all whitewashed or painted white.

There was no end to the flowers in the yard or at the grave. A wagon load of them went from the house. After the burial we came back with just as much pomp and ceremony as we went. I was sorry for the mother, and if she hadn't such an outlandish name I would give it. I have never tried to pronounce it, and not having seen it in print will give it up. That is the way with most all the names here. How they remember them is beyond me. I, for one, got very tired of hanging about. I gave up my diary after we came back from our gulf trip, but time hangs so heavy on my hands I have started it again and have caught up to this time the best I can. Colonel B. brought us here on the 16th and we have done nothing but loaf ever since. Brashear City is a small place on Berwick Bay. A small place just across the bay they tell me is Berwick.

Cattle and horses are brought down from the country to Berwick and made to swim across the bay to this place, where they are yarded and shipped to New Orleans for market. There is a store and a restaurant, and some large empty buildings that I suppose were used for storehouses. We came here by way of the Opelousas and Great Western R, R., which begins at Algiers opposite New Orleans, and ends here at Brashear City. This is the R. R. that the Twenty-Third Connecticut were guarding when the Rebels captured them, last June. A part of them were here as well as some other troops. The restaurant keeper told me of the capture, and showed me the bullet marks on his shop to prove they did not give up without a fight. He says the bravest fight of any was made by a New York man, whose grave he showed me near his shop. Just what we are here for or how long we are to stay does not yet appear.

Colonel B. says that part of Franklin's expedition that went up the Teche country by way of this place is somewhere along the Bayou Teche, and we are to wait here for orders. Last Tuesday I went to the city for our mail. I had six letters, all full of news I was rejoiced to hear. Our folks are well, and I begin to think they have more sense than their youngest son and brother, for they don't worry about me as much as I do about them.

Walt Loucks wrote about the 128th and Dave Cottrell wrote about his folks and his regiment. They are doing nothing yet, but resting up. When I got back I found our discharges from the 128th had come. As we have not been mustered into any other, I don't see why we are not just plain citizens again.

October 3, 1863.
Brashear City, La. Saturday.

Here yet and just as busy as ever, doing nothing. A week ago today I went to the city to be mustered into the *Corps de Afrique*. At the office I was told to come again on Monday, so I went to the old place on Gravier Street and spent Sunday writing letters. On Monday I went again to the mustering office and was told to wait until Tuesday.

Tuesday morning I made out to swear in. Our boarding master had sent by me for a half barrel of pork, and another of Fulton Market beef, and had given me two ten dollar bills to pay for it. I got the stuff across the river just too late for the train, and as another did not go until night there was nothing to do but wait. When at last the train was made up I settled down in it for an all-night's ride. It ran about a mile out and was halted by a signal. Soon after, the trainman said we must wait until morning, and I went to sleep. In the night it began raining and it ran through the car roof about as fast as it came.

I got out and went to the engine, where I went on with my nap, but in such cramped-up quarters that I soon woke up again, and then I went to the engine house and finished up the night, the most miserable one of any since that night on the *A. G. Brown*.

On my way back to the caboose I passed the car on which my pork and beef were the night before, and lo and behold the beef was gone. I saw tracks about the car where it had been taken off and traced it to a house not far away. I then went to the office of the provost marshal, who informed me that as it was not government property he could not help me. I then went back to try and help myself, but the people were all French and I couldn't even tell them what I was after. By this time the train was ready for a start and I got aboard hungry, dirty, and as mad as I could be. I told the man just how it was, and whatever he may have thought, he acted very nice about it, apparently believing every word I said. If I ever get ten dollars ahead, and am where I can do it, I mean to make it up to him.

Yesterday some of us went fishing and had good luck. We also got a mess of salt water crabs, which are new to me but which I found to be most delicious. Lieutenant Colonel Parker and four others have gone up the country towards Franklin, to see about new headquarters there. Colonel B. is in the city and the rest of us will wait here until he comes.

The last few nights have been cool enough to keep the mosquitoes down, so about all we do is to eat and sleep and grow fat. Unprofitable servants maybe, but we are obeying orders and that is what we agreed to do.

October 8, 1863.
Brashear City yet.

We have been expecting to go every day, but someway the order did not come. What money we had among us has played out and we have had to apply to the quartermaster for provisions. The cooking we take turns at, what little there is to do. We got all ready to go yesterday. The *A. G. Brown* tied up here and we bundled our belongings on board, only to take them off again. The captain says General Banks has the boat for a special purpose, what, he does not know, but had orders to meet him here, and to allow no one else on board. The general and a host of other officers came towards night and were soon on board and away. After they were gone the colonel and a part of his family took a walk up the Bayou Beuoff (pronounced Beff), to an island on which is a large sugar plantation. We got a boat and crossed over, strolled over the grounds, got all the oranges we could eat, and take away, and were handsomely treated by the people. They seemed real friendly, and I hope may have felt so. At any rate we had a pleasant time and got back tired enough to turn in and go to sleep.

October 12, 1863.
Monday. Nelson's Plantation, on the Bayou Teche.

Since my last writing we remained at Brashear City, eating, sleeping, playing cards and checkers, pitching quoits, running races and passing the time as best we could, until the arrival of the *A, G. Brown* just at night on Saturday, We went on board but did not get away until midnight. A large fire over in Berwick lit up the water almost like daylight. Captain Hoyt and Lieutenant Mathers were sent back to New Orleans on some business, otherwise our family was all together. We stopped at the mouth of the Bayou Teche until daylight and then went on as best we could. The Rebs had put every possible obstruction in the way. One tree had been fallen across it, for the Teche is narrow, in places not as wide as the *A. G. Brown* is long. Two old boats had been sunk in it, and these the *Brown* had to snare and pull around so as to get past. We arrived at Nelson's Landing about midnight. Unloaded and marched about a mile farther upstream and pitched our tents. This Bayou Teche I am told runs through the country and comes out into the Mississippi at Plaquemine.

So far as I have seen it, it is narrow, and in many places and for long distances is covered with the leaves of some sort of weed that grows up from the bottom. Being about on the same level as the land, it is for all the world like sailing over a green field. The water shows if you look down upon it, but not as you look forward or back. It is said to be deep enough for any sort of a vessel.

With all the obstructions to our passage, it was a much pleasanter one than the one we took in the Gulf of Mexico. After a late breakfast, there being nothing better to do, several of us went up the Bayou to where a lot of negroes were getting the wreck of a sunken boat out of the way. They worked from small boats, diving down and making fast to anything they could, and then with tackle hitched to a tree on shore would tear it loose and get it out of the way. One of them fell overboard and went down. Another dived for him, bringing up one foot which another in the boat took hold of, and without attempting to get his head out of water, rowed ashore with him, dragging him out on the bank by the one foot. The man was dead, but might just as well have been saved, for it was only a very few minutes from the time he went in until his one bare foot was in sight. They paid no attention to our advice or opinions of such work, and I soon found that they only understood French, and so did not know what we were yelling to them about.

We got a boat and crossed to the other side. We found a used-up cane field, which was hard to get through and which seemed to have no end. When we finally did get through we found a patch of sweet potatoes. Beyond seemed to be an endless open country with groves now and then, and everywhere, as far as we could see, were droves of horses and cattle. One flock of horses sprang us, came up close as if to investigate. They were small, but perfectly formed, and of almost all colours. Some were spotted, but the most were of one solid colour. Whether they are real wild horses or whether they have owners, we found no one to ask. Both the horses and cattle seemed to keep in droves separate from each other.

By the time we got back we were tired and hungry as if we had been on a forced march. We got hold of a nig who understood English, and told him what we were after. An even dozen immediately enlisted, so we have made a beginning, and feel encouraged. This country is beautiful. Not exactly level and yet no hills. I suppose it might be called rolling. A good road runs a few rods from the Bayou, and along next the Bayou are large live-oaks. These are covered with moss, almost every branch having bunches hanging down just like an old man's beard. It is a curious sight to me, and I cannot say I really like it. I would give more for a good look at Bryan's big maple than all of them. Our troops are said to be in or near Vermillionville, twenty-five or more miles from here, and that a battle may be fought any day. Lieutenant Bell is going back on the *Brown* tomorrow, and I will wind up this epistle and send it by him. Maybe he will bring me a letter when he returns.

October 13, 1863.
Tuesday.

We are to start for Vermillionville tomorrow. There is quite a gathering of odds and ends of regiments and detached parties that are to join the army there. We have been looking for horses today, and after a hard day have several, but not enough for all. While out looking for them we ran upon a squad of our cavalry, who ran down and shot a beef, of which they gave us a generous portion. We are cooking it now so as to have it to cheer us on the way tomorrow. Those of us who must walk will need all the encouragement we can get.

October 16, 1863.
Friday.

On Wednesday morning before we left Nelson's there was another try for something to ride, and by hook or crook we all made out. Colonel B. loaned me his horse to go and look for another. Along the Bayou about a mile below camp I found several horses hitched to the trees about a house, in which the owners were getting a breakfast. Only a couple of them had military trappings, the others having ordinary saddles and bridles. One of these was hitched to the upturned roots of a blown-over tree, the bridle being thrown over the root. I noticed this as I rode past, and as soon as I was out of sight I turned back, and riding close up to the stump I slipped the bridle off the root, and old sorrel followed me right along. Everything was ready for a start when I got back and away we went. I felt a little guilty, but I know by the trappings the fellow had stolen the horse, and the old saying, that it's no crime to steal from a thief, came to mind and comforted me.[1]

1. After the war. and after I was married, my wife and I went on a visit to relatives of mine in Albany County. While there it was proposed that we all go over into Green County and take dinner with some of my cousins whom I had never met. We went, and had the best sort of a time and dinner. It happened that one of the boys had been in the army, and naturally we talked of the war. He had been in the Gulf Department, as was I, and he was also in the, (continued next page),

We rode until noon and then stopped for something to eat and to let the horses fill up on grass. Then we went on across the prairie, which seemed to have no end. We kept an eye out for guerrillas, but saw none. About 4 p. m. I saw a cornfield a little off the way and went to it to get some corn for my horse. While I was gone the colonel decided to camp for the night in a grove near the road, and went there thinking to see me when I came along. But in some way we missed each Other and I kept on, finally reaching Vermillion Bayou. The guard told me no such party had come in. As troops were scattered all about I kept up the search until dark, when I crossed over into the village, stabled and fed my horse in an empty building, and spread my blanket on the *piazza* of a house close by. A woman came out, and although it was rather late to ask permission, I did so, when she flounced back inside and I heard her tell someone not to let such things lie on the stoop. I didn't take any such hints and was soon asleep.

An old dog acted much more friendly, for he sat by me until I went to sleep and was still there when I awoke. In the morning I fed the rest of the corn to old sorrel and then went on to Vermillionville, enquiring everywhere for Colonel B. and rest of the gang. Not finding them I came back, and on the way traded horses with a coloured gentleman who was having trouble, his horse going backwards in a circle, instead of straight ahead. She was a beautiful black mare, small, but wiry, probably one of the thousands that run wild on the prairies. After we got the trappings changed I had quite a time getting aboard my new craft, but by coaxing I finally mounted, and for awhile sat there, while the lady was considering whether to go or stay and fight it out. The nigger had tried whipping, so I tried petting, and she soon started to walk and in a short time was taking a gait that soon brought me to the Bayou, where I got some breakfast with the engineers who came in late last night.[2]

After breakfast I was about to start for headquarters to report the probable capture of Colonel B. and party, when in they came as sur-

Teche country. This led to my telling about stealing the horse, when he jumped up, declaring "You are the man who stole my horse!" He supposed the horse had got away, and having no time to look for him, rode through on one of the wagons of the Engineer Corps, of which he was a member. He described the horse, and some of the others, so I knew he was telling the truth. He said they had bargained with the people for a breakfast and were too busy eating to notice anything going on outside. L. V. A.

2. The man whose horse I had stolen the day before was of this company, and if I had not traded horses, no doubt I would have had some explanations to make. L. V. A.

prised to see me as I was to see them. They were going to report me captured, for they thought sure I had been. The engineers kindly offered a breakfast which the party was glad to accept, after which the colonel said we must go on to headquarters and report for orders. My "Black Bess" was afraid of so many people around her and kept as far away as the picket rope would allow. Whether she had a grudge against me I don't know, but as she swung around the circle she suddenly wheeled and with both her bare hind feet hit me squarely in the breast. My canteen had swung around in just the right position to receive the blow and that probably saved my life. As it was, one side of the canteen was smashed against the other and I was knocked flat on the ground. I was picked up and in a minute or so was as good as ever. The blow had knocked the breath out of my body, and as soon as I had recovered that I was all right, with not even a sore spot to remind me of the affair. We then pushed on about four miles beyond Vermillionville, where we halted to wait until our baggage wagon arrived. We encamped near a sugar mill on the Rebel General Mouton's plantation.

From among the negroes that came flocking about we found that many of them knew how to cook, so we divided our party into messes and each hired a cook. Lieutenants Gorton, Reynolds, Smith and myself were one, and we immediately set out for something to try our new cook with. Smith and I got after a pig which ran in General Mouton's yard and all the way round the house, but we finally got a shot in the right place, and had some of the most delicious fresh pork for dinner. After dinner we got hold of the English-speaking darkies and explained our mission among them. They were more anxious to enlist than we were to have them.

Even the women and children wanted to go, and we had more trouble to make them understand that only able-bodied men were wanted, than we did to get them to enlist. That night they built a big bonfire, and hundreds upon hundreds were dancing about it, until I got tired watching them and went to sleep. They have some good fiddlers among them, and many more that are not so good. Those that saw the thing out say they finally got to singing, "Glory to God," and "Abe Linkum," and wound up with a prayer meeting, in which Massa Linkum and the Linkum Sogers were the names most often heard.

October 17, 1863.
Saturday.
Today Lieutenants Heath, Reynolds, the quartermaster and myself

took a long ride about the country spreading the news of our head-quarters for recruits. The white people we met were civil, but their hatred of us could not be entirely covered up. I could not find it in my heart to blame them, and I much regretted that one of our party saw fit to trade horses with one of them and entirely against his will. But the blacks are wild with joy, and eager to become "Linkum Sogers."

In the afternoon a detail was sent out with the quartermaster's wagon for mutton or beef, for our family is getting so large they will soon eat up the government rations at hand. They came back soon with a choice lot of dressed mutton. The guides apparently knew just where to go. Later in the day Reynolds, Gorton and myself made another tour of the country towards the Mississippi River. We came to a house over towards the Great Cypress Swamp, as the folks here call it, and which is a belt of big timber lying between the Teche prairie and the Mississippi River, in which outlaws and wild beasts are said to abound, and in which bands of guerrillas have their hiding places. We have heard much of the Great Cypress Swamp and its terrors, and felt quite brave as we looked at it from a half mile distance. No one appeared to be at home, so we investigated.

The weeds were as high as our heads, but a path led back to a stable in which was the most perfect picture of a horse I ever looked at. He appeared to be scared out of his head at the sight of us, and plunged and snorted as if a bear was after him. The path continued and soon we came to a *mulatto* and his wife busy digging peanuts. We introduced the subject of enlistment and found he was ready and willing to go at once if he could take his horse with him. They could both talk English, and a jargon we supposed was French. When speaking to us they used English, but to each other they talked French. After a short confab he agreed to go with us, and his wife made no objection. He got his horse from the stable, and his saddle from the house and we set out for camp.

I thought it strange that either of them showed so little concern at parting for what might be forever, and wondered the wife did not ask to go also, as so many of the others had done. We reached camp just at night, where both the horse and man attracted the attention of all hands. Colonel Parker at once wanted to buy the horse, and a bargain was soon struck, the horse to be paid for on the next pay day, which was agreeable to the *mulatto*. He was so frank and open in all his talk, that when he asked if he might ride the horse home and remain till morning the colonel readily consented, telling him to be in camp by noon the next day.

October 18, 1863.
Sunday.

We lay about camp until noon and the horse and his rider did not appear. The colonel was mad clear through. He had been told the nigger would not come back, but he believed he would, and as the time went on little was heard but comments on the slick trick the rogue had played on Colonel Parker. After dinner he told Gorton and me to saddle up and show him the way and he would see whether he could find him. We went to the house but found no one at home. We then rode on towards the swamp. We saw a man running across a cleared spot and soon overhauled him. It was the fellow himself. He said his horse had got away and he was trying to find him, had been looking for him all the morning. The colonel drew his revolver and told him to march ahead of him to a big tree a short distance away, at the same time telling me to get my picket rope ready, for he was going to find that horse, or else find a dead nigger.

The nig was scared and began to beg, declaring the horse had gotten out of the stable in the night, and he and his wife both had been looking for him all day long. After he had got through, the colonel told me to throw the line over a limb, for he was going to keep his word. Whether he did really intend to hang him or not I don't know, but I thought he would stop short of the actual deed, so I proceeded to get the rope in position for a real hanging. Just then the rascal owned up. The horse was in the swamp where he had hidden him, and if the colonel would spare his life he would take us to him. We then went on and soon came to a beaten path that led directly to the dense forest before us. At the first turn in the path after we entered the woods the colonel dropped me off.

At the next turn he left Gorton, and he himself with revolver in hand followed the fellow on and out of sight. He was gone perhaps fifteen minutes when out they came, horse and all, and we made tracks for camp, which we reached about sundown. The next morning the man's wife came into camp, and they both acted as if nothing out of the ordinary had happened. Where I waited in the woods the undergrowth was so dense I could not see a rod in any direction except along the path. Squirrels, both black and gray, came out of the bushes and looked at me. I counted five black squirrels in sight at one time. They are not quite so large as the grays, and are a dark brown rather than black. I wondered if they were as plenty all through the woods as where I sat. Gorton says he saw as many as I did. If all the stories I have heard about the Great Cypress Swamp are true, I don't care for any closer acquaintance than I now have.

There are wild animals of all kinds common to this part of the country—bears, wildcats, opossum, deer and snakes as big as any in Barnum's menagerie. I can believe the snake part, for I have seen so many that I believe all the snake stories I hear. This same Great Cypress Swamp is said to be the home of outlaws, both white and black. That they have homes there where they live undisturbed by the laws made to govern other people. That runaway slaves find homes there, where they live and raise families which recruit the ranks of the lawless set living there, as fast as they are killed off by the lights they have among themselves and with the officers of the law that attempt to capture or subdue them.

Night. The work for tomorrow has been mapped out. Quartermaster Schemerhorn, Lieutenant Reynolds and myself are to start for Brashear City, taking with us the men we have enlisted. Two days' rations have been given out, and the darkies are having a farewell dance. This has been a busy Sunday, one I will long remember.

October 19, 1863.
Monday.
We were up early and found the dance still going on. These creatures have danced all night, and eaten up a good portion of the rations, in spite of the fact that they knew a hard tramp lay before them today. How they will get through, or what we will do if they give out on the way, is the next thing for us to think of. They don't care. Someone has always thought for them and will have to think for them for some time to come.

The quartermaster and Reynolds started off in good season but I was kept back for instructions until they were out of sight, and I did not overtake them until they had reached Vermillion Bayou. A drove of men, women and children, the families of the men we were taking away, had followed them until now. We had to wait for a wagon train to get off the bridge and this gave time for them to get through with the goodbyes, and most of them turned back. A half dozen or more of the younger women kept on and went all the way through. The day was warm, and the road was dusty, but we went through without accident or adventure, other than might be expected when all things are considered.

For several days the men had been in a state of great excitement over their new prospects. They had wound up by dancing all night, and eating up the provisions intended for us on this hard tramp.

As the day wore on the excitement wore off and they found themselves very tired and very hungry. Such few things as they had beside those on their backs was in a cart drawn by a mule, and driven by three wenches. When a man gave out we turned out a wench and put the man in her place. Finally all three wenches were on foot, and their places in the cart taken by as many men. Before long others gave out and the cart was loaded until that broke down. Then we held a council. We were outside the picket lines and night was coming on, and staying there in the road was not to be thought of. Three revolvers were the only weapons of defence we could muster in case of attack by a guerrilla squad. Capture meant death.

We explained the situation to such as could understand us, and they made it so plain to the others that they were all ready to hustle. We patched up the cart so the extras could be dragged along and away we went. The quartermaster rode on to find a place to stay at, and something to eat. I let one who was worst off ride my horse, and with Reynolds at the front to coax, and I at the rear to drive, we got up such a gait I had to do my best to keep up. The road had been graded for a railroad, and was wide and level as a floor. At dusk I saw the steeple of a church, and knew we were near our journey's end. Now that the end was in sight, the weariness all seemed to disappear. We passed the picket line and were soon in the town.

The quartermaster had got a schoolhouse for a stay over and had rations from the commissary. We made short work of these and expected to settle right down for the night. The men and women filled the schoolhouse full, and after being in there a few minutes, we three made up our minds the air was better outside, so we each took a board shutter from the windows and were soon settled down as comfortable as the circumstances would allow. Before we were asleep we heard a fiddle tuning up and in a little while a dance was started and was in full blast when I fell asleep. How long it lasted I don't know, but when I awoke about sunrise the inmates of the schoolhouse were sleeping like the dead.

October 20, 1863.
Tuesday.
I was nearly blind when I awoke. Something like an inflamma-

166

tion in my eyes had troubled me for some days, and the dusty tramp of the day before had made it worse. However, I soaked them open, and found that it had not affected my appetite in the least. While at breakfast Lieutenant Bell came and joined us. He was on his way to join the colonel and his party at the front. The colonel had given us an order to stop any boat going towards Brashear City, and with it I proceeded to the landing, leaving Reynolds and the quartermaster to pick up and bring on our party.

At the landing I met a party on their way to the front, and gave my horse to one of them who was in just such a fix as I was the morning I became a horse thief. In reply to his very profuse thanks I told him I would have to turn her loose if I didn't give her away, for I could take her no farther. I had long forgiven her the kick she gave me and sincerely wished her well. At Nelson's Landing I found a boat which was being held in readiness for General Banks and his staff, so that was of no use to us. Soon after the *A. G. Brown* came up and said she would be back that night, and take us. We went into camp near the sugar mill and very soon our small army was arranging for a sham battle. They talked French, so I could only judge what they were up to from what I saw. They divided into two squads and proceeded to fortify their positions by rolling the empty sugar hogsheads up in two parallel rows, behind which they stationed themselves, while the generals in command jawed at each other across the field. The men each had a hogshead stave for a weapon. For flags they used bandanna handkerchiefs, and for drums a piece of board upon which one man pounded while another held it up.

One of the generals made a speech which made the other side fighting mad, and they all jumped over the breastworks and met in the space between, batting each other over the head with their weapons, and yelling with all the power of their lungs. We thought sure they would kill each other, for the blows they struck broke some of the staves into splinters. Just as we were going to try and interfere, one side surrendered and were marched off, prisoners. There had been some blood shed, and the wonder is that no heads were broken. But the best part came after the fight was over, and when the final settlement was being made.

Through an interpreter we learned that the general who should win the fight was to kiss one of the young ladies that had marched with us all the way from Mouton's Plantation, and he now demanded his pay. She was led out upon the battlefield, and when the victorious officer came up to claim his reward she slapped his face, and then turned her back to him. He then gave some orders, when his men grabbed the dusky maiden and turned her about. I could not tell whether she blushed or not, but suppose of course she did. The general got down on one knee and then on both and jabbered French at her until she finally relented and stuck out her hand, which she allowed him to kiss. This soon led to a full surrender, and the battle was over, and peace declared.

We gave out the rations and began to get ready for a start as soon as the boat came along. We even filled a barrel with sugar, thinking it might come handy when we got to Brashear City. But night came and the *A. G. Brown* failed to appear. There were many here who like ourselves were waiting to get out of the country. Among them was a young mulatto woman, whom the others called Margaret, and who seemed of a higher order than those about her. She was willing to talk, and from her I have a story that has fully reconciled me to the wisdom of the President's Emancipation Proclamation. She has started for the North. Our coming among them has given her the chance she had long looked for. She has run away from her mistress, and her master is in the Rebel army. .She has a picture of her husband, and a fine-looking man he was. He was as white as I am. He was the son of his master, and her father she says is Judge ——, now in the Rebel service. Her husband picked up enough education to be head man on his father's plantation. He knew too much for a nigger, and when the Rebel army came through last spring he was taken out and hanged to a tree right before her eyes. After they had gone the slaves cut the body down and buried it. Margaret is in hopes to reach New York, and I wished I could land her there that minute. If she was dressed as well, and if she was educated, she would pass muster with any I have seen that go by the name of ladies.

No boat coming to take us away, we posted guards, giving each a stick of wood for a weapon. I remained up until midnight, and in going the rounds to see if the guards were awake, came near getting a club over my head as I turned the corner of the sugar mill. At midnight I called Reynolds, and rolled myself in my blanket and was soon asleep. The mosquitoes were about as thick and as savage as any we had met with. The horses and cattle had no peace for them. I rolled myself up head and heels in my blanket, and yet when I awoke found one foot had got out of bed, and the varmints had put a belt around my ankle between my stocking and trousers that looked like raw beef.

I don't suppose there was an atom of space that had not been punctured by a bill. But I slept right through, and as usual dreamed of home and home folks.

October 21, 1863
Wednesday.

Nelly, one of the women who came with our crowd, has volunteered to be our cook, and besides being a good cook has proved herself to be a good forager. When I woke up she had fresh pork and chicken cooked and we asked no questions about what price she paid for them. Quartermaster Schemerhorn rode up to Newtown for rations, and I went back to bed to finish up my nap. The mosquitoes had not quite finished their job on me, and some actually bit me through a thick woollen blanket. My leg was very sore where they feasted on it this morning. One of the men mixed up some mud for a poultice, which helped it wonderfully. I found out we could learn many things from these poor creatures, not the least being how to live on the fat of the land we are in.

Noon. The quartermaster came back and said the *A. G. Brown* would be along today some time. That it will make a landing one-half mile above here. Accordingly we pack up and move up to Mr. Nelson's so as to be sure of not missing it. Mr. Nelson, the owner of everything in this region, is here. He has been a merchant in New Orleans, but since Banks's order driving all Rebel sympathizers from the city, has been here at his plantation home. It is said he owns 20,000 acres of land, and all the necessary stock and tools to work so large a tract. After a supper of hard-tack and bacon. Lieutenant Reynolds and I went and called on the gentleman. He received us very politely, and offered us the best his house afforded.

The boat not coming we prolonged our visit, sitting on the broad *piazza* and smoking his cigars. He said he was a widower, with two children, a son in the army, and a daughter at school in Georgia. He told us of the outrageous wrongs he had suffered at the hands of the invading armies, how they had laid waste his land, torn down his buildings and fences, taking away his mules and horses, cattle and sheep, until he had nothing but the bare land to live upon, and no slaves left him to work even that. It was holding up the other side of the picture to our view, and in spite of ourselves we were sorry for him.

He evidently did not expect sympathy from us, for after reciting his wrongs he changed the subject of conversation around to topics we could all agree upon, and after a sociable chat he invited us to spend the night with him, agreeing to have us called in case the boat came during the night. He urged us to stay and we did. He gave us rooms, elegantly furnished, with beds so white and clean we were some time making up our minds whether after all we ought not to sleep on the floor, and leave the beds as they were. But the whole mosquito bars and a few nips from our ever-present enemies decided us. We undressed and were soon asleep, too sound even to dream of home. The boat did not come and the next thing we were aware of it was morning.

October 22, 1863.
Thursday.
We slept late, and when we came out, our host was waiting for us, to say that breakfast was ready, and would not listen to our going away until we had partaken of it with him. We sat down to a beefsteak breakfast, with all the extras. I did not think I was so hungry, but the smell of the victuals made us both ravenous. Our host seemed to enjoy seeing us eat and thanked us heartily for making him the visit, going so far as to say that in case the boat did not come that day he would be glad to entertain us again. In books and in other ways I had heard of southern hospitality and I now know it was all true. I wonder if it was ever put to a severer test.

We went down to the landing and found a guard of soldiers from an Illinois regiment, keeping watch over a quantity of sugar and molasses which the government has confiscated, and which the boat was expected to take away when it came. They invited us to make one of their party until the boat came, and we gladly accepted the invitation. They thought we had risked our lives in going to stay with Mr. Nelson, and eating food in his house, but we did not believe it, and did all we could to make them think better of him than they had so far done. The guards shot a hog, which made fodder for our folks for the day, together with the government rations we already had. The day passed and another night came on and still no boat. We crawled in wherever we could get and slept as best we could for the mosquitoes, which seems determined to eat us alive.

October 23, 1863.
A cold rainstorm that has been threatened for a day or two came upon us early this morning. A small flock of sheep came up the road

driven by a man on horseback. The negroes from everywhere have gathered here and the rations we give our men they give away to their friends and are always hungry in consequence. When the sheep came along they surrounded them and killed at least a dozen before we could stop them. The man hustled along with what was left and those killed were soon skinned and being cooked in various ways. We had mutton for dinner and for supper, and had enough left for breakfast.

The day finally passed and we began looking for better sleeping quarters. Reynolds and I with a part of the guard finally climbed a ladder and got into a loft full of cornstalks with the corn on just as it had been cut and stored away. The place was alive with rats and mice, which ran over and through the stalks, making a terrible racket, varied once in a while by a fight among themselves. We got used to the racket and finally were asleep. Just as we were enjoying ourselves, along came the boat we had waited so long for. We hustled to sort out the nigs that belonged to us and get them on board. In a little while we were off. The boat was crammed full of people—black and white, old and young, men and women all spread out on the cabin floor, or the tables. I never saw such a mass of people in so small a space. We poked around and after awhile found room to lie down, after which getting asleep was quick work.

October 24, 1863.
Saturday.
Another raw day. Now that the people are standing on end there is more room to get about. We made out to eat such as we had; while we wished for more, we had to content ourselves with what we had grabbed hold of the night before in the dark. At noon we passed Franklin, and about 3 p. m. reached Centreville, where there was a lot of sugar to load on the lower deck. The captain said if we would turn in our men to roll on the sugar he would undertake to fill them up.

I took advantage of the stop to see what the place looked like. On one of the streets I saw oranges on a tree and went in to see if I could beg or buy a few. As I went into the yard a young lady came out and, in a tone and with a look that almost froze me, asked what I was doing in her yard. To save me I couldn't think what to say, but I did after awhile come to enough to say I would like an orange. She turned to a negro and motioned towards the trees, when he went and picked his hands full and gave me. Then the madam pointed her linger towards the street and said, "Now that you have what you came after will you please go"—and I went. I don't know yet what I ought to have said or done, but the only thing I did was to get back to the boat as fast as I could.

I kept the adventure to myself, and gave the oranges away, for I think they would have choked me. That is a sort of southern hospitality I never read of in a book, or heard of in any other way. I never saw so much scorn on a face before. Why I stood there like a chicken thief caught in the act, and then carried off the oranges, I don't now know. If the Rebels were all like her I would resign and go home at once, for she did actually scare my wits all away from me. The sugar was on board and true to his promise the captain ordered a supper for our army, which must have made his stock of provisions look small. Rube asked me what I found the town like, and I told him it was different from any I had yet seen. We soon got settled down for the night.

October 25, 1863.
Sunday.

When we awoke we were in sight of Brashear City. We landed, formed in line as well as we could, and marched to our headquarters, where I found my old crony, Sol Drake. We found quarters for the men in an unused building, and in a little while their woolly heads were sticking out from every window.

The quartermaster drew clothes for them, and they were soon fitted out with suits of blue, just like the rest of the Linkum Sogers. The trouble was to fit them with shoes. I doubt if many had ever had a shoe on their feet. Their feet are wide at the toes and taper straight back to the heel. No. 12 was the smallest size we found use for, the most of them taking 14 or larger. They insisted on squeezing a No. 14 foot into a No. 10 or 12 shoe, but we, knowing what that would result in, got them properly shod after a long time. Then how proud they were! We then gave them their rations for the day, telling them through interpreters that if they wasted it or gave it away, they could have no more until tomorrow. We moved all our belongings from the boat and filled out the day visiting and talking over old times, and at early bedtime settled down for the night in a four-room house which has been taken for our headquarters while here.

October 26, 1863.
Brashear City, La. Monday.

On going out this morning who should appear to me but George Story of Company B, who was captured with General Dow at Port

Hudson last summer. He says he was well treated by his captors, and has no fault to find with them. They took him and the general to Richmond, and put them in Libby Prison. After a while he was paroled, and sent to Annapolis, Md. There he was kept until exchanged, and then sent south in charge of the provost marshal to be turned over to the 128th New York. Through a mistake at headquarters he was sent here, as the 128th was supposed to be at the front in the Teche country. If he had not met us as he did, he would have gone up the Teche on the next boat. As it is he will go back to New Orleans tomorrow, and look for his regiment up the river, probably at Baton Rouge, where we left them.

We commenced teaching our recruits the rudiments of soldiering. They are awkward, but very anxious to learn, and as that is the main thing, we look for little trouble in drilling them. By shoving them together, lock-step fashion, they soon got the idea of marching in time, and on the whole did as well or better than we did at Hudson, when we took our first lesson. The quartermaster has gone to the city for equipments, tents, etc., and when he returns we will soon be at the Manual of Arms. We expect Major Palon here today to take charge, and by the time Colonel B. and the rest get back, hope to have our recruits fit for turning over to any regiment that needs them.

October 27, 1863.
Tuesday.
It rained hard all day, consequently no drill or other work was attempted. Major Palon and the quartermaster came from the city, the latter with rubber blankets and shelter tents for the recruits. He also brought some letters. one for me telling about the draft at home. Those that are drafted can get off by hiring a substitute or by paying $300, in which case a substitute is furnished them. I am glad I enlisted. There have been times when I could hardly say it, but I can say it now with all sincerity.

More women and children have come, wives and children of the men we have. Poor things! I suppose they have nowhere else to go or to stay, so they have followed on after their husbands and fathers. I have heard that the government has provided camps for them, where rations are served to them just as to the soldiers. It is a very proper thing to do, and I hope it may be true that these helpless ones are thus provided for. This arming of the negroes is not such a simple affair as it seemed. This is a side I had not thought of, but I don't see how it can be dodged.

October 28, 1863.
Wednesday.

The rain has stopped, and the mud is now having its turn. It makes us just as helpless as the rain did. We have put in the time making plans for the time when the mud hardens. It does not dry up, as it does in the north, but the water seems to settle and leave the ground hard even if there be no sun or wind.

October 29, 1863.
Thursday.

After a council on matters and things in general, we have made some changes, looking to a more orderly-arrangement of our camp life in these quarters. The hangers on about camp have been driven away. The quartermaster's stores and those of the commissary department have been separated and placed in tents outside, where they can be found and got at. The most intelligent among the recruits have been appointed corporals and sergeants, and the screws of discipline turned on just a little more. Guards are placed, more for their instruction than for our safety, and things are putting on more the appearance of a military camp than a mere lounging place, as it has heretofore been.

Just as we had got everything to our notion, a boat came, and on it were Captains Merritt and Enoch with 120 more recruits. Tents and blankets were given them and quarters assigned them, which altogether has made a busy day for us. Discipline, what little there had been, went to the winds when the men all got together. They all seemed to be acquainted, and such jabbering French as they had. I suppose they had lots of news to tell each other. Some can talk English, but all of them can and do talk French when talking to each other. They came from Colonel B.'s headquarters at Opelousas, and were in charge of Colonel Parker, who got left behind at Newtown, and will be along on the next boat.

At night Dr. Warren, our surgeon to be, came from New Orleans, and tomorrow will examine the recruits. Sol Drake has been sent for to join Colonel B. at Opelousas and expects to leave on the next boat. Opelousas is beyond where I have been. I have posted Sol in getting as far as Mouton's, where we were, and beyond that he must find out for himself.

October 30, 1863.
Friday.

It has been a rainy day, but we have paid little attention to it. Dr. Warren finished up his examination and nearly every man passed muster. He was not as particular about it as Dr. Cole was at Hudson. As fast as examined and passed we gave them their new clothes, and a prouder set of people I never saw. Lieutenant Colonel Parker came at night with later word from Colonel B. and Drake does not have to go. For this he and the rest of us are glad. Colonel Parker brought eight men with him and about as many women. We have quite a respectable squad, and they are learning very fast—faster I think than we did when we first began. Those that were rejected by the surgeon as unsound are here yet, and what to do with them is a puzzle to us. We have each of us taken one, to do anything for us we can think of, and they seem perfectly happy.

Mine is named Tony, and is a great big good-natured soul, ready to do anything for me, if I will only let him stay. He came to me at first asking if I would write a letter to his wife, and when I asked him what I should write, told me anything I was a mind to. I wrote the letter, telling her where he was, and how he was, and put in a word for some of the others for Tony's wife to tell their folks. This pleased him so much that he hung around trying to do me a favour in return, and when he was rejected by the doctor he said I must keep him, for he would be killed if he went back home, because he had enlisted. The government allows us transportation and a daily ration for a servant, so I am nothing out, for he asks no other pay than his board and the privilege of staying.

October 31, 1863.
Saturday.

Lieutenant Colonel Parker and Dr. Warren left us to look for a healthier place, as many of the men are getting chills and fever. The ground is low and wet and I suppose is a regular breeding place for fever and ague. We are glad of a prospect of a change, but this country is all swampy and wet. The Teche country comes the nearest to dry ground of anything I have seen. We are getting into full swing. Companies A, B, and C are organized and assigned to Captain Merritt, Captain Hoyt, and Captain Enoch. There are thirty men left and these are turned over to Lieutenant Reynolds for drill. At night, a telegram from Colonel Parker says we must stay at Brashear City until our regiment is full. I have been out of sorts today and have laid up for repairs.

November 1, 1863.
Sunday.

Was detailed for officer of the guard, but not feeling well Lieutenant Reynolds volunteered to act for me, for which I am very much obliged. I put in another day trying to be sick, but toward night gave it up as a failure. However, I put in the day by staying indoors, writing letters for the men, some to their wives and some to their sweethearts. The more love I can put in the letters, and the bigger words I can use, the better they suit the sender. What effect they have on those that receive them I happily do not know.

November 2, 1863.
Monday.

I lay down last night thinking if only mother was here to fix me up a dose, as she has so many times done, I should be well right off. I soon dropped off, and the same thought kept right on going through my brain until I awoke this morning and found myself in the same position, lying crosswise of my bed just as I lay down last night. But my dream of home had cured me, and I was myself again, ready for whatever might come.

I found myself again on the detail for guard. After the new guard was posted I had but little to do, except to see to it that the reliefs were changed at the proper time. There was no enemy in sight, though the guards were just as watchful as if the enemy had been in the next yard. The worst was to remember the names of the sergeants, and that I got round by writing them down. Even then I had to guess at some. At night Colonel Parker came back from the city, on his way to join Colonel B., who is at the front with the rest of the gang. He brought me two letters, one saying father is sick and the other saying he is well again. I am glad the good news came with the bad, though I had much rather no news of that kind would come. I also had a list of names of those drafted from the town of North East. John and Perry Loucks and Amon Briggs were among them. Whether they will go or get substitutes the letter did not say.

Also that another proclamation from the President calls for 300,000 more men. I wonder if he knows what an army we are raising for him here. Report says an accident between here and Algiers last night killed twelve soldiers and wounded over sixty more. One train broke down and another ran into it, both loaded with soldiers. These roads are so straight and level it would seem that accidents of that kind might be avoided.

November 5, 1863.
Tuesday.

I made a raise of a postage stamp today and sent a letter home. The day has passed like all do nowadays, with little to do. But it has been pleasant, and that is an exception I am happy to make a note of. The quartermaster came in tonight with more tents, and more supplies.

November 4, 1863.
Wednesday.

The steamer *Red Chief* came down the Teche this morning with more recruits, in charge of Lieutenants Gorton, Smith, Heath and Ames. This will make more work and I am glad of it. Lieutenant Colonel Parker has been on the point of starting up the country again for several days, but has not gone yet. Today he has decided to move our quarters to higher ground. This is a wise thing to do according to Dr. Warren, for a great many of the men are sick with chills and fever. The site chosen is about a mile away. I am detailed to see that the stuff gets off, and the others are to be on the new site and receive it, and see to its proper distribution. I am temporarily assigned to Company D. By noon I had everything on the way, and after reaching camp helped to get Company D in as good shape as the others.

A regular camp is laid out and company streets made. It made me think of the laying out of Camp Millington. Grading the company streets and other necessary work will give us something to do for days to come. I put in so much time helping the others get fixed that I forgot my own tent, and as Captain Enoch invited me to sleep with him, I accepted, and after fighting mosquitoes until nearly midnight, I fell asleep and remained so until late the next morning.

November 5, 1863.
Thursday.

Tony was waiting for me when I woke up, and was feeling badly because I had to go to the neighbours to sleep. After our hard-tack and coffee were safely stowed away, I got my tent out and we soon had it up. Then Tony began skirmishing for furnishings. He had seen what the others had and set out to beat them all. He got hold of a board wide enough and long enough for me to sleep on, and soon had legs driven in the ground to hold it up. My modest belongings were put under it, and the deed was done. Colonel Parker gave a few parting orders and then took boat for New Iberia to join Colonel B., leaving Captain Merritt, in command. Captain Laird not yet having joined the command, I am curious to know what sort of a man I am to serve under. Company D is as yet made up of raw recruits, not yet having passed through the medical mill, so I have only to keep them within bounds until they are examined and sworn in as soldiers, when their education will begin.

At night Dr. Warren and Lieutenant John Mathers came from New Orleans. A cold drizzling rain began about that time and we were driven into our tents, where the hungry mosquitoes awaited us and war was at once declared. If I had a brigade of men as determined as these Brashear City mosquitoes, I believe I could sweep the Rebellion off its feet in a month's time. They make no threats as our home mosquitoes do, but pounce right on and the first notice you get is a stab that brings the blood. I have had at least one bite for every word I have written about them, and all in the same time I have been writing it. The only escape from them is in the hot sun, or under a blanket so thick they cannot reach through it.

November 6, 1863.
Friday.

This morning Lieutenants Reynolds, Smith, Ames and myself formed a club of four for mutual protection against starvation. We have a rejected recruit for a cook, and have made a draft on the commissary for salt horse, hard-tack and coffee. If he can't get up a meal on that, then he's no cook for us. My company was examined and almost every one proved to be sound enough for soldiers. A dozen at a time were taken into a tent, where they stripped and were put through the usual gymnastic performance, after which they were measured for shoes and a suit, and then another dozen called in. Some of them were scarred from head to foot where they had been whipped. One man's back was nearly all one scar, as if the skin had been chopped up and left to heal in ridges. Another had scars on the back of his neck, and from that all the way to his heels every little ways; but that was not such a sight as the one with the great solid mass of ridges, from his shoulders to his hips. That beat all the anti-slavery sermons ever yet preached.

But this is over with now, and I don't wonder their prayers are mostly of thanks to Massa Linkum. They are very religious, holding prayer meetings every night, after which the fiddle begins and dancing goes on all night, if not stopped on account of the noise they make, I don't know how they get along with so little sleep, or rest. After the examination we got blankets and clothes from the quartermaster and they were fitted as well as it is possible to fit from a ready-made stock.

Our cook, George, proved to be a jewel. He made salt beef taste so much like a chicken we didn't notice the difference. Major Palon came from the city at night, and brought some letters. One was for me and contained three dollars from my old crony, Walt Loucks. This will keep us in extras for a little while. We were some time deciding how to use it, but a majority thought a part of it should go for flour, so George could try his hand at pancakes.

November 7, 1863.
Saturday.

I have never described our camp, and may never have a better time than now. We are out of town, to the north, on high, hard ground, for this country—so high that there is quite a slope towards the water of Berwick Bay. Company streets are laid out and the camp kept clean by a detail made each day for that purpose. There are many large trees in and about our camp, and taken altogether we have never had a stopping-place quite equal to it. The sick list has shrunk already, though the hospital tent is pretty well filled yet. We have company drill every day and there is quite a strife among us to see which can learn his troop the fastest. The men are as eager to learn as we are to have them, which makes it much easier for both parties. Berwick, which is directly opposite, is quite a place from the looks, larger than Brashear. It is the shipping port for the great Teche country that lies beyond.

Just after dinner Colonel Tarbell's orderly rode into camp and inquired for me, handing me an order which read:

Lieutenant Lawrence Van Alstyne, commanding Company D, 90th U. S. C. L, at Brashear City, La. Captain Vallance, quartermaster, will furnish the bearer with a boat, in which he will proceed to Berwick and procure a sufficient supply of lumber to floor the hospital tent in said regiment.

Signed,   Tarbell, commander.

I took five men and such tools as we could find and called on Captain Vallance, who gave us a boat in which we rowed across the bay, which was still as a mill pond. We landed near a shanty which easily came apart, and which had good wide boards, enough to floor several hospital tents. We made these into a raft which we towed back, reaching camp without having seen a person, except a guard—who considered my order good enough authority for letting the boards go. We had boards enough for the hospital tent and all the other tents, which as soon as they are dry will be used for the comfort of all hands. At night Lieutenant Gorton arrived from the city to take the next boat for Newtown to join Colonel B.

Lieutenant Smith made me a present of a handsome pair of shoulder straps. The groundwork is dark velvet and the border of gold cord twisted and woven together. Altogether they are as handsome a pair as I have ever seen on anybody's shoulders. I shall lay them away until I get a coat fit to put them on, and that won't be until after pay day. Thank you, Matt, I'll try and not disgrace them. I presume he paid money for them that he needed for fodder; but that's just like Matt Smith. Major Palon also returned tonight, and made some changes. Lieutenant Ames, my partner in Company D. goes in the medical department as clerk, and Lieutenant Reynolds takes his place with me.

November 8, 1863.
Sunday.
On duty today as officer of the guard. Generally that is a light duty, but with these men it is not so much so. None of the men can read or write, and so the sergeant and corporal of each relief has to have the names of his relief repeated to him until he remembers them. Even then there are many mixups that have to be straightened out. The names are strange to me, and after writing them as they sound, I find it difficult to pronounce them.

I went the rounds during every relief, and never failed to find something out of joint. One at the major's tent, whom I had taken extra pains to educate, I found taking his gun apart to see how it was made. Another had his shoes and stockings off and was walking his beat with bare feet. Another had taken off his accoutrements and piled them up at the end of his beat and was strutting back and forth with folded arms. The only thing to do is to call up a man who speaks both French and English and through him straighten the matter out.

November 9, 1863.
Monday.
Today an order came to move to New Orleans. That is, all the companies that are full. That leaves Company D here until more men

come. There is a regular jollification over the order, as none of us are in love with this place. I suppose it would be a proper thing for me to introduce the officers of the Ninetieth to whom the readers of this diary may be, and as there is nothing to prevent I will do it now. If I ever get a chance to read it myself it will call them up before me as I now know them.

Colonel Edward Bostwick comes first, and anyone who will be apt to read this knows him as well as I. But as I want the list complete I will begin with him and work down the line. He is about five feet ten inches, light complexion, gray eyes, with brown hair and beard. He is rather particular about his own appearance, and also that of the men under him. He is always on the lookout for a higher limb to roost on, and after getting there himself, is very good about helping his friends up to him. He seldom drinks, never to excess, and on the whole is a good soldier. He came out as captain of Company B, 128th New York. Was promoted to major of the First Louisiana Engineers, May 2, 1863. He served at Port Hudson with them and had the name of doing well whatever he was ordered to do. In August 1863, was promoted to the rank of colonel, with permission to raise a regiment from the freed slaves in this department, and this he is now trying to do.

Lieutenant Colonel George Parker is from Poughkeepsie. Came out as captain of Company D, 128th New York. On Colonel Bostwick's recommendation he was promoted to his present rank. He is about five feet seven inches, light complexion, sandy hair and beard. Is well up in military tactics, and is afraid of nothing. Rushes right into anything, regardless of getting out again. Is kind to his men, but a strict disciplinarian. When his orders are obeyed he is all right, but when he gets angry he acts without judgment or feeling for anyone or anything.

Major Rufus J. Palon is from Hudson. Came out as second lieutenant in Company G, 128th New York. He has the army regulations and military tactics at his tongue's end. Is pretty strict on discipline, but never loses his head. Money has no value to him. He would give his last cent to any one in need, even though he might be just as needy himself.

Surgeon Charles E. Warren is tall, dark complexion, with dark sandy hair and beard. So far as I know he is a good surgeon. He is free with his money, and with the hospital whiskey. A real good fellow, though not in all things the sort one can pattern after with safety.

Quartermaster Peter J. Schemerhorn left home as orderly sergeant of Company G, 128th New York. Acted as second lieutenant of his company at Port Hudson, and was afterwards detailed as clerk at headquarters, where he remained until the formation of this regiment, when he was made first lieutenant and acting quartermaster. He makes a good quartermaster, seeing that his stock is kept up and ready for distribution.

Adjutant T. Augustus Phillips is one of the boys. He served in the Second Fire Zouaves in the three months' service and afterwards came out as orderly sergeant in the 165th New York. Was detailed as clerk at headquarters and in some way got a recommendation for adjutant in Colonel Bostwick's regiment. He is a New York tough. Gets drunk as a lord, and looks down upon anyone else who does not do as he does. He is not as popular in the regiment as he might be.

Captain Thomas E. Merritt was formerly sergeant in Company I, 128th New York. Was raised to acting second lieutenant of same company, and finally promoted to captain in this regiment. He has travelled a great deal and remembers what he has seen. He seems well fitted for the position he now holds and stands well with all hands.

Captain Charles Hoyt is as good an all-round man as is often found. He is fine-looking, a line singer, has a way of being everyone's friend, and making everyone a friend to himself. He is cut out more for society than for the army. He takes now and then a drink, but never gets beyond himself. Will share his last dollar or his last hardtack with anyone. Altogether, he acts as a sort of balance wheel to the rest of the machine, keeping some from going too fast, and helping others to go faster. He would be missed if taken away, more than any half dozen of us.

Captain Richard Enoch came out as first sergeant of Company I, 128th New York. He was wounded at Port Hudson, and did not again join his company, being recommended for promotion as first lieutenant in the *Corps de Afrique,* from which he came to us with a captain's commission. He has a jovial disposition, but has a very quiet way of showing it. He sometimes takes a little too much, and then is reckless of his money and of the good name he has gained. Everyone likes him, because they cannot help it. As a military man I doubt if he is ever heard much about. He had rather have a good time, and no matter what is going on he generally manages to have it.

There are several other officers who have not yet reported and of them I know nothing. One of them is Captain Laird, who will be captain of Company D, when he comes.

First Lieutenant Robert H. Clark was promoted from sergeant in the 116th New York. He is an excellent penman and would make a much better clerk in some department office than he ever will a soldier. He is rather hasty tempered, and has already had several jars with his brother officers, particularly with Adjutant Phillips, whose assistant he at present is. If Adjutant Phillips kicks clear out from the traces Lieutenant Clark will probably succeed him.

First Lieutenant Martin Smith was formerly an engineer on the Harlem R. R. He went out with a three months' regiment and afterwards as sergeant in Company G, 128th New York. He is open-hearted and outspoken. One can always tell where he is, for he is not deceitful. He is well liked by his brother officers. Just now he lies on his back on my bed making fun of a stove I have manufactured out of a camp kettle. He has no idea I am writing his biography.

First Lieutenant Reuben Reynolds is from Hudson, N.Y. He came out as a private in Company A, 128th New York. Was promoted to corporal, then to sergeant and then to first lieutenant in this regiment. He looks as if he had just been taken from a bandbox. No matter what clothes he has on he always looks neat and well dressed. He was on a three years' whaling voyage before the war, and tells some very interesting stories of his life on shipboard. Before he came to us he was detailed as clerk in the Y. M. C. A. at New Orleans. He is a professor of religion, and I think tries to make his profession and his army life jibe. We all respect him, though none of us feel as if we fairly knew him.

First Lieutenant John Mathers is from Fishkill, N.Y. He came out as a private in Company F, 128th New York. Was promoted to second lieutenant in the Third Engineers, and from that to our regiment as first lieutenant. For some unknown reason he and I took a dislike to each other while in the 128th, and used to pass each other by as one surly dog does another. Since we have been thrown together we have talked the matter over, and neither of us can give any reason for our mutual dislike. We are the firmest of friends now, together much of the time we can call our own. We are not a bit alike. He is a regular dandy in appearance but the commonest sort of a fellow when you get at him.

First Lieutenant Charles Heath was a sergeant in Company I, 128th New York. Was given a commission in the Third Louisiana Engineers, and afterwards given the same position in this regiment. In my opinion his head is not right. He acts strange at times. Sometimes he is as quiet and docile as can be, and in a little while as profane and foul-mouthed a man as I ever met. Is not ambitious, but seems to take what comes as a matter of course. He has no intimates, keeping mostly to himself. What influence ever brought him up from the ranks I cannot imagine.

First Lieutenant Garret F. Dillon was promoted from sergeant in Company H, 128th New York. He is a very small man, has a lisp, and a mincing walk. He looks and acts as if he was cut out for a dandy, but lacked the material for making one, and was thrown out in the shape he now is.

First Lieutenant Charles M. Bell was first sergeant of Company G, 128th New York. At the Battle of Port Hudson he happened to be nearest Colonel Cowles when he fell. He received the colonel's dying message to his mother and was sent home with the body. He is one of the most capable of the whole lot of us. There is no position he could not, fill, were it not for his liking for strong drink. This he does not seem able to control. I believe he tries to but lacks the strength to resist the temptations that are constantly placed in his way. Poor Bell, I pity him more than any other man here. With the right influences about him, what a different man he might be. He has more good traits than any of us can boast, but his one besetting weakness is strong enough to overcome them all.

First Lieutenant George H. Gorton enlisted in the 128th New York, as wagoner. Was promoted to commissary sergeant in the Third Louisiana Engineers, and from there he came as first lieutenant to this regiment. He is of a strange make-up. Is well liked by all, but not greatly respected by any. Is a good horseman and would probably make out better handling horses than he does men. Put him anywhere, and he manages to make money, and manages to spend it as fast as he gets it. Is free-hearted and obliging and I never knew of his having an enemy. Neither does he make any lasting friendships. He worked as teamster for Colonel Bostwick before going into the army, and it was through Colonel Bostwick that he got the position he now occupies.

First Lieutenant Henry C. Lay was a corporal in Company A, 128th New York. I knew him while in that regiment, but he has not yet reported for duty with us. He is on some special service and I suppose will sometime turn up among us. From what little I know of him I should say he will average well with the rest of us.

First Lieutenant George S. Drake was also with Colonel Bostwick before he entered the army. He was commissary sergeant in the 128th New York, and always in close touch with Colonel B. He and I have long been fast friends, so it will not do to say anything against him. But I couldn't if I would. There is nothing but good to say of him. He has been in a position that kept him off the field, so I cannot say what sort of a soldier he would have been, but he has always done well whatever he has had to do, and probably would have done the same had he been in the ranks. He is a fine penman, much better calculated for a business career than that of a soldier. He is no hand to push himself ahead, but all the same he gets there. Does not make friends as fast as some, but he keeps those he does make. He is all right, no one need worry about Sol Drake.

Second Lieutenant Jacob M. Ames came out as a private in Company K, 128th New York. He was for some time assistant hospital steward and afterwards promoted to sergeant in his company. From there he came to this regiment as second lieutenant. He has not much taste for a purely military life and I think he would have done better service as clerk in some department. He has fits of blues, when he is rather cross and surly, but when these go off he is good enough to make it all up. He seems to be out of place.

Second Lieutenant John Y. Keese was a private in Company H, 128th New York. Was made a corporal, and then a second lieutenant in this regiment. He has no enemies and few if any fast friends. He doesn't seem to have the knack of making either. Is not ambitious to get ahead. Some say he is lazy. At any rate it seems doubtful if he gets any higher than he now is. Still he may be like a singed cat, and come out top of the heap.

Second Lieutenant George N. Culver is another graduate from Company H, 128th New York. He has a habit of carrying his head high up and I have often wondered why he never stubbed his toes. He keeps rather to himself, not mixing with the others more than he is obliged to. Still he is a good sort of chap when one gets up close to him, and tends well to what he has to do.

Second Lieutenant Charles Wilson was a corporal in Company D. He is of German descent, rather quick tempered, and not real well calculated to get along in a crowd like this. Still he is a good fellow and I think will make a good officer when his patience has had time to grow.

Second Lieutenant William Platto is from the same company and regiment. He minds his own business and is well liked. So far as I know he neither smokes, drinks, or chews. If he has other bad habits I have not yet found them out. But he has good qualities enough to make him a favourite with all. He is tall and fine-looking and in all-round good qualities is above the average of us.

Second Lieutenant Orrin A. Moody has not yet reported for duty and so he goes free. I hope he won't lower the average.

Second Lieutenant Lawrence Van Alstyne was, like most of the others, from the 128th New York. He enlisted as private in Company B. Was appointed corporal, afterwards sergeant and acted as commissary of Company B until his discharge from the 128th and his transfer to this regiment. His spare time is mostly given up to writing letters either for himself or for others, and to keeping an account of his travels and adventures, which takes the place of letters to his folks at home.

So much for the officers, and now for the men. In colour they range all the way from ebony to a yellowish white. In stature they vary just as greatly, and so they do in intelligence and ambition. They are willing to learn and some of them learn very rapidly. But there are others that are quite the contrary, and that keeps the average rather low. In that respect they are like all other recruits, white or black, the quick to learn have to do a whole lot of hard work to make up for the stupidity of the rest. They look well in their uniforms and are tickled most to death with their outfit, especially their guns. Those that have been in the service long enough are good soldiers. When they have fought at all, they have fought like demons. If any were ever taken prisoners I have not heard of it, and quite likely they did not live long enough to tell of it. I have spent a lot of time over the descriptive list but am rather glad I stuck to it.

November 11, 1863.
Wednesday.

Yesterday I had to skip, or else break into my description of the Ninetieth, and that I did not want to do. Lieutenant Drake went to the city and I attended to his duties as well as my own. An order came for the Ninetieth to report at New Orleans, leaving a guard here to receive and forward such recruits as may be sent in from the front. It does not take soldiers long to move, and the entire outfit, officers and men, were off on the next train, leaving Lieutenant Smith and myself with Company D here to take care of the next squad that comes. Soon after they had gone who should appear but Colonel Bostwick, Adjutant Phillips and Lieutenant Wilson from Newtown with 130 more recruits. They were all hungry and we had quite a time filling so many empty baskets.

The colonel looks well and says he feels well. Wilson, however, is sick, and the colonel decided to go on to New Orleans, and to take everything with him except Smith and I, and ten men as guards. They got off on the 5 p. m. train. We had a hustling time getting them off, and after they were gone Smith and I sat down on the platform and smoked.

The weather is cold for the time of year and we lay and shivered till after sunrise. Having no tents left we took up quarters in the same house we were in once before. Had we been out in a tent I don't know how we could have slept at all. We put in the day preparing for another cold night. With the aid of an apology for a stove, a candle and a pack of cards, we passed quite a comfortable evening and night.

November 12, 1863.
Thursday.

I put in the forenoon writing and Smith in running around. After noon an orderly came with an order from Colonel Tarbell for us to vacate the house, as he needed it for his clerks. As he is boss we had no other way than to get out. But we took our stove with us. We got hold of a good wall tent which we put up and moved the commissary stores into it, and where we are about as comfortable as we were in the house with half the windows out. To make the matter worse, Lieutenant Keese came in just at night with another batch of recruits. He left Colonel Parker at Franklin, and he is about the last one left up the country now. We issued rations for the men, and got them in the depot for the night. We took Keese in with us and the stories he told of his adventures up the country made the evening pass quickly.

November 13, 1863.
Friday.

We were up bright and early so Keese and his recruits could catch the first train out. After that we went into our tent to talk over matters. This just staying here with nothing to do but think brought to mind many things we had not thought of for a long time. I told Smith what Ike Brownell said just before he died. "That if he had the power to do so he would start North with every man who wanted to go, and as fast as he passed over four feet of ground he would sink it." Matt said that expressed his sentiments exactly.

At noon the *A. G. Brown* arrived from Newtown and reported being fired on between here and Franklin. From the way she was barricaded with cotton bales about the pilot house and from the bullet holes through it, they must have had an exciting time. Lieutenant Reynolds before he left had got- hold of a pony, but as he could not take him with him, told me to sell or give him away. I found plenty of buyers but they had no money, so I let him munch government hay until today, when I saddled up and started for a trade.

I found a sutler a little way out of town who offered to buy if I would take it in trade. I made a rap with him, getting twenty papers of tobacco, twenty-five cigars, a pound of butter, a box of shoe blacking and a brush, and a glass of beer. That was the best I could do and it took me a long time to do that. Matt thought I made a good trade, and I hope Reynolds will think so too. A couple of sergeants from Colonel Tarbell's headquarters came in at night and we had a euchre party.

November 14, 1863.
Saturday.

For pastime today we went crabbing. We had good luck, and a feast to wind up with. The guards understand fishing much better than we, and they have all the fish to eat they care for.

November 15, 1863.
Sunday.

We kept in our tents nearly all day, writing letters and wondering when this dreary way of living will end. A man caught a big catfish which we traded some army rations for and have been living high tonight, besides having enough for some days to come. Our forces up the Teche are said to be working back this way. Droves of cattle and horses are being driven on ahead of them. They swim them across from Berwick, and when they get here are so tired out there is no trouble in yarding them. Then they are shipped to Algiers and slaughtered for the army. The horses, I suppose, are used in some other way, but am not sure, for I have seen bones in meat that I well know never grew in a cow, or a steer.

November 16, 1863.
Monday.

Tonight, Lieutenant Wilson came from the city with a couple of orders, one for Matt, to go up the Teche again and report to Colonel Parker, and the other for me, to pack up bag and baggage and report to Colonel B., at New Orleans. The *Southerner* came down last night with over two hundred holes in her cabin made by the bullets fired at her from the bushes along the Teche. Several passengers were wounded but no one killed. They have cut the telegraph wires. Our main force seems to have left the ground they have passed over, not well enough protected to keep the wandering bands of guerrillas from doing a lot of mischief. Wilson brought some papers which say Fort Sumter has fallen. I supposed that had happened long ago.

November 17, 1863.
Tuesday.

The colonel left his horse here when he went through and that is the reason I am here yet tonight. I could not get a transportation order signed in time for the only train that carries horses. Matt got left over for much the same reason. His order had to be countersigned by Colonel Tarbell, and before he could get his signature the boat had left. Colonel Parker came in today and went on to the city, leaving his horse at Berwick, and Wilson is to ride him back to Franklin. He has gone across the bay and Matt and I are here by ourselves, just as if none of these orders had come.

November 18, 1863.
Wednesday.

Am in Brashear City yet and alone. I couldn't get away with the horse, and not daring to leave him here kept the whole outfit. I wrote Colonel B. why I did not go. Matt had just the same trouble I did and he got mad and left on the s o'clock train for the city to find out what's the matter. It is a strange mixup. No one can leave the place with any government property without a pass signed by Colonel Tarbell, and Colonel Tarbell is out of town and no one left in his place. The report is Adjutant Phillips has resigned and his resignation has been accepted. Also that Lieutenant Clark has been put in his place. So much of my prophecy has come true, if this report is true.

Lieutenant Culver came down today. Colonel B. left him with no orders, and he has been loafing ever since. He came down intending to go on to the city and find out about it. Lieutenant Mathers came from the city on his way to the recruiting camp, which Culver says is at our first camping place near Nelson's Landing. They staid and took supper with me and then went on, leaving me all alone.

November 19, 1863.
Thursday.

Had a call from one of the Twelfth Connecticut today. Another man called and tried to sell me a map of Brashear City. I told him I had one printed on my brain already and did not care for another. I took out my ten men and gave them a drill so as to keep them even with the others, in fact did anything and everything I could to pass away the time. A large force came across the bay just at night, belonging to the Thirteenth Army Corps. They must have joined the Nineteenth Corps somewhere up the Teche, and their coming through this way shows the campaign is about to wind up. They are western men—great big, lusty fellows, and by the way they act are able to get a living anywhere, for they have been helping themselves to everything that is not nailed fast. No orders coming for me, I went and made a call on the Ninety-First fellows, who loaded me with oranges and other good things to eat. Some of them are from Columbia County, N.Y. and I being from Dutchess, we were neighbours right away.

November 20, 1863.
Friday.

Last night, after I was abed and asleep, I was pulled out by the heels and told I had company to entertain. It was Matt, with a couple of his old railroad cronies, all on their way to the front. One of them was an Irishman chockfull of fun and stories. The other was a lieutenant in the Second Engineers. After getting them something to eat we sat and smoked, and Matt got his Irish friend telling stories. The consequence was we all went to sleep with a grin on our faces. Matt had got the transportation business fixed up, and at 1 p. m. I left Brashear City with everything belonging to the Ninetieth U. S. C. I. The train was crowded, some riding' on top of the cars. One man, a soldier in the Ninety-first New York, had a chill that seemed as if it would shake his bones apart, and when that passed off had a fever that almost burned him up. Poor fellow, I pitied him, and that was all I could do. I hardly dare write it down, but I have never had a touch of that complaint that seems so universal in this country.

We got to Algiers at 8 p. m. I left a man with the colonel's horse and took the rest to the ferry and was soon in New Orleans, looking for the "Louisiana Steam Cotton Press," where Matt told me was now headquarters. I found the place, but it was so far from where I expected that I thought I would never get there. It was late, and after a handshake all around, I turned in with Sol and was soon asleep.

CHAPTER 12

The Louisiana Steam Cotton Press

November 21, 1863.
Cotton Press. Saturday.
I slept until called this morning, and was not through with my nap then. I had breakfast with the quartermaster and then set out to get acquainted with the place we are now in. The Steam Cotton Press is, or has been, quite an affair. It fronts on old Levee Street and is about 300 feet long, running back about the same distance, with buildings all around it. Except at the front these buildings all front inside, with a board shed or *piazza* roof along them, under which the cotton as it was brought in was stored until pressed. From Reynolds, who has inquired into its history, I learned that the four-storey front, except the space occupied by the press itself, was used for offices, and the buildings on the other three sides was for the help needed to do the immense amount of work connected with re-pressing the cotton for shipment to different parts of the world. Cotton was first pressed into bales about like hay bales, at the place where raised. Then it was brought here and sold to the cotton merchants, who re-pressed these bales to about one quarter their former size, thus enabling a vessel to take on a much larger load.

The press itself it a simple affair, but powerful. The bed is of railroad iron cut to the proper length, and the follower is of the same. Long levers, with a short elbow at the lower end, stand at each side. Over these, chains run to a drum which pulls the long arms down, and the short arm upwards, thus forcing the bed and follower together. The great square yard in the centre is graded smooth with sea shells, like the "Shell Road," and will make a capital drill ground. It is large enough for a whole regiment at a time. It is the best quarters we have ever had. Everything is dry and it should be healthy here if anywhere

191

is this flat country. My first job will be to help get the books and reports in shape. But today I am allowed to look around and I am doing it. The colonel sent me to the ferry landing on an errand just at night, after which I got something to eat, wrote this and am going to bed.

November 22, 1863.
Sunday.

On duty as officer of the guard. The duties in this bricked-in camp are light, and are more a matter of form than anything else. Still it must be gone through with. I find the men have improved wonderfully from what they were at Brashear City. Nothing at all happened worth writing about.

November 23, 1863.
Monday.

I came off duty at 8 o'clock, and after breakfast settled down for a nap, which was cut short by a call from Charley Ensign of Company B, 128th, who has just been discharged and is on his way home. We went out for a walk, and a talk about the boys of Company B. He says George Drury has got an appointment to come to us as hospital steward. Let them come. We are pretty much made up of 128th boys now, and if they keep coming we will get all of them.

In the afternoon I took Company D out for an hour's drill. I found a great improvement since I last had them out. Once the hard shell of stupidity is broken through they learn fast. The best of it is they are anxious to learn and one can afford to have patience. John Mathers came in last night with twenty men, which will about make up another company, then our regiment will be half full.

November 24, 1863.
Tuesday.

The twenty men brought in last night were turned over to me to uniform and equip. Dr. Andrus from the 128th called on us today. He is on his way home on a visit. How I wish he could be with us all the time. Of all the men I have met since leaving home, there is none I admire as I do him. I wish all men were like him. A few might have to come down a little, but the most would have to jump up to reach his level; and some of them would have to jump high. At any rate it would raise the average wonderfully. Sergeant McArthur, also of the 128th, made us a visit. It seems as if everyone that can get a pass to come to town are sure to fetch up here. We are glad to see them and they act as if they were glad to see us. The rainy season is about due now, and from appearances it is about to begin. A year ago today I was sick, on board the *Arago* off Fortress Monroe. It is a good thing I don't know where the next 24th of November may find me. I had rather leave it as it is than to know.

November 25, 1863.
Wednesday.

Drilling the men, and getting settled in our quarters, has kept me busy all the day. Borrowed five dollars and bought a stove with it. Have had plenty of help and advice about it and expect to have plenty of company, for we are great on visiting each other. We are in the most comfortable quarters for winter we ever had and I hope we may not be called out again until warm weather comes. The weather is not cold, that is, water does not freeze, but we do, almost. There is a chill in the air at night that goes right through a blanket.

November 26, 1863.
Thursday.

Thanksgiving-day, as sure as I live! I never thought of it, until someone mentioned the fact to me. How the good things will abound at home. I suppose we should give thanks for what comforts we have, hut it would be much easier if we had more of them. The day goes by like all the others, drilling our men, eating our rations, and sleeping in our tents, which are pitched under the sheds nearest the press,

November 27, 1863.
Friday.

A sergeant in Company K, 128th, who deserted while we were at Fortress Monroe, has been arrested and sent on here. He is in the Parish Prison, and Ames, who knew him, has gone up to see him. I don't know what they do with such, but from the fact of his being sent on I suppose it will be nothing more than reduced to the ranks.

November 28, 1863.
Saturday.

Colonel B. issued his first general order today and it reads like this:

Roll call at half-past 5 a. m. Immediately after the sound of the bugle the men will arise and arrange their knapsacks, blankets and overcoats in neat and compact order. The bunks swept, the blankets folded in the knapsacks, shoes polished, clothes brushed, muskets stacked and accoutrements hung on them.

The company, except the police, will form and march to the river and wash face and hands. Breakfast call at 7 a. m. Doctor's call at 8 a. m. Guard mount at 9 a. m. Drill 9 to 11 a. m. Roll call and dinner at noon. Cleaning of muskets and accoutrements from 1 p. m. to 2 p. m. Drill 2 to 4 p. m. Supper 5.30 p. m. Roll call at 8 p. m. Tuesday and Friday evenings a recitation in tactics from 6 to 8 p. m. A detail of one man from each company and one corporal from the regiment for policing camp. A pass to two men from each company each day, to visit the city or call upon friends, time of leaving" and returning to be written on pass. Saturdays to be spent in cleaning up camp and getting ready for Sunday morning inspection. Officers in command of companies will be held responsible for the carrying out of this order and accountable for any neglect of duty by the men or officers under them.

By command of

Charles E. Bostwick,

Colonel commanding 90th U. S. C. I.

Good for you, Colonel B. It has given me something to write in my diary if nothing more. But I think the order a most sensible one. We know what to do now and when to do it. Besides it will keep us busy and that is what we most need. Some sort of deviltry is sure to be hatching soon after we get out of work. This being Saturday we have everything in apple-pie order. Oh dear! how I wish I had some. Just writing the words "apple-pie" makes my mouth water. I never saw a camp so spick and span as this is tonight. An order has just come for 130 men to be turned over to the Fourth Engineers. That cuts us down nearly half. Colonel B. gave me a handsome inkstand today. I suppose that would be as appropriate a present as he could make me, considering my constant use of one. He also asked me if I needed money. I told him I needed it badly enough, but did not want it enough to borrow just now; but all the same I thanked him and am glad to know I can call on him if necessary.

November 29, 1863.

Sunday.

Just two months since I was mustered into this regiment. Consequently I have two months' pay, $211, and am as poor as a church mouse. I am just as handy with a hard-tack and a cup of coffee as ever, and I presume feel better than if I could have anything I want. We have a way of telling what we will have for our next meal, fretting up a bill of fare that would beat the St. Charles Hotel. After we have ordered the meal from George, our cook, we pick up a hard-tack and nibble away on it and are just as well satisfied, and all the better off. A letter from home tells me they are all well, and "the world it wags well with me now."

The chills and fever keep at the men. Every day one or more comes down. I suppose they brought it with them from Brashear City. It doesn't seem as if they could get it here, for we are in the dry all the time, and everything about camp is as neat as can be. In my short army life we have never been in a place where we were so comfortable as here.

December 2, 1863.
Thursday.

For the past few days I have been too busy to even keep my diary going. We have been making out transfer papers to go with the men. We have to enumerate every article of clothing and equipment that goes with each man and they must all be made in duplicate. An officer from the engineers has been here and looked at the men, and seen them at drill. He decided to take Companies E, B and D. That cleans me out of a job, but I suppose Colonel B. will find me another. Charlie Ensign and Henry Y. Wood who have been visiting us until their discharge papers were made out and transportation secured are to leave for home on the *Cahawby* tomorrow. Charlie has left me his profile, and says he will go to Sharon and see the folks in my place. We are all on a quiver, for someone has got to go on another recruiting tour, and no telling where it will be. Adjutant Gus Phillips, who has been under arrest for drunkenness for some time, was released today and started right off on another and a worse spree. This so exasperated Colonel B. that he put him under arrest again. I don't know what the outcome will be, but hope it will clear him from us for good and all.

December 4, 1863.
Friday.

Officer of the guard today, in place of a sick man. I once had the favour done me, and I am very glad to pay it back. Still more glad am I that I am well and able to do it. We expect our pay tomorrow and then hurrah for some new clothes, and a full stomach. Also a photograph to send home. Another steamer in and no letter for me. What's the matter up there? I guess I'll send them some stamps when I get the money to buy them.

December 5, 1863.
Saturday.

After guard mount this morning I started for the paymaster's office, and got pay up to November 1st, 31 days. It came to $110.15, several times as much as I ever before got for a month's work. With it I bought a coat, $30, a pair of pants, $10, a vest, $4, a couple of shirts, $5, four pairs of socks for $1, a cap for $3, invested another dollar in collars and a necktie, $4.50 for a trunk, paid the balance due Mrs. Herbert for board $2.50, had a dinner that cost twenty cents, a cigar that cost five cents, and a paper for five cents more. Paid a hack driver seventy-five cents to bring me home, paid George the cook $8.50, Lieutenant Gorton $7.65, borrowed money, for half a dozen handkerchiefs, ninety-five cents, and had $31 left over. I owe others for borrowed money, and by the time I get round I fear my pile to send home will be small. When next pay day comes I hope to make a better showing, for I won't owe so many and have so much to buy.

December 6, 1863.
Sunday.

Lieutenant Gorton and myself took a walk up town this afternoon, and at the Murphy House who should we meet but Charlie Ackert, one time editor of the Pine Plains *Herald*. Fresh from good old Dutchess County, he was able to tell us all about the folks we so often think of. He looks and acts just as he did, just as full of fun as any boy. We walked about the town for a couple of hours and finally stopped at a picture-taking place and sat for photographs. We hardly expect they will be hung outside with the show pictures, but I have my new clothes on, and that may be an inducement. We came back through Rampart Street, which from the looks is where the F. F. V.'s live. I wrote a couple of letters, wrote the above in my diary and am now going to bed.

December 7, 1863.
Monday.

At home I was called a jack-at-all-trades and I find they all come in play here. The addition to my family by the arrival of Lieutenants Gorton and Smith made additional sleeping arrangements necessary. They both helped about making the beds, but not liking their work I drove them both out and made some that they owned up were much better. I also made a rack to hang our clothes on, for now that we no longer sleep with them on, we have need of something better than the floor to hang them on. We get good news from the North, nowadays. Grant is up to his old tricks again. The Army of the Potomac is on the move also.

Towards night Colonel B. came round and said he had orders to turn over the rest of our men to the Engineers and to start out after more. An expedition is being fitted out for some place, supposed to be Texas, and probably that is where we are to go. I only hope we won't go by way of the Gulf again, for I would dreadfully hate to get my thirty-dollar coat wet. If General Banks will leave us as we are now until warm weather comes again, I will vote for him to be our next president, provided he can get the nomination.

December 8, 1863.
Tuesday.

After a bed, the next thing was to manufacture a table, and from that I went to chair making. I made some little saw-horses, and across the top stretched a piece of canvas, and we each have a very comfortable seat. Smith says they should be patented. One end up they are chairs and turned over they are sawbucks. He says a man with one of them could saw wood until tired and then turn it over and have a good chair to sit on and rest up. Matt always has something to say, but we try to endure him. It has been a rainy day, but all being under shelter we care but little. No further news about Texas comes and we hang our hopes high.

The photographs came today. Gorton doesn't like his and is going to try again. Mine are all right, except that Matt says the nose is crooked, but I don't care for a little thing like that, and shall hurry one of them home by first mail. At night we all gathered at Colonel Bostwick's tent, to show him how much we remembered of the army tactics that were worked into our noddles at Camp Millington. We filled his tent too full for comfort, and he decided to put off the school until he found a better place to hold it. He told us what lines to be prepared on and after visiting awhile we all went to our own homes, I to write and the rest to bed and asleep.

December 9, 1863.
Wednesday.

Officer of the guard again; was detailed, but soon after excused and another put in my place, all due to a mistake the adjutant had made. I went and had more photos made, as I found I had more friends than photographs. We exchanged with each other, and are each getting up a collection that will remind us of each other, when we again go our different ways. The officers that have horses are each trying to get the fastest one. This is a great place for horse racing, and everyone seems to catch the fever. Dr. Warren has the fastest one and Lieutenant Colonel Parker and Major Palon thought if they couldn't beat him alone, they might do it together. So on a back street they tried the experiment this afternoon. The doctor and the major started together.

At the half mile post Colonel Parker struck in and the major dropped out. It turned out to be no race at all, for the doctor's horse beat them and didn't half try. Colonel Parker's horse is the one we searched out from the Great Cypress swamp. lie is a beauty, but he can't run as well as he looks. The judges said the doctor's horse made the half mile in fifty-eight seconds and the mile in two minutes. We think the judges may have had a drink of the doctor's whiskey.

December 10, 1863.
Thursday.

Staid in my tent all day and wrote letters. I won't tell how many I wrote or to whom. At any rate there are none that I know of who can accuse me of owing them a letter. At night we went again to recite tactics to Colonel B. He said we knew our lesson, and I suppose we each got a credit mark. After that we went back to our tents and yarned it until bed-time.

December 11, 1863.
Friday.

Today, after posting the letters I wrote yesterday, I regulated things in my trunks, getting rid of the letters I care the least about, and having a general house-cleaning time. Some of the letters I have read and re-read until they are nearly worn out. If the senders knew how I prize them I think they would send them oftener. It is rumoured that Grant has been cutting up more didoes. If half the victories we read of were true the Rebellion wouldn't have a leg to stand on. Consequently we only believe such as are reported several times, and let those that are printed only once go for lies, which they generally prove to be. Still it gives us something to talk about, and to think about, and that is something we are always glad to get. How such stories get started is a wonder to me. Someone must make them up out of whole cloth, but if they knew how we hunger and thirst for the real naked facts I don't believe they would do it. At night Colonel B., Gorton and I went for a walk. We went up to the stable where the colonel has his horse kept, which is way up beyond Canal Street.

After looking at the horses we went to the Murphy House and filled up on oysters, washing them down with beer. After an hour or two of this we returned by a roundabout way to the Cotton Press, our home. I found my name on the bulletin board for officer of the guard tomorrow. As that meant no sleep tomorrow night I turned in, and the very next thing I knew it was morning.

December 12, 1863.

Saturday morning, and almost time for guard mount. Lieutenant Reynolds pulled me out or I would have lost my breakfast. I reached guard headquarters just in time to march the new guard out for inspection. Then the colonel reminded me that I was not dressed according to regulations, and excused me while I returned for my dress suit, sash, sword and cap. Not having a sash I took the colonel's and was soon on hand, "armed and equipped as the law directs." I met with no other adventures, and had little to do, for the men show the training we have given them and are not the awkward things they once were. At 3 p. m. an officers' drill was had on the parade ground. Colonel Parker was drill-master, and had everyone out.

Being on duty, I had only to look on, and enjoy seeing the awkward work done by some of them. It was not all fun for the drilled, for the driller seemed determined to get the last drop of sweat out of them. He afterwards said he did it for the good of the service, that enlisted men were looking on, and he wished to set them a good example. For that same reason none of them dared to make any objections until they were back in their quarters and then the drill-master got his medicine. He claimed he wanted to find out just how long it took to wilt a paper collar. I presume if another drill of that kind comes off Colonel B. will act as drill-master and the lieutenant colonel will get as good as he gave.

Midnight. Some of the shoulder strappers have gone to the theatre and the others are snoring away in their tents. In order to keep awake I am writing up the day's doings. A prayer meeting has been going on in the men's quarters since dark and is in full blast yet. It would be laughable only for their earnestness, which beats all I have yet witnessed. They sing more than they pray, and their hymns I have never seen in print. One of them I can repeat the first and last lines of, the middle being made up of variations. It starts "This lower world's a hell for us," and closes with "Where Jesus rides on a big white boss." It was not funny, they were too much in earnest. Matt, who has just got in from the theatre, says he hopes it sounds better in heaven than it does here, and I haven't a doubt that it does. Abe Linkum comes in for a full share, his name being used as often in their praises as that of the Deity.

December 13, 1863.
5 a. m. Sunday.

The prayer meeting continues. I have found out that a negro preacher of great fame among them is present and conducts the services. If he does it for pay he is certainly earning his money. Reveille sounded before the meeting was over. After guard mount, a breakfast and a wash up, I turned in for a nap. In the afternoon I set out to go to church. Where, I had no idea, but after following the sound of bells, and finding some of them on fire engine houses, and some on steamboats, I turned and followed some people who had books in their hands and had every appearance of church-goers. They finally brought up at a church and I followed them in. The church was crowded, and the service was in a tongue strange to me, so as soon as I could I got out and came back home. Home—what a place to apply the blessed name of home to! Still it is my home.

Any place, that a soldier leaves, expecting to return to it, is his home. If asked where my home is I should say at the Louisiana Steam Cotton Press. It's my only home now. That's what I say, but yet my heart says "in the little brown house under the hill, where the old folks stay." Shall I ever get over longing for that home? It is very humble but there is no other place on earth that I would rather see. Just as I was about turning to indigo, the postmaster came in and gave me a letter from Jane. Dear old Jane! If she could have seen me grab it, and watched me read it, I know she would write oftener. She is the scribe for the whole family. She is a fast writer. She knows just what to say for the others as well as herself, and the very worst thing I can say against her is that she does not write oftener. Still, the pile of letters in my trunk, all from her, are a witness that I am selfish to ask or expect her to write oftener. I will drop you, my diary, and answer this letter before it is cold from my hands.

December 14, 1863.
Monday afternoon.

Lieutenant Colonel Parker and Lieutenant Heath went out for a ride, and it was whispered about that they were going out on Montague Street for a horse race. Gorton and I followed them up and found them already at it. A horse-car line crosses Montague Street a few blocks' from the Cotton Press, and a car came across just as they were almost to it. Heath just missed and the colonel ran plump into it. His head hit the edge of the roof, which laid his scalp-lock right back on his head. We picked him up and got him into a nearby drug store, and by that time he was coming to. But he didn't know where he was or what had happened. We got a doctor, who said he should go to the hospital, and he is there now with a very sore head, and the prospects of a big broad scar to remember his ride by.

If some of them don't get their necks broken it will be a wonder. Gorton has taken one of the rejected recruits to wait on him. Someway he had got past the doctor who examined him and was sworn in. But he is lame and was afterwards thrown out. His name is Henry Holmes, and says he enlisted at West Baton Rouge under an officer whose name he has forgotten. He was brought to New Orleans for transfer into a regiment, and was finally thrown out. He is very anxious to go north, and Gorton has promised to take him along when he goes home. He and my Tony are chums already and I am teaching them their letters.

My time not being my own, I have no regular school hours, but they are always ready and really try hard to learn. As there is no prospect of our leaving our present quarters, and being of small account here, several of us have applied for leave of absence to go home. It is not expected each will get one and several bets have been made for and against any of us getting one. But wouldn't I be a happy boy if it should happen to be me.

December 15, 1863.
Tuesday.
Our hopes for a furlough are gone. Maybe we had no reason to hope, but all the same we did. Just a few minutes ago the colonel got orders to start at once for Matagorda Island. Where it is or what we go for, the order does not say. We are all in a fluster about it, and wondering what we will do with the housekeeping outfits we have collected. We certainly can't take them along. Some think Matagorda Island is off the Texas coast and others say off the coast of Florida. Matt Smith is sure it is on a mountain in Mexico. We expect to know when we get there. The best thing I can see in the move is that it will give us

something to do, and me something to write about in my diary. I do hope another mail will come before we go. I feel now as I did the night we were marching on towards Port Hudson, when the mail carrier ran along the lines giving out the letters, and besides a letter gave me a photograph of dear old father and mother. I felt then as if I could storm Port Hudson alone, so much good did they do me. It has been my constant companion every minute since, and will go with me to Matagorda Island when I go. But I would like another letter. We are packed up, and the colonel is off looking after transportation. Goodbye diary, for a spell.

December 16, 1863.
Wednesday.

Yesterday and today we have waited for the word "March," and are still waiting. Colonel Parker has come back. He has an ugly scalp wound, and his head is covered with bandages. But the prospect of active duty has brought him around sooner than anything else could do. We know no more about our destination than the order, to "go at once," says. We are ready, and that is all we can do. I have got out my writing traps, but it won't take me long to stow them away when the word comes. The stories we hear about the place we are going to are wonderful, but as none of them are likely to be true I won't waste paper putting them down. I am quite an authority on the times and places we have visited and am often called in to settle some disputed question, but my notes all look backwards and are good for nothing when asked about the future. We are still hoping for letters before we start.

December 17, 1863.
Camp Dudley. Thursday.

I have never thought to tell the name given our camp here at the Cotton Press. All camps have a name, so orders can be sent to camp so-and-so, and someone with the proper authority named the Cotton Press, "Camp Dudley." We are here yet waiting for further orders. The trial by court-martial of Adjutant Phillips comes off today, and several have gone as witnesses. The story goes now that Matagorda Island is off the mouth of the Rio Grande River. If I only knew how long we are to be gone, I could tell what to take and what to leave, and would be better satisfied. Dr. Warren has given me a book for keeping up my diary. It is a physician's visiting list, just right to carry in my side pocket and I am just beginning in it, having packed up and sent off my diary up to this date. We had a hard thunderstorm last night, but it is cool today, and I have stuck up my stove again and have a good fire in it.

Noon. The court-martial was adjourned and our family is together again. Our marching orders have been changed and now we are to start for Bayou Sara, just above Baton Rouge. We are going tonight. I have been trying to be sick for a day or two, and the colonel says I am just the one to stay and keep house. Dr. Warren came around in a little while and agreed with him, so I am to stay. It is the first time since I came out of the hospital last spring, and I hate to break such a record, but I do feel miserable for a fact. A steamer called the *Northerner* has just pulled up opposite camp, to take us up the river. She shows the marks of a skirmish with the Rebs, having a lot of bullet holes to show, and a big hole through her wheel house, where a cannon ball went through, taking off the head of a man in the cabin. They say the guerrillas are very troublesome.

At night I had a letter from my sister, Mrs. Loucks, and in it was a picture of her own dear self, looking just as she did a year and a half ago; also a dozen stamps from father; they are all well, and so am I, now that I have heard from home, and have this little reminder of my sister to look at. A part of the regiment has gone, leaving the rest to keep house.

December 18, 1863.
Friday.

I was awakened this morning" by a terrible commotion in the tent. It was full of smoke, through which I could see Gorton flying around and splashing water over everything. It appeared he had got up and built a fire and such a hot one that a spark flew out and set fire to the tent. Colonel Parker has got off some of the bandages and he looks as if he had been to an Irish wake. I have been writing letters and am all caught up now. George, the cook, has mended the tent so we are comfortable again. My letter and picture didn't cure me entirely, for I feel almost sick today. Dr. Warren is dosing me with something" and I expect to be better or worse pretty soon. Goodnight.

December 19, 1863.
Saturday.

We heard a gun in the night, and are looking for letters today. We have got the President's message and have read it through and through. He has no notion of giving up the ship yet. He must be real game, for as near as I can make out he not only has the whole South to fight, but a part of the North as well. I wish he would send the Copperheads down here where they belong. Sim Bryan, the mail-man of the 128th, is here, waiting for a boat. He says the boys of Company B are in fine spirits, and are still at Baton Rouge. If I had staid with them all this time I should surely have died with the blues. Besides, what would I have had to put in my diary? My stomach has a trick of throwing up the good things I eat as fast as I put them down. The weather keeps cool, and I do nothing but sit over the stove and shiver. We hear no more of going anywhere, and I begin to think we shall put in the winter right here.

December 20, 1863.
Sunday.
Today has been my well day. That is I felt so much better I got out for a walk and took in a church on the way, where I heard a part of a sermon in English. The walk has made me feel almost like myself. If I don't get another setback tomorrow I will be all right again. I got hold of a New Orleans paper today, printed October 22, 1861. It is amusing to us, but it cannot be so to the Rebels, to read what they then planned to do and then to look about and see what they have done.

December 21, 1863.
Monday.
Reported for duty this morning, and call myself well again. There was nothing for me to do however, but I am no longer reported on the sick list. Gorton says I was scared at the thoughts of going away and so played sick. But he says so much I pay little attention to him. Four different mail steamers are now due, and two of them have been due for a week. Have been in camp all day, keeping things shipshape against the return of Colonel B. and the rest of the regiment.

December 22, 1863.
Tuesday.
The *Evening Star* came in some time during the night and this morning I had business at the post-office. I took my stand by box thirteen, opening it every little while to see if anything had got in. This I kept up for a long time, and then went across the street, bought a paper and read the news. When I next opened the box there lay two letters, and both for me. I came back to Camp Dudley, hardly touching the ground, and was soon visiting with the folks at home. They are all well and seem to be enjoying themselves. So am I.

December 23, 1863.

Wednesday.

Have been making out the company returns. Also wrote some letters. Nothing new to report.

December 24, 1863.

Thursday.

Expecting the colonel back any time, and wishing to show him what good housekeepers we are, we got the drummer boys at work to sweep out the quarters and slick up the whole camp. Like boys everywhere, they started in well, but soon got tired. Gorton and I then took hold and helped them finish, and we are ready for anybody's inspection. We gave the boys each a pass to go outside, and after dinner went out to the race track, to see if any races were being run. Nothing much was going on, and after looking at the stables and the horses we came back. As tomorrow is Christmas we went out and made such purchases of good things as our purses would allow, and these we turned over to George and Henry, for safe keeping and for cooking on the morrow. After that we went across the street to see what was in a tent that had lately been put up there. We found it a sort of show.

There was a big snake in a show case and a tame black squirrel running around, and sticking his nose into every one's pockets. Then there was another show case filled with cheap-looking jewellery, each piece having a number attached to it. Also a dice cup and dice. For $1.00 one could throw once, and any number of spots that came up would entitle the thrower to the piece of jewellery with a corresponding number on it. Just as it had all been explained to us, a greenhorn-looking chap came in and, after the thing had been explained to him, he said he was always unlucky with dice, but if one of us would throw for him he would risk a dollar, just to see how the game worked.

Gorton is such an accommodating fellow I expected he would offer to make the throw for him, but as he said nothing I took the cup and threw seventeen. This the proprietor said was a very lucky number, and he would give the winner $12 in cash or the fine pin that had the seventeen on it. The fellow took the cash, like a sensible man. I thought there was a chance to make my fortune and was going right in to break the bank, when Gorton, who was wiser than I, took me one side and told me not to be a fool; that the greenhorn was one of the gang, and that the money I won for him was already his own. Others had come by this time and I soon saw he was right, and I kept out. We watched the game awhile and then went back to Camp Dudley and to bed.

December 25, 1863.
Friday.

Christmas, and I forgot to hang up my stocking. After getting something to eat, we took stock of our eatables and of our pocket-books, and found we could afford a few things we lacked. Gorton said he would invite his horse- jockey friend, James Buchanan, not the ex-president, but a little bit of a man, who rode the races for a living. So taking Tony with me I went up to a nearby market, and bought some oysters, and some steak. This with what we had on hand made us a feast such as we had often wished for in vain. Buchanan came, with his saddle in his coat pocket, for he was due at the track in the afternoon. George and Henry outdid themselves in cooking, and we certainly had a feast. There was not much style about it, but it was satisfying. We had overestimated our capacity, and had enough left for the cooks and drummer boys. Buchanan went to the races, Gorton and I went to sleep, and so passed my second Christmas in Dixie.

At night the regiment came back, hungry as wolves. The officers mostly went out for a supper but Gorton and I had little use for supper. We had just begun to feel comfortable. The regiment had no adventures and saw no enemy. They stopped at Baton Rouge and gave the 128th a surprise. Found them well and hearty, and had a real good visit. I was dreadfully sorry I had missed that treat. I would rather have missed my Christmas dinner. They report that Colonel Smith and Adjutant Wilkinson have resigned, to go into the cotton and sugar speculation. The 128th is having a free and easy time, and according to what I am told, discipline is rather slack. But the stuff is in them, and if called on, every man will be found ready for duty. The loose discipline comes of having nothing to do. I don't blame them for having their fun while they can, for there is no telling when they will have the other thing.

December 26, 1863.
Saturday.

The steamer *Yazoo* came in this morning and brought me four letters, one of which was from father. He wants me to come home for a visit, for he has been told I can come now if I want to. Dear old soul, I wonder if he knows how much I want to. I hope now my application for a furlough may be approved. It has been so long now that I had given up thinking about it. I saw Colonel B. and told him how the case stood, that I had neither asked for nor received any special favours since I came out, and would not now if there was anything to do. He says he approved the application I made some time ago, and that he would help me by trying to trace it and see what had become of it. He says there are so many applications for leave of absence that there is nothing strange about their not being heard from, but he will try and find mine and will also try and have it allowed. Good for you. Colonel Bostwick. But what shall I say to father about it? I finally decided to write him just how it is, that I will come if I can get away and that I want to see him as much as he wants to see me, but I did not dare say how many chances there are against my getting away.

December 27, 1863.
Sunday.

A heavy rain began early this morning and kept up until 3 p. m. Consequently we have not been able to do more than visit each other in our tents, or ramble about the Cotton Press. After the rain, the lieutenant colonel of the 25th Connecticut came and preached to the men. Another officer came with him, and also spoke. Altogether it was an interesting meeting. After this I settled down to write some letters, for a New York mail goes out tomorrow, and I don't allow any to go without one or more letters of mine. I met with a singular mishap while writing.

Lieutenant Gorton had thrown his hat on the table and gone out to visit his neighbours. To get it out of my way I put it on my head and it having a wide brim, my candle set it on fire. The thing did not blaze, but just ate its way across the brim. I smelled it all the time and even looked about to see if anything was on fire, but never thought of the hat, until I felt the heat and then the hat was ruined. Colonel Parker held a meeting in the hospital tonight and promises to have services in camp now right along. That looks as if our trip to Matagorda Island had been indefinitely postponed.

Father's letter has completely upset me. He needs me for something or he would not have written as he did. But there is just nothing at all that I can do more than I have. If Colonel B. can't bring about my going home I don't know of anyone who can. Goodnight.

December 28, 1863.
Monday.

I had another talk with Colonel B. today and as he gave me several messages to take to his folks in case I do go, I am wild with hopes that he sees a way for me to go. I didn't suppose I could be such a fool. If I fail, I think less of what the disappointment will be for me than for "the old folks at home." But I shall keep right on hoping until my application comes back with that awful word "Disapproved" written across it.

December 29, 1863.
Tuesday.

I put in a miserable night. I simply could not sleep for thinking about my application. I traced it from headquarters to headquarters, all the way up to G. Norman Leiber, A. A. A. General, and watched to see what he wrote across the back. It was approved at every stopping place up to his office, and I thought he merely glanced at the endorsements and then wrote "Approved." I found myself sitting up in my bed with the sweat pouring off my face, and Gorton and Smith both yelling at me to know what was the matter.

So it seems I did sleep enough to have that blessed dream, but I was about heart-broken to find it only a dream. Smith says he shall tell the colonel to ask that my application be approved for the good of the service, and if that doesn't work will ask for another place to sleep in. After breakfast I was sent with a detail to get some material for brush-brooms, to sweep the quarters with. This was something I had long recommended, for I had learned from the men that they could make them if they had the material, and that could be found in any swamp.

We went out Montague Street and followed it mile after mile till we were out of the city and into the Little Cypress Swamp, so-called to distinguish it from the Great Cypress which we saw when in the Teche country. We found acres of the stuff, and soon had all we could lug back. We got back in time for dinner and then the broom manufacture began. Some of them are fully as well made as any in the market, and all look as if they would do good service.

After dinner I went at the company returns so as to be ready for January 1st, when we expect to get our pay. What if my leave of absence should come before pay day? I don't suppose there is money enough in the whole outfit to pay my fare to New York. Jim Brant from Company B, 128th, came in tonight. He has a furlough and is going home by the first boat. Recitation came again tonight and we all had good lessons. I am going to try and sleep tonight, for I need it.

December 30, 1863.
Wednesday.

Rain all day, and at it yet, 10 p. m. Have been getting my company affairs settled up so as to be ready to turn over in case I go home. Have also been looking up so as to be ready for the tactics recitation tomorrow night.

December 31, 1863.
Thursday.

The last of the year 1863. A year ago we were at the quarantine station seventy-two miles below here, hardly any well ones among us, and from one to three deaths every day. All were discouraged and ready for any change, no matter what, for nothing could be worse than the condition we were in. We were about as hard hit as any regiment I have yet heard of. What a heaven our present quarters would have been to us then! Then we came up to Chalmette, just below here, where several more died, and then on to Camp Parapet, where I was so sick that Colonel B., then Captain B., wrote his father I would probably be dead before the letter reached him. But God was good to me. The next the captain knew I was better, and I have never seen anyone get well as fast as I did. Before I was discharged from the hospital I followed the regiment on a scout to Ponchitoula, and that completed the cure.

We then went to Port Hudson and through the siege of six weeks before the works there, and were rewarded by being one of the seven regiments to go in and receive the surrender. Then after marching back to Baton Rouge, we went to Donaldsonville, and then by easy marches up the river to Plaquemine, and from there to Baton Rouge again. Then came the split up, the 128th to remain where they since have been, and a few of us sent back to this city for discharge from the 128th and for muster into the *Corps de Afrique.* An exciting trip to the mouth of the Sabine River and back, and then a run up the Teche country and back here, brings me round to the present time and place. Thus I have summed up the most eventful year of my life. I have captured no medals for bravery, neither have I had a single reprimand for cowardice or lack of duty in any place I have been put.

This much I am telling you, diary, and don't you ever tell how many times I have been scared most to death in the making up of this record. It is not one to brag" about, neither is it, from my standpoint, one to be ashamed of. I have been on duty as officer of the guard today, but the duties are so light, and the sergeants so well drilled, I have found plenty of time to write. One of the officers—I won't mention his name, but will say he is the one responsible for our muster rolls being' sent to the paymaster—got on a spree and forgot to send them. Colonel B. has talked him sober and he has gone to deliver them personally. If he don't get going again on the way, we stand a good chance of getting paid off tomorrow.

Tonight is recitation night, but being on duty excuses me. However I have the lesson at my tongue's end, for we have not yet got beyond what Colonel Smith pounded into us at Camp Millington. I shall never forget how, as knowledge rolled in, the sweat rolled out while in that hot and dusty school camp at Millington. Goodnight, 1863,

January 1, 1864.
Friday.
Good morning, 1864. How do you do, and have you a leave of absence for me on or about you? This is the coldest day I have seen in Louisiana. Ice formed on every puddle. The natives say it has not been so cold in seventeen years. Good! I have seen ice once more. Now for a snowstorm and then it will begin to seem like home. What are our folks at today? It is easy to guess, that they are together somewhere, probably at home to eat some of the good things mother knows so well how to cook. Then after dinner they will talk the afternoon away and then go home. But I forget that the roads may be blocked with snow, and the mercury too low for comfort in going out.

At any rate it is safe to say they will have a good time somewhere and somehow. This idleness is going to be the ruination of us, I fear. Three officers are absent without leave, and Gorton was sent to round them up. He came back first and I mistrust he came on after giving them a caution. Soon after the runaways came back and were placed under arrest by Colonel B. and they now have only the limits of the camp. As nothing more is likely to happen tonight I will stop writing and try and plan how to sleep warm.

January 2, 1864.
Saturday.
As might have been expected, our half-burned tent kept out but little of the cold. Today we have drawn a new one and put it up in a place more protected from the wind, and have left the old one standing for a store room. It has been a busy day in camp, for all hands have been trying to make themselves comfortable in any way they can

think of. Tactic school again tonight, and that is all there is to say for the miserable day it has been.

January 3, 1864.
Sunday.

There was preaching in the quarters as promised. After a good sermon by an old man whom Colonel Parker had got hold of, the colonel gave a first-rate talk to all hands. I wrote several letters to home folks and had to tell them I had heard nothing more about my leave to go home. Goodnight, all.

January 4, 1864.
Monday.

Pay day today. I had $205.25 due me, and now let the furlough come. I am ready for it and if it had come before this I could only use it by walking.

Gorton has said so much about a fortune teller he has several times consulted, that I went with him and had my fortune told. I found the fortune teller to be an old woman, whether white or black I am not sure. She was black enough, but her features were not like an African's. Whether Gorton had given her any points about me or not I don't know. He says he didn't tell her a thing. She took me in to a room dimly lighted and sat me down at one side of a table while she took the other. Then she spread out a pack of common playing cards, and began. First she said I had received a letter from a near relative that had caused me trouble of mind. That this near relative had also seen trouble on my account. That brought to mind father's letter and I thought, and wanted to say, "Go it, old gal, for you are correct so far."

Next she told me I was going on a journey and would start within nine days. That it was partly by water and partly by land, but mostly by water. Also that I was going to meet with a great disappointment soon. These are the things I remember, and are the ones I feel most concerned about. The journey, provided she can read my future, and which I don't yet believe, may be the long expected trip to Matagorda Island. That order has not been countermanded yet. Or it may be I am really and truly going home. Either one would be by water and land both, but mostly by water. About the letter that had caused both myself and a near relative trouble, it must have been the letter from father, and Gorton may have told her of it.

The disappointment is what troubles me most. I know of nothing on earth that would be a greater disappointment than the disapproval of my application. Gorton knows all about that and may have told her, though he swears he did not. He says there is another fortune teller he knows about, but has never seen, that has a greater reputation and charges a greater price. My old woman charged a dollar and the other one has five times that, but all the same I am tempted to see her just to see how they agree. If they should agree I would have to own up they knew something, and if they disagreed I would throw the whole thing off my mind, that is, if I can.

Lieutenant Reynolds wanted to go to the theatre tonight and I have taken his place on guard. A white regiment has moved in with us for winter-quarters. There is room for several regiments, and provided we agree, it will be pleasanter for all.

January 5, 1864.
Tuesday.

We had a cold wet rain this morning and then the rain stopped. The cold, however, kept right on and we are expecting to shiver all night. Sol, our commissary, had to go up town on business, so with his authority I went to the post bakery and drew bread for the regiment. Towards night Sol, Jim Brant, who is still waiting for a boat, and myself went up town and filled up on raw oysters, getting back in time to say our lessons to Colonel B. The run home, or the oysters, or both, warmed us up so the weather seems much milder, and we had a much more comfortable night than we looked for,

January 6, 1864.
Wednesday.

Another rainy morning, and so cold the water freezes on the trees and looks real homelike. The natives say it will kill the orange crop and the bananas also. Also that the sugar-cane crop will be a failure. From all I can learn this is very unusual weather for this part of the country. What about the soldiers that are out in tents, lying on the ground. They say nothing of them, but I cannot help thinking of and pitying them.

Colonel B. has been to headquarters today and heard that our Texas trip is likely to come off yet. Just how soon he did not find out, but it is not given up. I suppose it would really be the best thing for us, for camp life is a very demoralizing life for soldiers. What we will be by spring if we stay here is hard to tell, but deviltry of one sort or another is sure to get a good start. Just at night I went to the post-office to have a look in box thirteen. There were some letters, but none for me. But I always think no news is not bad news, and then go to looking for the next mail. Sergeant Brant is here yet waiting for transportation. His furlough will run out while he waits, but he doesn't seem to care. I am sure I would be an uneasy mortal if I was in his place.

January 7, 1864.
Thursday.

Officer of the guard again and in camp as a natural consequence. The weather is quite mild. Rain keeps coming. It is the rainy season for this country, and we must put up with it. Lieutenant Ames is celebrating his full pockets. I am saving mine until I hear from my application and maybe then I'll celebrate.

January 8, 1864.
Friday.

The anniversary of the Battle of New Orleans, and a great day for the place. They tell me it is nothing to what it used to be before the war. Still there is lots of noise and the bands are all playing as the people march by on the way to Chalmette.

At night I went to the first show I have attended in New Orleans. It was at the Academy of Music and was fine. There was a troop of trained dogs that did everything but talk, and I expected that would be the next thing. Some were dressed like ladies and were posted around the ring on little chairs. A coach, drawn and driven by dogs, and with other dogs inside, came round making calls on the ladies. The coach would pull up opposite a lady, the footman would jump down and hold the horses while the lady inside got out and rubbed noses with the lady in the chair, and then on to the next until the circuit was completed. People could not have acted the part better. All that was lacking was the chatter and the smack that would have been heard if humans had acted the part. The rest was good but the dogs suited me best.

January 9, 1864.
Saturday.

Two letters today. Aunt Maria and Jane were the senders. They had just got my letters, written Dec. 9, so it takes just a month for a letter to come and go. I went up town and had my phiz taken again. Jane didn't like the one I sent her. Coming back I met with a strange adventure, and although there wasn't much to it, it someway impressed me so I have thought of little else since. A fairly well-dressed man, old and venerable looking, tapped me on the shoulder and asked for five cents to buy some crackers. He did not look or appear like a beggar, and something about him and his manner struck me as no other such plea ever did. I had spent nearly all the money I had with me, but what I did have I handed over, and was going on when he stopped me to know if I would receive an old man's blessing.

I stopped, not knowing what to say or do, when he raised his hands above my head, and as near as I can recall the words said, "God Almighty bless and protect you and yours. The Cross of Christ shall stand between you and all harm, a bullet shall never hit that head; you have helped a poor old man, and as you have helped him so shall you be helped. You have cast bread upon the water and though it be late in life, your reward shall come." I thanked him and hurried away. Quite a crowd had collected while this was going on. I was all togged out in my new uniform, having been to have my picture taken, and I suppose the sight was a little unusual. I haven't told a soul but you, diary, for anyone but you would laugh at me.

But you and I are confidants and you have never yet betrayed me. Lieutenant Gorton is about sick tonight, and I have been doctoring him up the best I know how. Have got him to bed and given him a part of my covering, for though the night is cold he needs it the most. I don't feel a bit like sleep. In spite of me I can't get the old man and his strange conduct out of my head.

By way of experiment a squad of sergeants was sent out tonight to try their hand at recruiting. They have come in with about sixty good-looking negroes. This shows they can beat us at the business, and if they are kept at it we will soon have a full regiment.

January 10 1864.
Sunday.
Sergeant Brant thought sure he would go today and after a good-bye all round started for the boat. He came back soon after, saying he had given up the trip for today. It seems the boat is held back for some reason and will sail tomorrow. That will give me time to write some more letters. The quartermaster and I went to church today. He knew where to go, and though it was a long walk there and back, I felt well paid for going. As near as I could tell it was a Methodist church. At any rate the language used was United States, while those I had before attended used Latin. We were seated in a pew with a handsome young lady, who gave us a hymn book, even finding the place for us. I was never more sorry I could not sing.

After church she invited us to come again, saying how glad she was

214

we had come today. We promised her we would, and came back. If I can find the way there I certainly mean to go again. We now expect to start for Texas this week sometime. Only a part are to go and we are all impatience to know who will be taken and who left. If I knew my leave of absence wouldn't come I should want to go, but suppose it did come and had to follow me up, the time would be up before I could get started. I am very often thankful for the things I don't know.

January 11, 1864.
Monday

I sneaked off this morning, and hunted up Madam Black, the "Great Indian Astrologist," as the papers call her. I had been boiling over with curiosity to know how near she and the other one—I have forgotten her name—agree as to my future. I found her without trouble, and was surprised to find her, not a squaw, as I expected, but one of the sweetest-looking and most motherly-acting old women I have seen since I saw my own dear mother. She simply took me by storm. I couldn't disbelieve her if I tried. I had always been an unbeliever in fortune telling, but in the state of mind I was in I was ready to catch at any straw she held out. She took me into an elegantly furnished room, and the only question she asked about myself was the day and month of my birth. This I told her, and she sat down before me and closed her eyes as if going to sleep. Soon she began, and gave me as good a history of my past life as I could have told her, without going into particulars more than she did.

Of course I was then ready to gulp down anything she might say, and was tempted to run away and leave my future as it had always been to me, a closed book. But my desire to hear about my going home, or going to Texas was strong upon me, and I held my breath while she continued. She told me I was born to disappointment, that my plans had been upset as fast as I made them, and this would continue until after my forty-fifth birthday; that happily for me I was also born with a disposition that did not allow disappointments to sink in as it otherwise would, and for that reason I had never been so discouraged as not to try again. After my forty-fifth birthday things would change and I would wind up rich and contented. As she said this she added, "but it won't take as much to make you rich and contented as it does most people." She told me I was to have two wives (she didn't say both at one time) and five children.

Then she said, as the other one did, that I was going on a journey in a few days, from which I would return to New Orleans again; that inside of seven months I would go on a journey from which I would never return to this place; that after that I would be happy and the world would be kinder to me than ever before. Aside from a chat we had on other subjects, that was all I got for my $5. I believe now I am to go somewhere very soon, but whether to Matagorda or to Dutchess County I know no more than before. I came back and went to work getting ready for a start, because that was what the others were doing, but to save me I couldn't put much heart in my preparations. It rained today, as usual.

Altogether it has not been a cheerful day for me. I am five dollars poorer and the little knowledge I swapped it for does not cheer me as I hoped it might. Goodnight, diary. Remember you are not to tell a living soul of this, and when Gorton next proposes my going to consult my future, I shall tell him I don't believe a thing in it, and that the whole thing is a swindle. The question, Texas or home, is still unanswered.

January 12, 1864.
Tuesday.
"Glory, Hallelujah!" I'm going home. Just as I was crawling under my blanket tonight, after a miserable cold, wet day of routine duty, the colonel's servant came and said the colonel wanted me to come to his tent. I got up and dressed, wondering what it could mean. Just then I recalled hearing a horseman ride in and out, and I said to myself—that means Texas sure. I found pretty much all the colonel's family packed in his tent and all with long, sober faces on them. The colonel asked me what sort of a caper I had been up to when out on a pass yesterday, adding, before I could reply, that I was the last one he expected to get such a report about from headquarters, at the same time handing me an official-looking document and requested me to read for myself. In a sort of a daze I opened it and at a glance saw it was my leave of absence. I came to life then.

Whether they are glad to be rid of me for a while, or what, I don't know, but they all appeared as glad as I was. Appeared, I say, for it is not possible they could feel as I did, and do, about it. We kept the colonel up until he drove us off and then the most of them went home with me, and we kept up the clatter of talk until almost morning. The errands and the messages I have promised to do and deliver will make a hole in my vacation, but I don't care, for anyone of them would do the same for me. The day had been so dull that I was not going to write a word about it, but the wind-up was too momentous not to mention it on the day and date thereof. And now for a nap, or a try for one.

January 13, 1864.
Wednesday.

In spite of late hours last night I was up early, and as soon as I had eaten, was off to look up the matter of transportation. If a transport is to sail soon I can go through for nothing. I found it was barely possible one might go this week, but it was quite uncertain. Knowing how very uncertain these army uncertainties are, I went to the office of the *Creole* and found she sails on Friday. I engaged passage and came back and have since been getting ready to go. Gorton wants me to take his Henry Holmes along to help Mrs. Gorton, and says I can pass him through as my servant free of cost. I told him if that was the case I would take him along, and the darkey is almost as glad to go as I am. Marching orders came today, and preparations for a move are already under way. Two regiments of mounted infantry have come in to camp with us and this makes neighbours pretty close.

January 14, 1864.
Thursday. Night.

Camp is torn up, and the men and officers have gone. Part started for Franklin again, for recruits, and Colonel B. with the rest have started off towards Lake Ponchartrain, what for, nobody here knows. If I have the good luck that was wished me, I shall certainly have a fine time. I have got my ticket, and my baggage is on board the *Creole*. She sails at 7 a. m. tomorrow morning. I am back in camp to stay with Sol and the quartermaster, who are left to go on tomorrow with the stores. Colonel B. rode in for some final directions. He says they encamp at Lakeport tonight, and will receive orders in the morning what to do or where to go. He says there is a prospect of our being transferred to the quartermaster's department.

January 15, 1864.
Friday.

On board the steamer *Creole*, at South West Pass. Have taken on a pilot and will soon be across the bar and into the Gulf. We left at foot of Toulouse street at half past eight this morning. Gorton had managed to get in, in time to swing his hat as we started down the river.

Whether he had something of importance to say I don't know, for he was too late for anything but the farewell swing of his broad-brimmed hat. The boat is so nice I don't feel a bit at home. The table and staterooms are likewise. However I shall try and endure it. The most of the passengers are army men with a sprinkling of men and women, some of the latter being Sisters of Mercy. No place would look right without them, for they seem to be everywhere. We are in the Gulf now, and the pilot has just left us. The sea is getting rougher every minute and my dinner and supper seem to be quarrelling about something. I did not expect to be seasick, but the symptoms are all here and I think I will go below.

January 17, 1864.
Sunday.

Yesterday I did not write. I had other business to attend to. Friday night I went below, thinking I might the better escape an attack of seasickness, which I felt coming on. But I did not. After a night as full of misery as one night can be, I found myself alive at daylight, but perfectly willing to die, if I only could. The stateroom was first swinging around in a circle, and then going end over end. First I would go up, as if I was never going to stop, and then sink down until it seemed as if I must strike bottom. My clothes, hanging across from me, were going through the same motions. I was soon gazing at my breakfast, dinner and supper of the day before, and I think I saw traces of my New Year's dinner.

Life or death, York State or Louisiana, peace or war were all the same to me then. Whether the ship was on its way to New York or to the bottom didn't interest me a particle. Anything would suit me. After a while of this I fell asleep, and about 3 p. m. I came to life again, and began to take stock, as Sol says. I felt like a dishrag, thrown down without being wrung out. Soon a knock came at the door, and I was surprised to find I could say "come in." A coloured individual with the boat's uniform on came in, and after a look at me and then at the floor went after the necessary tools for house-cleaning. There were two berths, one above the other, and I was in the lower one. He helped me into the upper berth and began operations on the one I had occupied.

After a while he claimed things were once more shipshape, and left me saying I would soon be all right. I soon after got out on the floor and managed to get into my clothes. From that I ventured into the cabin, where I sat down in a chair I could not possibly fall out of, and soon got into conversation with a man, whom I found to be a sea captain, on his way to New York to take out another vessel. He didn't seem to be worried about me, and said there were many others on board that had been sick and had not yet showed up. He got me a cracker, which I ate, more to see if my stomach was still there than because I was hungry. This helped me wonderfully, and after visiting a while I went back and slept sound all night.

Today I have been on deck almost all day. The water is not smooth, but it is nothing to what it was night before last. I looked up Henry Holmes, and found he had been as sick as I, and that he was not over it yet. His colour had changed to a gray, which did not improve his looks at all. All I could do was to tell him how sorry I was for him, and that he would soon feel well again. But he said he would "never live to see the Noff, he just knew he couldn't." The day was perfect, almost everyone was on deck, and though some were rather pale, all seemed to enjoy themselves.

January 18, 1864.
Monday.
I was all over my sick spell this morning, and although there was quite a breeze, and the water quite rough, it did not disturb me. Henry was still sick, and wished himself back on the old plantation. I wished I could help him in some way, but was told there is nothing to do but grin and bear it. About 10 a. m. we saw something they called Florida Cape, but if it had not been pointed out I should not have seen it at all. Altogether the day passed very pleasantly for me.

January 19, 1864.
Tuesday.
The same thing today. Henry is sick yet, though I think I see some improvement. We don't seem to move, but I suppose we do. There is nothing in sight but water, and it seems to go up hill in every direction. The *Creole* keeps chugging away, but there is nothing by which I can tell whether we move or not.

Night. The captain says we are off the coast of Georgia, but how he knows I don't know. If we were near enough, I would feel just like jumping off and going on foot to New York and telling them the *Creole* is coming.

January 20, 1864.
Wednesday.
Today the wind has been against us. At noon we were said to be off Charleston. The sea-captain passenger has had fun with the lands-

men about staggering as we go about, but he is laughing no more. This afternoon he was getting up from a nap in his room, when a sudden lurch of the vessel pitched him head first against a mirror opposite, and smashed it fine. He called all hands up for something at his expense. We have spent the evening playing euchre and had a very pleasant time.

January 21, 1864.
Thursday.

The day has been warm and pleasant, we are past Cape Hatteras and with good luck will be in New York by tomorrow at this time. Henry is coming round all right but he has been dreadfully sick and shows it.

January 22, 1864.
Friday.

Was up early, for at night, or before, we were to reach New York. I saw that Henry was ready to grab his little bundle, and then kept an eye out ahead. The first I saw was Sandy Hook, and soon we were in sight of land and numberless other vessels. At 2 p. m. the *Creole* tied up at pier 13, North River, and not long after, Henry and I were in an express wagon bound for the 26th Street depot. I had to call at 197 Mulberry street to deliver a message for John Mathers, and his people urged me to stay all night and tell them about John and the war. From there we went to Brook Brothers to do an errand for Colonel Bostwick and then on for the station. A man jumped on the wagon and wanted to hire Henry for a cook in a restaurant, but Henry had all the job he wanted, and refused. He offered him $25 a month and board, but Henry said no.

At 26th Street we found the train would soon start and I hustled for tickets. I had given Henry a dollar, telling him to get something to eat at a place opposite the station and looked all around for him after I had my ticket and trunk check. I went to the restaurant and hunted all about until the cry "All aboard" came, and then giving his ticket to a policeman, to send him along on the next train, got on board, and at 8.20 p. m. landed at Millerton. No one knew of my coming, and the people gazed at me as if I had risen from the dead. I was still five miles from home, and as the roads were it might as well have been fifty. There was no one in the place from our way, and as I had to be there when the train came next day to look for Henry, there was no other way but to stay all night. This I did, at Sweet's Hotel.

January 23, 1864.
Saturday.

I visited about until train time, and managed to send word home that I would be there at night or before. I took dinner at Jenks' and was scolded for not coming right there the night before. At 2 p. m. when the train came I was on the platform, but no Henry got off. I then gave him up as lost in New York somewhere, but for what reason he had left me as he had I could not imagine. I had seen him enter the Dutchess County House after a lunch, and in ten minutes I was back there looking for him, but he was gone. That is all I could tell Mrs. Gorton, or the lieutenant, when I saw him again. I jumped in with Joe Hull, stopped at the Centre and told Mrs. Gorton about Henry, went on, stopping at Mr. Hull's for a short call, and was soon after at home.

I found little change in the dear old couple. I thought they looked a little older, but it was the same father and mother who had never been absent from my thoughts since I left them a year and a half before. They had been told I was at Millerton, on my way home. There had been no time to notify them by letter for I left New Orleans before a mail steamer did, after my furlough came. What was said and what was done concerns only us three, and we are not likely to forget it. It is enough to say we were all happy, and that we talked until late bedtime. I found my room just as I left it. So far as I could see, nothing had been disturbed. It was a long time before I slept, but I did at last, and I suppose they did also.

February 27, 1864.
Saturday.

From January 23 on I was too busy, visiting and being visited, to do more with my diary than keep notes enough to remind me, when I got time, to write up again. Time was too precious to even write about, I had the free run of everything. Horses and wagons, or sleighs as the case might call for, were free, and the houses of my friends were all open for me either night or day. Many times the younger set met somewhere for an evening and in that way I did much wholesale visiting. I feel ashamed now, as I look over the list, to think I spent so much of the time away from home. But there seemed no other way.

The main object of my coming, that of getting a place for father and mother to live after April, was accomplished by buying the place opposite Mott Drake's, with which they are well pleased. They will be among old and tried friends, and about central for the girls to visit them—near the church and store, and where the mail passes every day. With land enough to keep the cow, and to raise all the vegetables they need, they have never been so comfortably situated since my time began. Through Mr. Bostwick's kindness I was able to accomplish all this, and I go back to my task with a lighter heart and a heavier debt of gratitude then I came home with. I cannot mention all the people I visited and that visited me. It would be easier to tell those I did not meet. Those who had dear ones in the South that I could tell them about were never tired hearing about them. Some whose dear ones lie buried where they fell were the hardest for me. I could not tell them the worst, and the best seemed so awful to them I was glad when such visits were over.

Almost at the last I got track of Henry Holmes, and left him with John Loucks to pass along to Mrs. Gorton. He told me the man who tried to hire him in New York followed him into the restaurant and told him I had left a trunk on the *Creole*, and that I wanted him to go and get it. He jumped in the same wagon that had brought us there and was taken down town to a recruiting office, where he was asked to enlist. His being lame prevented that, and he was turned out in the street again. He asked everyone where the depot was where Lieutenant Larry went for tickets. Finally he told his story to someone who was humane enough to help him, and in that way got back to the 26th Street depot. There the policeman to whom I had given his ticket saw him, and, as there was no train that night, sent him to some place for the night, and saw him on the train the next day. He was asleep on the train when it reached Millerton, and was taken through to Albany, where he kept up the search and inquired for Lieutenant Larry. Some kind-hearted people then set about quizzing him for my last name, and hearing the name Van Alstyne, which is common in Albany, he at once said it was Lieutenant Larry Van Alstyne.

After a while he recalled Major Palon and Colonel Bostwick to mind. As neither of these names were of Albany, and as the Palons were known to live in Hudson, he was sent there. The Palons got him a place with a farmer at Johnstown, below Hudson, and also put an advertisement in the paper giving the particulars as Henry had given them. One of these papers fell into the hands of Colonel Bostwick's mother, who sent for me. John Loucks then went to Johnstown and found Henry, who had a good place with people who were good to him, and he refused to go, saying he had been fooled so many times he had rather stay where he was. As John was about to leave he happened to say in Henry's hearing, "I don't know what Larry will say."

At the name Larry, which it appears had not been spoken before, Henry at once asked if he meant Lieutenant Larry, and upon being told he did, he said, "If you know Lieutenant Larry, I'll go with you." And so it came about that we came together only the night before I was to start for the South again. I was certainly glad to see Henry, and if actions are any guide, Henry was glad to see me.[1]

---

1. After the war I became a citizen of Sharon, and soon after Henry Holmes came there to live and so conducted himself that only good can be said of him. In the book of Sharon epitaphs, published in 1903, appears the following:—
Henry Holmes
Died May 19, 1887
Free at last.
Henry Holmes was probably about seventy years old at the time of his death. He was born a slave and so remained until freed by the Civil War. He was last owned by a cotton planter in Louisiana from whom he took his name. He came north in the winter of 1864-5 and lived nearly all the remainder of his life in Sharon. He was a Methodist, and was buried from that church. The ministers from both the other churches attended and requested the privilege of taking part in the services. They each in turn gave testimony to the help and encouragement they had received from the words and example of this good old man. He was entirely self-supporting and at his death it was found he had laid by a sum sufficient to defray the expenses of his burial, and to pay for the enduring monument which marks his grave in Hillside Cemetery.

CHAPTER 13

On Board the "McClellan"

I reached New York on my return journey Feb. 23, and sent my trunk to the *Creole*, which was to sail the next morning. Returning to the Washington Hotel for the night, I found Daniel McElwee, who told me if I would wait until Saturday he would send me through free of expense. This was inducement enough for me to send and get my trunk and wait. Sixty dollars saved in three days was not to be missed even at the risk of a slower boat and poorer accommodations. John Thompson was also there. With a letter from Daniel to George Starr, the head of the transportation department, we went and gave him a call. He seemed glad of a chance to do his friend McElwee a favour, telling me to be on board the transport *McClellan* on Saturday morning and he would do the rest.

I had promised Mrs. Gibson to call on my way back and tell her more about her brother, Lieutenant John Mathers, and we next went there. From there to Brooks Brothers to find out about Colonel B.'s clothes, and then back to the Washington, where I met several old acquaintances and spent a very pleasant evening. The next morning I got to thinking of a donation party that was to come off at the city that night, and how nice it would be to drop in and surprise them. By train time I had figured out a programme that would cost no more than waiting in New York, and at 8 p. m. I was in Amenia, and in one of the worst storms of the whole winter. Rain, snow, and hail, and a high wind to drive it. There was nothing to do but go to Putnam's and stay over.

The next day I took the stage to the city and found out the donation party did not come off. The storm continued and for all I could do it would not stop. I put in the day as best I could and the next morning went back to Amenia and took the train for New York, having been within five miles of home, when they supposed I was some-where on the Atlantic. I put up at the Washington but found no one with whom I was acquainted. I spent a dull enough evening, and went to bed disgusted with everything, but mostly with myself for putting such a miserable finish to the vacation which I had so longed for and had so much enjoyed.

February 27, 1864.

I was on board the *McClellan* at 10 o'clock, as agreed upon, and found Mr. Starr already there. He introduced me to the captain, the surgeon, and the purser, as his friend, whom he wished them to give as good as the boat afforded, and to land me safely in New Orleans, as a personal favour to him. They appeared to know him well, and seemed glad to do him the favour. I told Mr. Starr I felt under great obliga-tions. He said as he could not fight for his country himself, he was happy to help those who could, and said: "If you ever get the chance, just give the Rebellion one blow for George Starr." But after all said and done, the McClellan is not the *Creole*. It is a government transport, much after the pattern of the *Arago*. There are a dozen or so of military officers on board, one of them with an eagle on his shoulder, several with one and two bars, and the rest like myself, second lieutenants, with their bars to get. I was given a stateroom to myself, but not very much like the one I had coming home.

However, beggars must not be choosers. The cargo so far as I could see was commissary stores and other warlike material. We went a little way out into the stream and anchored, and soon a smaller vessel came alongside with the toughest-looking lot of people I had ever seen together. There were four hundred of them, and they were counted as they stepped on board, as sheep are, running through a gate. They were stowed in below, just as we were on the *Arago*, only there being so few they had plenty of room. I had never seen such evil-looking faces on human beings as some of them had. The purser told me they were conscripts, deserters and bounty jumpers; that they had been in close confinement, and for safety were not brought on board until we were away from the dock.

Their language was as vile as their faces, and they seemed to have neither fear nor respect for the officers who had charge of them. Not all were like that, but there was quite a sprinkling of them. There was perhaps a company of soldiers in uniform and with arms, which I found to be men who had been sick or wounded, and were now returning to their regiments. The last to come on board were a couple who it appears had gotten away while on their way from prison to the boat, and had been rounded up by the police. One of these was accused of robbing another of a hundred-dollar bill, and as the accuser had some proof the fellow was stripped on deck, but no money was found on him or in his clothes. Just as he was to be released, one of the soldiers I have mentioned stepped up and running his finger in the thief's mouth hooked out what I supposed was a chew of tobacco, but which proved to be the hundred-dollar bill. He was then allowed to go below.

Then we started for Dixie. The wind blew like a hurricane and we were soon in rough water. Rain kept falling, and altogether it was a most dismal setting out. Soon a great rumpus was heard below, and something that sounded like shooting. The officers in charge of them paid more attention to a demijohn of whiskey they had than to the men. So it went till night. Cries of murder were heard and such cursing and swearing and quarrelling I never heard even in the army. A man came in the cabin with a broken arm, and told who broke it, but nothing was done about it. A little Dutch doctor undertook to set it, but both the doctor and the patient were drunk and got to quarrelling, and the man was hustled back with the broken bone unset. Altogether it was the blackest picture I had ever looked upon. I shut myself in my little coop wondering how it all would end, and hating myself for deserting the *Creole*, for a free ride on this old tub. If I had a chance to swap the $60 I had saved for a berth on the *Creole*, the bargain would have been made then and there.

February 28, 1864.
Sunday.
The wind continued strong and against us, and all was quiet below. The whiskey had given out. The man with the broken arm was sober now. He had suffered all night, and his arm was swollen badly. The Dutch doctor was seasick, as were many others. The ship's surgeon fixed up the broken arm as well as it could be done in the condition it was. The day passed off after a while, and nothing worth noting happened.

February 29, 1864.
Monday.
The last day of winter. The wind kept dead ahead and blew strong. The waves were higher than any I ever before saw. I got acquainted

with a Captain Reynolds, and was surprised to find him a brother to Captain Reuben Reynolds of our regiment. He was much surprised to find I knew his brother and to hear so direct about him. He is so much like his brother I seem to have known him a long time. The performance below has begun again. The officers have but little influence over them. One of them, a captain at that, went down to quiet them and was hit with something and his eyebrow cut open. There is so little light below, it is dangerous going about among the devils down there. Some have money and the others steal it like highwaymen.

A man who looked and acted like a crazy man came in the cabin and declared he was afraid for his life. As the day wore on the deviltry grew worse. Captain Gray told the officers in command that unless they could control them he would stop at the nearest port and land them. He is afraid of fire, as they smoke and have open lights all the time. Several of them are known to have revolvers, and to have fired them. The officers I think are afraid of them and I don't know that I wonder. There are six or eight ringleaders, and the peaceably inclined have to submit to anything they say. At least a dozen complaints were made today and all were against a few, of whom they are in terror.

March 2, 1864.
Wednesday.

After breakfast, and as we were mostly on deck smoking, a man rushed up from below and went out upon the guard in front of the wheel house as if to have a wash up from the tub standing there. His manner, and the look upon his face, attracted the attention of several. He pulled off his coat, and throwing up his hands sang out, "Goodbye, all," and jumped off directly in front of the wheel. We rushed to the rail in time to see him come up behind the wheel, and strike out to swim. He had hit something, for his head and face were bloody. "Man overboard," was yelled by everyone, and chairs or any other thing handy was thrown towards him. The vessel was stopped, but by this time the man was far astern, and only to be seen as he rose on the waves, which were quite high.

A boat was lowered and put out after him, and that, too, was hidden from view about half the time. The man, as near as I could judge the distance, was a half mile away by this time, though by watching the place he could be made out every time he came up in sight. Those who had glasses watched him until the boat seemed almost to him, and said that as he lay in plain sight on the uphill side of a wave he suddenly went down.

One of the crew said sharks were always prowling about near a ship at sea, watching for anything thrown out, and if one of them crossed the trail of blood which the man must have left, it would follow him like a streak of lightning. He thought it strange he had been let alone so long, and had no doubt that a shark was the cause of his going down so suddenly. The *McClellan* had come round so as to face the wind, and waited for the boat to come back, which it did just before noon. A rope was thrown out and caught, and after several times trying, the boat was got close enough to be hauled up, men and all. While this was going on, nearly everyone on board had come on deck.

A few, with the best-looking faces, were brought to the quarter-deck and questioned, and the stories they told of the doings below could hardly be believed. Everything short of murder had been done. The worst of the lot had so terrorized the rest that they dared not report them for fear of what might happen to themselves. The man who jumped overboard had been so abused for coming to the cabin the night before, that he took the only other course to get rid of it that seemed open to him.

Now that the whiskey was gone, the most of them were willing and anxious to be decent, but were in such mortal terror of the ringleaders that they dared not make a move to bring them to justice. After hearing the stories, which were all of one kind. Colonel Zotroski (that's the way it sounds), being the ranking officer on board, took command and declared martial law. He summoned every military officer and the armed soldiers to the quarter-deck. These soldiers had, by the way, kept apart from the others and had not been molested. After taking the names, he appointed an officer of the day, and I was almost paralyzed to hear my name called as officer of the guard. A guard was detailed from among the armed men, and then I got orders to station them at different places below, and to arrest and put in irons any who created a disturbance or disobeyed an order given them. Also to allow no smoking between decks.

Scared most out of my wits. I took the first relief and went below. I posted them where they could see all parts of the room they were in, and one on the next deck below, in a smaller room where the cooking was done, giving them the orders I had received from the officer of the day. I then started back up the ladder, when someone caught me by the feet, just as I had my hands on a brass railing that ran beside the opening to the deck above. That hand-hold saved me. I yanked one foot loose and with the heel of my boot jammed the knuckles of the hands holding me so they let go and I was free. I said nothing, out loud, but went straight to my room for my revolver. I came back just in time to see the guard I had posted in the kitchen tumble out on deck, all spattered with hot potatoes which had been thrown at him, some burning him severely. He was mad clear through and was ready to shoot, and I wished we were in the open where loaded guns could be used.

I took him back to the same post and told him to bayonet the first man that attempted to lay hands on him. A great big hulk of a fellow stepped out from the crowd and coming close up, said, "Good, old hoss, if you want any help just call on me." I made all the allowance I could for his manner of speech, thanked him, and went where I could see what went on without being seen by him. Pretty soon he started as if going past the guard, and when opposite him made a quick grab and got hold of the gun barrel, and the fight was on. Before I could get there the guard was down and ready to be tumbled on deck again. It was just what was needed to bring my Dutch up to the fighting point.

I grabbed the tough by the collar with one hand and with the other jammed the muzzle of a cocked revolver against his ugly face, telling him to climb that ladder or die. He was a coward after all and went on deck as meek as you please, where I handcuffed him to the rigging and went back after more. Another was pointed out and when I beckoned to him he came right along. The well-disposed took courage and in a little while had two more on deck, where I handcuffed them fast in different places. I now had four, but the worst one of the lot could not be found. He was said to be the leader in all the deviltry that had been going on. The men said they would watch for him and let me know the minute he was found. I went on deck, where I found several men who had been robbed by the man yet at large, of sums totalling $211. Another said the one I got first had stolen a shirt from him and was then wearing it.

My orders said nothing about restoring stolen property, so the matter was carried up to Colonel Zotroski, who told me to act my pleasure about it. It was my pleasure to take off the handcuffs and let the owner of the shirt take it off the thief's back. After locking him fast again, I went on with the search for the missing one. I wanted to find him while my gritty spell lasted, for, from all accounts, he was a desperate character and the leader of the gang. Just before dark one of the watchers came and told me they had located him under a berth, and they thought he was asleep. Sure enough he was, sound asleep between the floor and a lower berth. I took him by the leg and had plenty of help to haul him out. He had a revolver and a cheese knife with him, but in the narrow quarters, and in the jiffy of time it took to get out, had no chance to use either.

There were as many hands as could get a hold, and by the time I reached the deck he was there. A madder man I never saw. The men he had robbed were there and I told them to go through him and see what they could find. Although he was handcuffed, he was so handy with his feet that shackles had to be put on before the search for the money began. Wrapped around one ankle was the money, just two hundred and eleven dollars. As that amount was what the victims claimed to have lost, it was given back to them to divide up. As I fastened the villain to the pump, the handiest thing there was, he swore all sorts of vengeance on me, saying he would see my heart's blood if he had to wait twenty years for it. Besides the knife found on him, his revolver had three empty shells, showing he had used it, and probably would have used it again if he had been found while awake. I was mighty glad sleep overtook him before I did, for if it had not the day's doings might read differently.

All was quiet now, and at the supper table I found myself to be quite a somebody. Some with whom I had not spoken before took pains to speak now and to congratulate me on the result of the day's work. But if they had known how scared I was when I went at the job, and how little bravery was really necessary to arrest four cowards and one sleeping bad man, they might have thought differently. But I hope never again to feel as I did when I arrested the first man. There was murder in my heart, and the man's wilting as he did is all that saved me from being a murderer. If that is bravery, I am glad I have so little of it.

After supper Captain Gray asked me to use his room on deck for my headquarters, and as I must be up all night I was very thankful for such a nice place. The captain's bunk was in a room adjoining and he turned in, leaving me alone. A map of the ocean's bottom lay on a table. The depth of water all along the coast and for a distance from it was marked on the map. The wind came up between nine and ten o'clock and howled terribly. The captain came out and looked at the barometer hanging on the wall. He said it was all right yet, but if it got to a certain point, which he showed me, it would mean a much bigger blow. I went the rounds about once an hour, and found it very difficult to walk on the deck. The prisoners were where I put them, and in spite of all I began to feel sorry for them. But not knowing what to do with them I left them to suffer a little, thinking it would be no more than they deserved.

To stop smoking between decks was not so easy as it might seem. On every round I made I had smelled tobacco smoke, but had not located a single smoker. Finally I saw what I knew was a lighted cigar in an alley along the outside tier of bunks, and where the light from the lamp did not reach. It was after midnight, and all but those on duty were supposed to be asleep. This fellow did not see me until I was right upon him. I took the cigar from his mouth, dropped it on the floor and put my foot on it. Neither of us said a word, and I found no more smoking after that.

At midnight the wind was something awful to hear or feel. After one of my rounds I came in and found the barometer pointing to the very place the captain had pointed out. When I told Captain Gray of it, he jumped up and pulled a bell handle. Soon another officer came and they consulted together. A change of direction was decided upon, and then there was more pulling of bell handles, and they both went out. Soon after this the ship seemed to be going over. A tremendous thump, a smashing of timber, and a great rush of water all came together. I thought the ship was sinking or had run afoul of something.

I started out and was glad to get under cover again. The deck was wet and water was dripping from everything. The deck was so high from the water I did not think it possible the waves could reach it, and yet as it was not raining I had to think they had been very much higher, for the water was running down from everything. The prisoners were alive yet, for I could hear them yell and swear. After a little the ship stopped rolling and only pitched and dove. I ventured out and found it raining and the wind blowing harder than ever. The poor wretches fast to the rigging were repentant now and begged for some better place. I looked about and found a sheltered place, and with the help of the sergeant of the guard moved them to it.

Morning finally came, and with it better weather, though the sea was something awful to look upon. What I heard in the night was now explained. A great wave had gone clean over the vessel, taking every loose thing with it. It also smashed some of the timbers that form the guard in front and back of the wheel-house. These had gone clear over and out on the other side. They looked to be six inches square and solid at that. The rail was broken where they struck it going over. I thanked my stars I was inside when that happened. Such waves I had never seen. As the bow climbed up one, the stern would sink down in another, until a solid body of black water stood up all around it, and seemed ready to fall upon and sink the ship, but instead, the bow would go down and the stern go high up in the air; at the same time a sheet of water would come swashing over the deck, and running off at the sides.

I had often wished I might witness a storm at sea, and here I was right in one. I asked Captain Gray if this was the real thing and he said it was "pretty stiff weather." Eight o'clock came and I was relieved. After a wash-up and breakfast I turned in and slept till dinner, and since that have been writing up my diary. Everything is quiet on board. No more cutting up between decks has yet happened. I am glad now I had just the part I did in bringing about this state of affairs, but to tell the honest truth I didn't suppose it was in me to go through the part I did. There was a whole lot of good luck, as well as some good management. As I look back over the last twenty-four hours I see much more to feel thankful for than to feel proud of.

March 3, 1864.
Thursday.
Before the wind for the first time since leaving New York. The sea is still rough, the vessel pitching and diving all the time. Everything quiet and well behaved in the lower regions. At night the captain says we are off Savannah, Ga.

March 4, 1864.
Friday.
A fine day and fine weather. Have spent the day on deck, smoking, reading and thinking about my two homes, the one I am going to, and the one I have so lately left.

March 5, 1864.
Saturday.
Have been in sight of Florida all day. The day has been plenty warm enough for comfort, the water smooth and I suppose a good run made.

March 6, 1864.
Key West, Florida. Sunday.
We stopped here for coal about 9 a. m. I have been on shore and looked about. To me it is like being in another world. Everything I see

is different from anything I ever saw before, unless it be the people, and they talk a language I never heard, even in the French quarters of New Orleans. Cocoanuts grow here, and pineapples. The place appears to be the tip end of Florida, as the sea shows in all directions but one. The buildings are low, squatty, wooden buildings, but the streets are clean and the people look so. A few can speak English, but the most of them, black or white, talk more like geese than anything else. I saw a great many strange sights in the markets and shops.

Nearly every building is a store on the ground floor. Great turtles, some of them a yard long, were sitting up on end in the markets and helplessly waving their feet, or fins rather, for that is what their feet look like. So much misery made me sorry I had seen the place. I suppose they are kept that way until they are sold, or die. Last night there was a quarrel among the men, and Colonel Zotroski interfered and got some talk back that made him mad. He ordered the man to be brought on deck, and to be bucked and gagged. This was done, and when it was time to release him he was not to be found, and has not since been found. It is supposed he rolled overboard, but I don't see how that was possible. More likely his friends got him and have hid him away.

March 7, 1864.
Monday.
We left Key West about ten last night. We are now out of sight of land, and I suppose are in the Gulf of Mexico. The weather is hot as blazes. So hot an awning has been put over the quarter-deck, and it is now a most delightful spot to sit and watch the porpoises play.

March 8, 1864.
Tuesday.
Another perfect day. A shower passed over just at night and sprinkled the boat with warm water. I have been off my feed for several days, but begin to be myself again and think I will be able to crack a hard-tack by the time I get into camp. My vacation, or leave of absence, that seemed so like heaven to look at, is over now, and the stern realities of a soldier's life are looking me right in the face. Well, I have a lot to think of that I didn't have then, and a whole lot of things to talk about, too.

March 9, 1864.
Wednesday.
When I woke up this morning, we were outside the bar, waiting

for a pilot. About six o'clock one came and we were soon steaming up the river on the last stage of our journey. I was again detailed as officer of the guard, and so it came about that I was the first and the last to have charge of the prisoners, who were still in irons. The fellow who threatened me with such dire vengeance was quite docile, and said no more about killing me.

At quarantine we were halted and a medical man came on board to look us over. He must have found us all right, for he soon went overboard and we proceeded up the river. It called up sad memories as we passed the little graveyard where so many of our boys are lying.

I wondered if such a used-up mess had ever struck the place before or since. About noon a sharp shower came upon us, and drove every-one under shelter. It lasted nearly all the afternoon. At 8 p. m. we tied up at the foot of Josephine Street. I turned the prisoners over to the provost marshal and I suppose they were soon in jail. I wonder what their punishment will be. I was soon relieved from duty and went ashore. I went first to the Murphy House, where I found Dr. Warren's and George Drury's names on the register. They were out, but I se-cured the room next to them and went out to see if I could find any one I knew. I went to 184 Gravier Street and found the house shut up. Got a shave and then went to the St. Charles. Coming out I met a fellow passenger looking for a place to stay and took him with me to the Murphy House. There I found Drury and from him got the first trace of Colonel Bostwick and family. He said they were at Lakeport, nine miles away.

CHAPTER 14

The Red River Campaign

March 10, 1864.
Thursday.

Was up early, and after breakfast started for the *McClellan* to get my trunk. I bargained with an expressman to take it and myself to the Ponchartrain Railroad, where I met Hallesay, our sutler. He said the boys had heard of my arrival and were on the way to meet me. Soon after this we were together again, and such volleys of questions as were fired at me was a caution. They didn't give me time to answer one before several more were asked. The train was ready for the return trip and we soon reached Lakeport, where I found Sol and Matt Smith both having a tussle with the chills and fever. The regiment had been across the lake at Madisonville nearly all the time I had been away. Had had some cases of smallpox among the men, but no deaths.

Tony was overjoyed to see me, and almost the first thing wanted me to write a letter to his wife. I was kept so busy answering questions I hardly had a chance to ask any, but I found out that the regiment was under marching orders and expected to break camp that day. I felt quite flattered to think every white man, not sick or on duty, had gone out to meet me. After dinner in camp, we all hands took train for the city again. Sol and I switched off and went to do some errands on our own hook, after which we joined the regiment at the foot of Poydras Street and went on board the *Laurel Hill*. I put in the rest of the day and evening, when not answering questions, writing letters to the home folks, for I had a long list I had promised letters to.

March 11, 1864.
Friday.

I kept right on scribbling, but was so bothered with questions, I finally gave it up and talked till hoarse. After dinner I was detailed for guard duty, but as there was only one guard to post, I had next to nothing to do. We had the whole great boat to ourselves, and were in the finest kind of quarters. As soon as I had a chance I began to ask questions and found out that the muster rolls were sent for before I returned, and I had been reported as absent without leave. I then figured up and found I had over-stayed my time, owing to the long time it had taken to make the trip. Had the rolls been called for a few days sooner or a few days later I would have been all right. Colonel B. says it will all be made right next time. But in the meantime I must live on borrowed capital, for I had come back skin-poor.

March 12, 1864.
Saturday.

I managed to write some letters before I was relieved and after the new guard went on I fairly made them fly.

March 13, 1864.
Sunday.

Started for church with the quartermaster and brought up at a fire on St. Charles Street. Nearly a whole block was burned. I saw fire engines at work for the first time. There were several of them. They threw water enough to float a ship, and still the fire kept bursting out in a new place until all that could burn had been burned. The side streets were full of families and their belongings. At night we went again and saw a sailor from one of the boats baptized. After the sermon, a trap door was raised and under that was a space filled with water, into which the minister and the sailor walked by way of steps at one end, and where the convert was dipped just as they do it in the brook at Stanfordville.

March 14, 1864.
Monday.

Two cannon were brought on board today and mounted on the forecastle. This looks like business, but none of us know as yet where we go or when. The *Evening Star* came in with a large mail this morning. I had one letter, from my never-failing correspondent, sister Jane. Was glad to hear that all's well at home.

March 15, 1864.
Tuesday.

The *Laurel Hill*, our present habitation, cut loose from foot of Poydras Street this morning and tied up at the foot of First Street. Forage for man and beast soon began to come on board and kept it up by spells all day. The paymaster came and paid everybody but Ames and Van Alstyne. The one is under arrest for drunkenness, and the other has been "absent without leave." We looked on with wistful eyes, but the paymaster never took the hint. Whether out of pity or not I don't know. Colonel Parker invited me to go with him and Captain Hoyt to the theatre. We went, and enjoyed what we saw of it very much.

At what seemed to me the most interesting part, the captain of the *Laurel Hill* came in and said he had orders to go to Port Hudson as soon as he could get up steam. The officers and many of the men were out on pass and we started out to round them up. I found Major Palon at the St. Charles, and he knew where others were likely to be found. He went one way and I another. I found it easier to find them than to get them started for the boat. Some refused to go; thinking it a ruse to get them back on the boat. I did get one started and we double-quicked it to the foot of First Street just in time to get on board. Upon counting noses we found sixteen officers were left behind, Colonel Bostwick among them.

March 16, 1864.
Wednesday.

Woke up opposite Donaldsonville, passed Baton Rouge a little after noon, and reached Port Hudson at 4 p. m. Here we received orders from General Andrews to land in the morning, as the *Laurel Hill* is needed for another purpose. So we settled down for another night of comfort, not knowing what the next may be.

March 17, 1864.
Thursday.

We unloaded ourselves and our belongings, and teams soon carted them to the high ground above. We settled in the quarters just vacated by the 22nd C. D, A., borrowed some tents and in a little while were living like soldiers again. I could not help thinking how different was our coming this time from what it was almost a year ago. Then it took us six long weeks to get inside, and now not as many hours. As we had no orders, we looked about the place for awhile and then settled down, I to my everlasting task of writing.

March 18, 1864.
Friday.

Same old story. With no idea when I can mail a letter I kept right on writing them, and by night was where I could begin to see the end. No news from the missing ones yet.

March 19, 1864.
Saturday.
We found a ball and had a game, which helped to pass the time. Colonel Parker tried to find Colonel Bostwick by telegraph, but did not make out. At night was detailed for guard tomorrow.

March 20, 1864.
Sunday.
On duty and in camp all day, of course. An order came for us to go on board the *Illinois*, which was tied up under the bluff, but before teams came for us the *Illinois* cut loose and went down the river.

March 21, 1864.
Monday.
We were ordered on board the *Laurel Hill* again until further orders. That suited us much better than lying on the ground in camp, and as soon as teams came we loaded up and were soon in our old comfortable quarters again.

Major Hill's sentence was carried out at noon on the parade ground, and in as public a manner as possible. He is to forfeit a year's pay, and spend the next ten years on Dry Tortugas at hard labour. His straps and buttons were also cut off.[1]

The *Laurel Hill* has orders to take on 4,000 sacks of grain and then drop down to Baton Rouge for a part of Grover's Division, after which she is to go to Alexandria, somewhere on the Red River, I believe.

March 22, 1864.
Tuesday.
Oats kept coming on board all day, and by the sound all night as well. The *Errickson* came up and unloaded two regiments of coloured troops at night.

March 23, 1864.
Wednesday.
Left Port Hudson at 4 a. m., and at 6 were at Baton Rouge. I hustled off for a call on the 128th. Found them breaking camp to go with us, and at noon we were all together on board the *Laurel Hill*. At

---

1. I have no recollection at this time of this affair more than is here given.

1 p. m. we started upstream again. I had to go all over the story of my going home, for it was very interesting to all of Company B. But they had little to tell me, for they had been in the one place ever since I left them. Dr. Andrus had also been home. He is the same good soul he has been all along. No wonder the boys all love him well enough to die for him if it were necessary. Any man that can first get, and then keep the profound respect of the 128th New York's officers and men alike, is truly a wonderful man, and one perfectly safe to pattern after. If I die in the army I hope it will be with Dr. Andrus near me, for it would be so much easier. He has spoken for another game of checkers as soon as we can find a place and a board to play on.

We kept on past Port Hudson, going first one way and then another, on account of the many crooks in the river, and by night entered the mouth of the Red River. I have found out why it is called red. The banks are a reddish clay, and enough is all the time washing away to colour the water so it shows plainly after it joins the Mississippi.

March 24, 1864.
Thursday.
Still going up the Red River. We passed a fort, called Fort Derussey, which was until lately in possession of the enemy. General A. J. Smith, with portions of the 16th and 17th Army Corps, took it with everything in it. These troops were with Grant at Vicksburg, and are now ahead of us on the way to Alexandria. These with the 19th Corps under Banks make a big army. The Red River is mostly crooks. Now and then a straight place gives a look ahead and backward, and boats of all kinds cover the water. They are mostly transports loaded with troops and their equipments. It is easy to tell about moving an army, but the amount of stuff that must be moved with them is another thing. By water it is a question of boats enough, and by land a question of enough mules and wagons.

Where all these things come from is what I often wonder at. Mules and wagons are constantly giving out, and yet there is never any lack. And I have never seen any repair shops for wagons or hospitals for mules. Once they give out their places must be taken by others. The wonders performed by the quartermaster's department are not mentioned in any reports I have seen, and yet it is what the life and success of the army most depends on.

A man hailed us from the bank and was taken on board. He proved to be one of those captured at Sabine Pass last fall when Franklin's expedition undertook to land there. He escaped, and has been living with the negroes most of the time since. From all I can learn we are on the way to Shreveport, where the Rebels are said to be waiting in force. Shreveport is said to be the gateway between this state and Texas.

March 25, 1864.
Friday.

We reached Alexandria about midnight. The 128th went ashore, but we of the recruiting squad remained on board. We hear nothing of Colonel Bostwick and the others that were left behind. After breakfast I went ashore and looked up the 128th, and also looked about the place. It is a pretty place, not quite so large as Baton Rouge, but in every way a much better place to live in. A broad street runs along next the levee, and appears to be the principal business street. The Court House, a large brick building stands on a square by itself, and is the finest building I saw. Alexandria is rather a big village than a city. The streets are wide, and the houses are not crowded up against each other. Nearly every house has a yard and one or more shade trees in it. I saw no fortifications. If there are any they are outside. Altogether it is the finest place to live in I have seen in Louisiana. General Smith had taken possession, and we had only to walk in and enjoy ourselves. Towards night the negroes began to flock in and we enlisted quite a number. Dr. Andrus staid with us. The pilot let us in his house, where we rigged up a checkerboard and played till most morning. Neither of us had anything to brag about when we finally gave it up.

March 26, 1864.
Saturday.

The boats cover the water as far as can be seen both up and down the river. There are rapids a little way above town and the gunboats have trouble in getting over, there only being places where the water is deep enough for them to clear the rocks. The 128th, which went into camp a mile or so out, moved back in town for provost guard duty. Colonel Bostwick and the other missing ones came up and our family is all together again. Captain Laird, who has not before been with us, came with them. He was assigned to Company D, and if ever we get a regiment, I suppose he will be my captain. For that reason, I have looked him over pretty closely, and without being able to tell why, yet there is something about the man I don't like. I hope I may be mistaken in him, as I sometimes have been in others. At any rate we won't have much to do with each other for a while, so I am not going to worry over it.

It was expected that the 19th Corps would take the lead from this point, but General Smith has gone on with his army. The *Laurel Hill* got sailing orders and we had to leave our pleasant quarters. We took a large brick house, where we have all the room we want. The dining-room was so large we all ate at one table. Dr. Andrus came and staid with us again, and we had another tie game of checkers. The last tenants took all the furniture with them, so we had to sleep on the floor, but we don't mind a little thing like that.

March 27, 1864.
Sunday.
Colonel Bostwick sent all hands out to look up recruits and we are to make that our business from this on. We are to report every night what success we meet with. Not one of us got a recruit, but we all got a lecture.

March 28, 1864.
Monday.
Colonel B. didn't like the house we were in, and we all moved into another that he liked better. Moving day at home used to be a busy one, and so were several days before and after, but we have improved on the old order of doing such things. We just pick up what belongs to us, walk out of the old house into the new one and throw them down—and the job is done.

Lieutenant Bell and I were set at making out reports, and we managed to smuggle in a letter or two apiece. After that, Sergeant House from Company B came in and we all walked up the river as far as the Falls, as the rapids are here called. It was very interesting to watch the ironclads feel their way over the rocks into the deeper water above. The hospital boat, the *Woodford*, hit a rock and sprung a leak. She was run ashore on the opposite side and the gang plank run out. From the way the sick people hurried off I don't think they were very badly off. The boat began to settle down, as if the damage was serious.

March 29, 1864.
Tuesday.
Was detailed for officer of the guard, and was in camp all day. There are men coming in every day that have escaped the conscript-officers and have been living in the woods like wild beasts. They opposed secession and would not serve in the secession army. Many of them are

owners of property in this place, but they left their homes and their families and herded together for protection against small bands of pursuers, scattering again when a larger force was sent after them. Now that the coast is clear, they offer to act as scouts or to fight in the ranks for the Union cause. Nearly enough for a regiment have reported. They are well armed and are ready to use their guns against the common enemy. They are not the poor whites, who are as ignorant as the blacks, but are intelligent men, and the stories they tell of the wrongs they have suffered and the sufferings they have endured have made my blood boil with sympathy for them.

They swear Alexandria shall never again be in possession of their enemies, for they will burn it to the ground before that happens. They call themselves "Jay-hawkers" and seem proud of the name. It seems wicked to doubt their sincerity, and yet I can't help thinking what a slick trick it would be for the Rebels to cut these men loose from their army and send them among us with just such a story as they tell. Now and then one could slip away and not be missed as regular enlisted soldiers would, and so every plan and every move we make be carried straight to them.

Rumour says Colonel Bostwick has been detailed at headquarters, and Lieutenant-Colonel Parker has been appointed superintendent of recruiting service in this department.

March 50, 1864.
Wednesday.

New orders already. Major Palon, with Lieutenants Bell, Dillon and Van Alstyne, is to go to Natchitoches for recruits. The Jay-hawkers say every one of the recruiting squad is known by name to General Mouton, and that he also has a pretty good description of each one. He has had this ever since we camped on his plantation last fall. If any are captured we are to be tried by the civil authorities for "nigger stealing," the penalty for which is death. How General Mouton got all this information the Jay-hawkers say they don't know, but if what I have been mean enough to hint at should be true, then it all becomes plain. It seems to me they should be watched until they prove their sincerity by their works. We begin to think we are somebody after all, to be mentioned in general orders, even if it is only to advertise us as "nigger stealers."

We boarded the steamer *Jennie Rogers* at noon. I tried to get Tony to stay back, telling him the Jay-hawker story and that if he was caught in our company his fate would be as bad or worse than ours. At first he decided to stay, but as we were going on board he changed his mind and would go, saying, "If the Rebels get you, then I'm going to die wid you." We ran up to the rapids and stopped. The gunboat *Ozart* had got fast in the mud by going too close to the opposite bank. A big rope was run across the river to a tree and made fast, and the machinery on the *Ozart* went to winding up on it, thinking to pull herself loose.

Next, another rope was tied to the middle of the big one, and a tugboat began pulling on it, the *Ozart* all the time winding up the slack. The big rope, or hawser as they call it, was finally pulled high enough so the tug could go under it, and then it went up stream as far as the rope would let it, and then, with a full head of steam, came down under it, fetching up with a tremendous yank on the hawser, which made the water fly from it in all directions. This was done several times, but the *Ozart* was still there. Then a tree was cut and one end brought on board, the other resting against the bank. In some way, tackles were rigged so that the tree was made to push, and the tug giving one more pull, the *Ozart* came loose from the bank and seemed none the worse for the tugging she had had. The line across the river was then taken in and the *Jennie Rogers* went on for ten or a dozen miles and tied up for the night.

March 31, 1864.
Thursday.
We started at daybreak and had gone perhaps twenty miles, when we overtook General Smith's army, which was stopping every boat that came along, until enough were had to carry his army. We tied up and I went ashore and mixed up with the western soldiers to see how they differed from the eastern troops. They are larger men on the average, and more on the rough and ready order than ours, but on the whole I liked them first-rate. They were at Vicksburg, and if they told the truth about the siege of Vicksburg, we of Port Hudson hardly know what war is like. As I could not match their stories, I told none, more than to give an outline of the siege, which they thought must have been pretty tame.

From an old man, a native, I was told an interesting story about a hill that is in sight. He said it is called "The Hill of Death," so named by the Indians, who fought a Kilkenny cat battle there until all were killed but a few women and children. It is not much of a hill, not more than half as big as Bryan's "Sugar Loaf," but otherwise much like it. Boats kept coming and tying up. Those that came later brought news of the capture and destruction of the *Lacrosse*, just below Fort Derussey yesterday. Also that the *Mattie Stevens* was fired on and her pilot killed. Sim Bryan, our mail carrier, was on the *Mattie*, and if the Rebs got Sim and the letters he carried they know what our opinion of them is.

April 1, 1864.
Friday.
Moving day at home. Our folks will get into their new home to-day, and I wish I was there to help settle them down in it. It will be their first move without me since I was big enough to help.

I slept late this morning, till long after breakfast, and then, having nothing to get up for, lay and dozed until dinner time. Tony had my clothes brushed and my boots blacked and felt much worse than I did because I had lost my breakfast. I told him I would make it up for dinner, and I did. The river is full of boats now.

April 2, 1864.
Saturday.
About noon General Smith and staff went on board the *Clarabelle* and at 2 p. m. we started up the creek. A copy of the code of signals that are to govern us was sent to each vessel. The river is so narrow we must go Indian file, and are to keep 400 yards from each other. One long whistle while tied up means "Get under way." One long whistle while under way means "Tie up." Three short whistles, "Close order." Four short whistles, "Open order." Five short whistles, "I wish to communicate." One gun from the flagship, "The enemy is in sight." Two short whistles and a long one. "I want assistance." Three short whistles and a long one, "The enemy has a battery." Four short whistles and a long one, "The troops will land." One gun and a long whistle, "All right." We got under way and everything went well until dark when, in rounding a short turn in the pesky little rivulet, another boat bumped into ours and stove a hole in below the water line.

The *Jennie* was pointed for shore and by the time she struck there, there was such a panic among the Vicksburg heroes as I don't believe eastern men ever thought of. At any rate none of our party so much as thought of joining in. They rushed for the side and began jumping from the upper and lower deck at the same time, landing on each other and some of them in the water, and then began quarrelling and fighting over the hurts they had got. The rush to one side tipped the hole out of water, and as soon as the men could be got on the boat again it was held in that position until the damage was repaired. The whole thing was amusing from our point of view, and after a good laugh over it we went to bed.

April 3, 1864.
Sunday.

The leak was stopped and the water pumped out, and at 4 a. m. we took our place in the line and went on. An idea of the number of boats is had from the fact that they had been passing all the time this was going on, and the end was not in sight when we started again.

At noon we stopped for wood, and to relieve the neighbours of their surplus chickens. The western men are all right on a chicken raid, for I don't think one escaped them. At 6 p. m. we were under way again, but the *Jennie* ran onto a sand bar soon after and it took a lot of puffing and blowing to get loose from it, and to catch up and take our proper distance again. This makes thirty out of the last thirty-eight days I have been afloat. One in New Orleans, four at Port Hudson, and three at Alexandria, is all the time I have been ashore. At that rate I will soon be a sailor.

April 4, 1864.
Grand Ecore, La., Monday.

We reached Grand Ecore sometime in the night without further mishap and found ourselves tied fast to a tree on the bank when we awoke this morning. About noon the *Jennie* untied and went a little above the town and made fast again. We did nothing but watch the unloading of the troops. About 10 p. m., just as we were about to turn in, an order came for us to report at once at Alexandria for further orders. We were told that the *Luminary* was to start at daylight, and Major Palon told me to see if I could verify the report. Between us and the *Luminary* was a creek, without a bridge or other visible means of crossing. Tony found a boat and we were soon on board the *Luminary*, where we found the report about her sailing at daylight was true. In the meantime, someone had taken our boat, and we had to go away along the bayou until we could hear the challenge of the picket guards before we could get across.

We legged it down the opposite side, and in the darkness mistook the *Hastings* for the *Jennie Rogers*. From her we got our bearings and were soon on board the *Jennie* and reported. The *Jennie* had a small boat, the *Little Jennie*, and with this we crossed the bayou and were soon on board the *Luminary*, only to find that since I was there her orders had been changed and she was to go up the river instead of down. By this time it was almost morning and we went back to the *Jennie Rogers* and to bed. I had had exercise enough to make me ready to sleep almost anywhere, and I was soon sound asleep.

April 5, 1864.
Tuesday.

We were glad we left the *Luminary*, for she ran into a nest of Johnnies, who fired on her and killed six men. Heavy firing was heard in front and skirmish firing much nearer. Smith's troops had gone in that direction and had probably met some opposition. I went ashore and fell in with an old resident who told me that Grand Ecore proper lies four miles back in the country now, though it was once right on the river bank. It being on the inside of a bend, the water kept washing the earth from, one side and leaving it on the other, until now the village and river are four miles apart. At every time of high water the river moves on a little farther, leaving a strip of new made ground on which young Cottonwood trees immediately sprout up. This makes the top look like a great green stairway, the first step of which was made by the last freshet, the next by the freshet before, and so on to the top.

The firing grew nearer and there was more of it. By ten o'clock it was plain that hot fighting was going on, and not very far away. The dense growth of cottonwoods cut our view down in that direction to a little strip along the river, and out of this wounded men and small parties of prisoners began to come. By noon it seemed as if the whole of Smith's army was coming back and coming in a hurry, too. Batteries from below were rushed up and planted in the young cottonwoods right in front of us. Artillery horses, with their traces cut, came out by the dozen, and there was everything to show that a part or the whole of Smith's army was retreating. Soon the woods were alive with choppers, and the trees began to fall.

In a time so short I hardly dare tell it the road and a strip each side of it was uncovered for at least a mile. How men could live where trees fell as they did there is a miracle. All the time men, horses and mules kept coming by the hundreds, and maybe thousands. Boats began loading with them. Forty-seven were put on our boat, three of them commissioned officers. A guard of negro soldiers was on the boat and the idea of being put under them made them howl with rage. Such swearing as one captain did would be hard to beat anywhere. The trouble in front began to quiet down. Not a shot had come our way, and not one had been fired in that direction. Whatever had happened was too far away for us to more than guess at. But it was plain that General A. J. Smith had run afoul of something that was a match for him, and what we were looking at was a genuine retreat.

From the way boats were loading up and moving down stream it looked as if the "nigger stealers" were to have plenty of company on the way to Alexandria. From an artillery sergeant who was not so scared but that he could tell what had happened I found out this much. That the road ran through the woods for a long way and finally went diagonally across a large cleared space and into the woods beyond. That they were not molested until, while crossing this opening, they were fired upon and a panic was the result. The road was full and reinforcements could not get at them from either direction, and they cut loose and ran for it. The infantry caught some of the bolder of the enemy and brought them in. They could not stop the retreat. They had to get out of the way or get run over by the crazy men and horses that filled the narrow road.

One of the prisoners is a Captain Todd. He was quite willing to talk. He said he was a cousin to President Lincoln's wife, and that he should now take the amnesty oath and try to get a job as clerk in some department.

Captain Faulkner, another prisoner, is as full of venom as a rattlesnake. He brags of what he has done and tells of what he will yet do. If he carries out his present intentions we had better skip for the north before he gets loose. He said he led the force that riddled the Black Hawk at Morgan's Bend, and I think he told the truth, for the pilot on the Black Hawk at that time is now pilot on this boat. They knew each other at sight. Captain Faulkner said, "Captain Frayer, I had four shots at you at Morgan's Bend, and all I ask for is one more."

The main force is somewhere in advance, but a good bunch of the rear guard is here. Everyone is blaming everyone else for what happened, and I expect all hands are ashamed of it now. When General Smith gets at them I expect they will feel worse yet.

Captain Faulkner's horse came in with others, and as soon as the captain saw him he begged to have him taken on board. He called him up close to the boat by whistling through his fingers. The coming of his horse changed the captain wonderfully. If he hated us, he certainly

247

loved his horse. I felt sorry for him and told him so. He asked me to take off his saddle and bridle and perhaps he would find his way home. I stripped him and found a bullet had grazed his back and the flies were already at work. The saddle had also galled him.

More out of pity for the horse than the captain, I took him to the river and washed his sore back clean, and at the captain's suggestion got some bacon fat from the steward and rubbed it well in. The captain said that would stop the flies. He was very grateful and told me all about the horse, how intelligent he was and how he hated to leave him. Said he never needed training, for he knew more than most people. He had raised him from a colt and no other white man had ever handled him as much as I had just done. Among the soldiers I found one that was a fellow passenger on the *McClellan*, and that brought up the subject of the rough passage and the rougher passengers. He said the ones I had arrested were tried and sent to the Dry Tortugas, which is an island in the Gulf of Mexico off the Florida coast.

April 6, 1864.
Wednesday.

Captain Faulkner was up before I, and had called up his horse. The pony, for he was nothing else, tried to get up the gang plank, and would have come on board if the guard had not driven him back. I wished I could see them together. I had never seen so much affection shown by a horse, and I felt almost as bad as the captain did to see them kept from each other. I gave him a good washing with soap and water and another greasing with bacon fat. About wood. The pony followed, and when the gang plank was run out he again tried to come on board. This was too much for me. I went to the captain and offered him the only five-dollar bill I had in the world to take him on. But it was of no use. He resented my offering him money to disobey orders, and the door against the pony was closed. The last I saw of him he was running off across the country as if a new idea had struck him. But Captain Faulkner was most grateful to me, and I hope if the enemy ever gets hold of me Captain Faulkner will be among them, for he says he would just like a chance to get even with me for what I have done.

Another of the prisoners had been overseer on the plantation where we were taking on wood. His wife, with their little boy, came on board and pleaded for his release on parole. This, together with the pony affair, made the day a miserable one for me. Someway that sort of suffering hit me in a very tender spot. I could have seen the overseer and Captain Faulkner both shot and not have felt as badly as I did to think of that wife and child mourning for their husband and father, and the pony looking for his master, and perhaps falling into the hands of someone who would be cruel to him without ever knowing how near human he is. It is lucky for the government that I am not president, for such things as I have seen and heard today would tempt me to pardon Jeff Davis himself.

When the wood was on board we started down the river for Alexandria, having done nothing more to earn our pay than to spend a few days as spectators of the stirring times at Grand Ecore. At a bend in the river by a woodyard an old darkey, mounted on an old gray mule, hailed us and said the Rebs were waiting for us in the woods about a mile below. A boat behind us had some guns on her forward deck, and began shelling the woods as soon as they came within reach, and we went past without a shot being fired at us. The river was lower than when we came up, and also narrower, in places not much wider than the length of the boat.

At 11 p. m. we reached Alexandria and went to headquarters to report. We found the family all abed and asleep. A whiskey bottle standing on the table relieved us of any embarrassment we might otherwise have felt for calling at so late an hour. We soon had them all out of bed to receive us in a manner more fitting to the occasion. Dr. Warren got mad and used some improper language, for which he was soundly spanked and put to bed again. Thus ended our trip to Natchitoches, a place we never saw.

April 7, 1864.
Thursday.
There being nothing to hinder, I went to visit the 128th. Found that Charlie Travis had died while we were away. He was one of the best of the lot, and Company B was feeling pretty sober over his sudden taking off. They were going to have chicken for dinner and I had to stay and help out. After that I came home and wrote a letter. The *Polar Star* came up with 500 prisoners on the way to the front to be exchanged. They were delighted at the prospect of a chance to fight us again. Those we brought down with us, on their way to prison, didn't seem to feel so happy.

April 8, 1864.
Friday.
While we were up the river the rest of the squad have enlisted over

300 men, and have gone in camp just out of town. Colonel Parker is in command. After breakfast I went to see them. Found Sol shaking yet; cold one day and hot the next. From his looks he has been real. badly off. I visited them until noon and then went back to headquarters, where I found a lot of writing had been saved up for me. I wrote till night and then made Sol another visit, after which I came home and went to bed.

April 9, 1864.
Saturday.
Orders for up the river again. The same four go, with Major Palon in command as before. Some way this trip smells stronger of danger than any we have taken. We have packed our trunks, keeping out an extra shirt apiece, and left the keys, with directions what to do with them in case we don't come back. At 1 p. m. we boarded the *Laurel Hill,* our old favourite, and set out. As we were turning about to get under way another boat almost touched us, and on it was Lieutenant Manning, with a bundle of letters in his hand for us. Was ever anything more tantalizing than that? To go off, not knowing for how long, with those letters almost in our hands, was worse than not seeing them at all. But there was no help for it and we went on, swallowing our disappointment as best we could. We reached the rapids and got over them without mishap, and in a little while had tied up for the night. We sat on the deck and smoked, wondering if any of the letters were for us, after all, and when we would see them in case they were.

April 10, 1864.
Sunday.
We started at daylight and met with no adventures worth telling of on the way. At 6 p. m. we were at Grand Ecore again, where we learned that a hard battle had been fought at Mansfield Plains and at Pleasant Hill—a two days' fight and nobody claiming the victory. Some say the Rebs had the best of the first day's fight and that our folks had the best of the last, which was yesterday. A large body of men and animals is here—cavalry, infantry and artillery—all mixed up in no sort of order. Wounded men are lying on the ground and wounded horses and mules hobbling about. I looked until dark, and then listened to the sounds of suffering until sleep overtook me.

April 11, 1864.
Monday.
We went ashore and put up our two tents as much out of the way

as possible, and waited for things to settle down. Wounded men were all the time being brought in, some on stretchers and some on foot. General Ransom went past on a stretcher, with one knee bandaged and bloody. Right behind him walked a man with one arm gone, and who was joking with another who was carrying his cut off arm in his hand. I got out among them to try and hear what had happened and what I heard was not altogether complimentary to General Banks. But it was Smith's men who were talking and some allowance must be made for that. They say it has all come of poor management on the part of General Banks. If Grant had been in command this would never have happened, from all of which I judge the Rebs have given them a dressing out and they are mad at General Banks about it.

A strong rear guard is all that keeps them from coming and finishing up the job. Lieutenant Bell has been out taking notes and upon a comparison, we have both the same story to tell. Everything is in a mixed-up condition. Everyone is full of trouble but the recruiting squad, and we have nothing to do but look on. The process of unravelling the tangle is very interesting to me, but so much suffering on every hand makes me sick, and I cannot help wondering if it pays.

April 12, 1864.
Tuesday.
Having no orders to do otherwise, I kept out among the stragglers to learn what I could. The wounded have mostly been sent down the river for better treatment than can be had here on the hospital boats. It is said that several boats are above here, some aground and others helping them off, while all the time the Rebs are firing on them from the shore. One story is that reinforcements are being hurried up the river from Alexandria and other points below.

April 13, 1864.
Wednesday.
Things have been lively here today. Firing was heard up the river this morning, and a pontoon bridge was thrown across here and troops hurried across and gotten into position. The Colonel Cowles came down and reported the boats above here to be in an awkward situation. Troops have been going up on the other side all day. They soon go out of sight around a turn and are hid by the woods. We certainly are having the soft side of soldiering now. There is nothing we can do but look on, and we do that all the time. But we are obeying orders, and that's all any of them are doing.

April 14, 1864.
Thursday.
The stranded boats began coming down this morning, and were greeted with cheers from the soldiers and whistles from the steamers. Several were riddled with bullets, and quite a number of dead men were taken off and buried. The wounded were taken on board the hospital boats. The Black Hawk, as usual, came in for a full share, getting the worst shooting up of any. This is the third time she has got it on this expedition. The land forces brought 300 prisoners with them. We are still watching proceedings, being too light handed to do anything more. No recruits are here, and they won't dare come in as long as the enemy holds the ground all around us.

April 15, 1864.
Friday.
This has been an interesting day. An attack was expected and preparations were made to receive it. Troops were shifted from one place to another. The pickets on the Nachitoches road were driven in. The woods were chopped away to give the artillery a chance in that direction. A negro came running out of the woods saying the Rebs were within three miles and were coming on the double-quick, but this report was not believed, for someone besides him would have found it out. At any rate no attack was made and the day passed and left things very much as it found them.

April 16, 1864.
Saturday.
Another day of doing nothing. This looking for trouble is worse than finding it. The troops have been shifting about all day, as if it was hard to decide what was the right position. There were no more signs of trouble to come than the getting ready for it. The recruiting squad helped all it could by looking on and wondering what it is all about.

April 17, 1864.
Sunday.
Reinforcements having been coming in for some days. I set out this morning to look them over and see if the 128th was here. Sure enough, I found them about a half mile out on the Natchitoches road, feeling fine and ready for business. I staid all day with them, getting back in time for supper and to talk over the hard times we are having doing nothing.

April 18, 1864.
Monday.

For pastime today. Lieutenant Dillon and I borrowed a skiif from one of the boats and explored the country along the river above here. We went ashore and looked for something to vary our diet of hard-tack and coffee. After dinner we moved our tents back into the woods, where we will have shade all the day long. Our duties are so laborious it is necessary to have a cool spot to work in. For exercise we run, jump, box, or do anything we can think of to keep up circulation. We have made the acquaintance of a stray mule and take turns letting him tumble us off over his head in the sand. He is gentle as can be, and lets us do anything with him except riding him beyond a certain distance. When he has gone far enough he gives a quick jump, stands on his head, and the thing is done.

April 19, 1864.
Tuesday.

Just before daylight the "Long Roll" sounded and such getting up nothing else could have brought about. Batteries limbered up and took position. The horses were taken back and left with harness on. Men took their stations at the guns. Ambulances were placed in convenient places, and every preparation made for a fight, but no one appeared to fight with. The excitement, which was great at first, grew less until it was all gone and the same lazy feeling that had been with us for days came back. I have been doctoring a wounded horse for the last week, and the beggar has got to depending on me for his rations instead of hunting for it himself. He eats hard-tack much better than I can, and appears to like them better than grass. I have to go across the river for grass, and mow it with my knife. He eats it without as much as a thank you, and as he is about cured I am going to take him across the river and leave him soon. Tonight we had a grand gymnastic performance and are going to bed.

April 20, 1864.
Wednesday.

On board the *John Warner*, bag and baggage. When we got up this morning we found everybody pulling up and getting ready for a move. We watched and waited for orders to do likewise. The major, who had gone to investigate, came back and said the Red River campaign had been given up and all hands were going back to Alexandria. He secured passage for us on the *Warner* and here we are. For fear someone would press him into the service and forget that he was only a convalescent, I took the horse I had patched up, and after stuffing his wound with bacon fat, I took him across the pontoon bridge and turned him loose in the big grass on the other side. When I came back Tony had my few things picked up and ready to go on board. The bulk of the army goes by land and a portion of it is already on the way to Alexandria, our first stopping-place. Major Palon says the expedition had to be abandoned on account of the falling of the water in the river, and if the boats get over the rapids at Alexandria they must do it right away. At any rate a retreat is now in order and the major says I will have plenty of filling for my diary before it is over.

Night. Four thirty-pounder Parrot guns have been mounted on the forward deck, and the men and ammunition necessary for their use is on board. Every preparation for trouble is being made, whether we have any or not. The cause of the retreat is common talk now among the officers. Banks is blamed for the failure of the expedition, though I fail to see how he is to blame for the falling of the water in the Red River.

A man fishing from the boat this afternoon hooked onto something which when pulled up proved to be a dead soldier with his skull smashed in. The boatmen remembered him as one who had a quarrel with a deckhand last night, and as he, too, is missing, it is thought he killed this soldier and after throwing him in the river cleared out. I could not get his name or regiment, but am sure he did not belong to the 128th. It is easy to die here and there are many ways of doing it. A dead man was found on the upper deck of the *Mattie Stevens* yesterday. He was thought to be asleep until a comrade went to wake him up and found he was sleeping his last sleep. He was shot through the heart, but as no shot had been fired on the boat it is supposed it came from some distance away, missing the thousands that are here and finding only this sleeper. He was of the 33rd Massachusetts.

What I have seen today would fill a book. The major's prophecy that I would find plenty of filling for my diary is coming true. I had noticed a prisoner handcuffed fast to a post in the cabin, but had paid no attention to him until some loud talking in his neighbourhood led me to it. A soldier, one of the Western men, with a bloody bandage around one leg, was giving this prisoner the biggest kind of a tongue-lashing, and was with difficulty kept from clubbing him with his cane. I finally got at the Westerner and found out what it was about. He said his regiment was waiting in the road below here for the line to be made up. Noticing a house and other buildings in a grove not very far away, he and two of his comrades set out for some eggs and perhaps something else good to eat. They were met by this prisoner, who acted very friendly, giving them milk to drink and to fill their canteens. When they asked for eggs he told them there were none in the house but plenty in the loft, pointing to a loft with a ladder reaching to it.

Without a suspicion of treachery they set their guns up by the side of the building and went up the ladder after the eggs. When they started to come down they found their own guns pointed at them, in the hands of this prisoner and two other men they had not seen before. There was nothing to do but surrender, which they decided to do. They came down and were marched into the woods for some distance, stood up in line and fired upon. One was killed instantly, my informant was shot through the leg and fell more from the expectation of certain death than from his hurt. The third man was missed clean and started to run with the three devils after him. That gave this fellow a chance and he legged it for his regiment and fell fainting from terror and the loss of blood.

When he came to, his comrades were returning with this prisoner, the only one they could find. They did find the man that ran away, lying where he had been overtaken and stabbed to death with bayonets. The wonder and the pity is they ever brought this murderer away with them. Why they didn't shoot him full of holes instead of taking him prisoner is what none of us can understand. I suppose he will live on Uncle Sam for a while and then go free. This must do for one day's record. It is late and I am almost blind from writing by the light of a lantern.

April 21, 1864.
Thursday.
We were loaded up and ready for a start early this morning. We dropped downstream to our place in the long line of steamboats, gunboats and most every kind of boats. Got onto a sand bar and had to be pulled off. A gunboat got fast just below us and getting that loose took the rest of the day.

April 22, 1864.
Friday.
We got another start at about daylight and kept going until noon, when we struck bottom and had to be pulled loose again. We could plainly see that the bottom of the river was much nearer the top than

when we came up. We stopped at the same landing for wood where the old contraband warned us of trouble on our last trip down. Sure enough, he was here again and with another warning. He said the woods below Cane River were alive with sharpshooters, of which he had warned the boats ahead, and would warn those to come. We heard firing long before we reached Cane River, and as we neared the woods the guns on our boat began a raking fire on each side and kept it up until the woods were passed. It was dark by this time and the boats went little if any faster than the flow of the river. We reached the rapids above Alexandria about 10 p. m., and so far as I know, not a person was hurt on the way.

April 23, 1864.
Saturday.

When we awoke we were glad to hear it raining hard. This will at least stop the river from going any lower, and may raise it. We left the boat and took a four-mile walk to Alexandria, where we found our folks well and enjoying themselves. The regiment is nearly full. If we had remained here we might have filled it. As it is, our two trips to Grand Ecore have amounted to nothing more than seeing some stirring times in which we had no other part than spectators. Sol had nine letters for me and a basketful for the others. It took me quite a while to read so many. After reading them I began writing a reply to each one. I had had a grumbling toothache for some days and today it has taken hold for sure, I suppose my walk in the rain gave it an excuse. At night we were relieved from recruiting service and ordered back to the regiment, I reporting to Captain Laird for duty. Lieutenant Bell and I were ordered to report for fatigue duty in the morning at 7 a. m.

April 24, 1864.
Sunday.

Agreeable to orders. Bell and I reported to the quartermaster at 7 o'clock and were given 134 men and sent to the rapids to unload boats and load up wagons for transportation below the falls. One was to check what came off the boats and the other what the wagons carted off. Someone else checked again as the stuff" was loaded on the boats below the falls, and if anything was lost it was easy to tell who was to blame. My tooth ached so badly that the quartermaster put another in my place and I went back to camp to try and get rid of it. Dr. Andrus talked me off the notion, and gave me something to put in it, which helped it so much that I went back and finished out the day. When we reached camp at night I felt as if I had earned my pay, having walked sixteen miles, done a lot of writing, and had suffered severely with toothache nearly all the time.

April 25, 1864.
Monday.
The army begins to get in from up the river. The 128th had a brush at Cane River and lost one man. I put in the day writing, and at night went and visited with Sol.

April 26, 1864.
Tuesday.
Kept right on writing. Sim goes in a day or two and I want to get even with my correspondents.

April 27, 1864.
Wednesday.
Heavy firing up the river. By the sound it is ten or more miles away. The gunboats are up there holding the enemy from getting their artillery within reach of the transports. The Rebs are closing in around Alexandria and the pickets begin to clash. Went for a walk with Captain Enoch, after which I called on Dr. Andrus to get him to do something with that tooth. He put me off with some more medicine, but says if it doesn't stop tonight he will pull it tomorrow.

April 28, 1864.
Thursday.
On duty as officer of the guard, and next to nothing to do. So many of the men are helping unload the boats, the camp is almost empty. The enemy is fighting his way along day by day. The roar of artillery is heard almost constantly. Our lines must hold the country for ten miles all round us, for that is as close as the fighting appears to be. We hear of wrangling among our leaders, one blaming another for the fix we are in. A dam is being built below the falls to raise the water so the gunboats may slide over. A Colonel Bailey is the engineer in charge of the job, and it is quite a job. too.

Night. A ring of fire surrounds Alexandria tonight. It is said our forces are working in and burning everything as they come. Lieutenant Ames, who has been under arrest since last winter for drunkenness, was today dismissed from the service.

April 29, 1864.
Friday.

No fighting here yet. The firing outside is constant now, but what it amounts to we don't know. Was relieved from duty at 8 o'clock and went for a walk before turning in. On a back street a terrible commotion broke out as I was passing a backyard with a high slab fence around it. I peeked through a knothole and saw a shocking sight. An old sow had a little child down on the ground and was trying to eat it. Two women, one with a broom and the other with a mop, were hammering the sow and screaming at the top of their voices, while the old sow was making such a noise as only a hog can make when raging mad.

Just as I had taken in the situation, something struck the top of the fence with force enough to shake it from end to end. One of the ugly-looking dogs called bloodhounds had jumped and caught his fore feet over the top and was scrambling for a hold with his hind feet. Just as I looked up he got a toe hold, and quicker than I can tell it was over the fence and had the old varmint by the back of the neck. The women ran in the house with the child, and whether the child or the old sow lived I don't know, but I shall always think well of the bloodhound after this. I went back home and slept the day away.

April 30, 1864.
Saturday.

Five letters today. All from good friends at home. They are all well and know nothing of the predicament we are in. Every loose board about town is being gathered up for use at the dam. The water is already up so many of the lighter draught boats are floated over the rocks. The gunboats, our main dependence, are there yet.

May 1, 1864.
Sunday.

My tooth bothered me yet, and I went to the hospital this morning determined to get rid of it. Dr. Andrus was out, but Lew Brooks, the hospital steward, said he could do the job just as well. He got a good deep hold and pulled on it, but the tooth stood firm. After a second trial and a second failure, he called in a man to hold my head still and tried it again with both hands. The tooth simply wouldn't come out. But the character of the pain was changed, and that was a little satisfaction. Dr. Andrus gave me some chloroform liniment which helped some, but has taken from my mouth what little skin Brooks left on. I have been in agony all day. The tooth sticks out so I can't shut my jaws, and is getting sore every minute.

May 2, 1864.
Monday.
I don't know what has been done today, and I don't care. I have had troubles enough of my own. Dr. Warren has excused me from duty. Tony made me a stew that needed no chewing, and I drank it without asking what he made it from.

May 3, 1864.
Tuesday.
Have felt worse today than any day. My neck and shoulders are so lame and sore I can hardly roll my eyes. My mouth is better, and I can begin to use it.

May 4, 1864.
Wednesday.
I found myself this morning feeling much more like myself. Tony stole a chicken and cooked it so I could suck the meat off the bones, and it made the whole world seem better. I got out among folks, and hope by another day to be able to manage a hard-tack. The Rebs are coming, for the firing sounds plainer than any day yet. There is much discussion of, and more cussing about, the situation we are in. A party of unarmed men was seen on the other side of the river, and a boat was sent over. They proved to be all that is known to be left of the 120th Ohio, which was on its way to join us. They were fired on from the shore and their boat crippled. The men jumped overboard and swam ashore, and while the most were captured, some got away and have found their way here. Others may come if not picked up on the way.

Sergeant Nace, who said he belongs to the 176th New York, found me today and almost claimed relationship. He knows the folks in Rowe Hollow, and from his talk and actions was very glad to see me. I never heard of the man before. He was a good talker, and if the ears of the people in Rowe Hollow didn't burn it wasn't because they were not talked about.

May 5, 1864.
Thursday.
Reported for duty and was put on as officer of the guard. The 128th got in touch with the rebel skirmish line and Casey, of Company I, was shot through the mouth. The dam is being pushed in every

possible way. Trees are cut and dragged in the river, and bags filled with earth are thrown in to fill up the spaces. Stones are so scarce that brick houses not in use are torn down and used for ballast. I bought a horse, saddle and bridle today for four dollars, and he is now eating government hay with the mules. He may come handy when we skip out, which we expect to do as soon as the gunboats are over the falls.

General Smith fought quite a battle above here today and took some prisoners. It is reported tonight that the *John Warner*, the boat that brought us from Grand Ecore, has been sunk in the river below here, and Sim Bryan captured. He had our mail, and if the Rebs read our letters they know about what we think of them. I'd like to hear the comments they make. The tables have been turned, and we are now the besieged, instead of the besiegers.

May 6, 1864.
Friday.

"*It never rains but it pours.*" About noon Lieutenant-Colonel Foster of the 128th and about thirty others came in. They are all that are known to have escaped from the *John Warner*. They report the river blocked for anything short of our ironclads, which at present are lying above the rapids waiting for the dam to be finished. Colonel Foster thinks Sim may have destroyed the mail, but the time was rather short for it. Our pay rolls and the monthly returns were in his bag, and five letters from me to different friends. If the captors get any comfort out of them they are welcome. Colonel Foster had some dispatches with him, but managed to get away with them. As a reminder, he brought with him a ball in the calf of his leg which Dr. Andrews cut out with his jack-knife. It was just under the skin and popped out at the first cut.

Just at night more came in. They had escaped in the confusion of the attack and our cavalry scouts had found them and brought them in. These say that Captain Dane was hung, but we hardly think they had time to see all they tell of. However, it may be true, for he left the Confederate service when Butler took New Orleans, and has since been in our service, and true to it. He is the one who ran the *A. J. Brown* on our Texas trip. He has made several trips to Grand Ecore, the last of which was when we came down with him. The 128th had another brush with the enemy last night and took several prisoners.

May 7, 1864.
Saturday.

The 128th and another regiment captured and brought in a wagon train loaded with corn and other stuff the Rebs had picked up for their own use. They are skinning the country below here, so we will have to board ourselves or go hungry when we leave Alexandria.

May 8, 1864.
Sunday.

A very hot day. The men are being examined and any not fit for a hard tramp are put on the boats. The dam is nearly completed. All but the deepest draught boats are below the rapids waiting for the dam to be blown up so they can come down and load up for the run down the river. From all I can learn the plans are for the gunboats, provided they get over the rapids all right, to protect the left flank, which is to follow the right bank of the river and go as fast as infantry can possibly go. General Smith is to take care of the rear and as much of the right flank as he can. General Banks is to open up the way and also to look out for the right flank. No hard fighting is expected, but skirmish fighting is looked for all the way down. I went up to the dam just at night. The water rushes over it and through it like a young Niagara. It is a big job, and the engineers deserve great credit, whether it does all it is expected to or not.

May 9, 1864.
Monday.

The dam broke away in the night; all the boats near the break were swept through by the rush of water and are now where they can be used. The accident brought out a new idea, which is to repair the break and to build wing dams from each side towards it, and to depend on the rush of water pulling the whole outfit through.

Marching orders were issued this morning and every effort is being made for a sudden start. I have only my blanket and my diary to carry. Everything else besides my sword and revolver is on the *Rob Roy.* The troops have been moving out, getting in position, and everything betokens an early departure from Alexandria. We have a regiment of unarmed negro soldiers to get away with. They can be handled fairly well in camp, but how they will act in case of an attack is not yet known.

May 10, 1864.
Tuesday.

A rainy day, a rare thing nowadays. Colonel Parker succeeded in getting arms for our men, and they are wild with delight. Few of them ever had a gun in their hands before, and are as awkward with them as can be. We have been drilling them in the manual of arms and they did as well as could be expected. The army is getting straightened out for a start as soon as the ironclads are released. The wagon train is said to be fifteen miles long now, and the final start will add miles to it.

May 11, 1864.
Wednesday.
We put in a solid day of drilling in the manual of arms. No loading has been attempted, but the times and motions have been drilled into the woolly heads, so that a very encouraging improvement is the result. Captain Laird, my captain, is missing, and whether he has run away or been carried away, no one seems to know. At any rate, the care and conduct of Company D now comes upon your humble servant.

May 12, 1864.
Thursday.
Another day of the same. While the most of them do as well as can be expected, yet the ignorance and stupidity of the others is enough to try the patience of a saint. A boat came up today and was only fired on at one point. This looks as if the Rebs are planning some new move which will develop later. The moving preparations go steadily on, and the dam is progressing finely.

May 13, 1864.
Friday, Eight miles below Alexandria.
The Jay-hawkers kept their promise to burn the place rather than have it go into the hands of the enemy again. About daylight this morning cries of fire and the ringing of alarm bells were heard on every side. I think a hundred fires must have been started at one time. We grabbed the few things we had to carry and marched out of the fire territory, where we left them under guard and went back to do what we could to help the people. There was no such thing as saving the buildings. Fires were breaking out in new places all the time. All we could do was to help the people get over the levee, the only place where the heat did not reach and where there was nothing to burn. There was no lack of help, but all were helpless to do more than that.

Only the things most needful, such as beds and eatables, were saved. One lady begged so for her piano that it was got out on the porch and there left to burn. Cows ran bellowing through the streets. Chickens flew out from yards and fell in the streets with their feathers scorching on them. A dog with his bushy tail on fire ran howling through, turning to snap at the fire as he ran. There is no use trying to tell about the sights I saw and the sounds of distress I heard. It cannot be told and could hardly be believed if it were told. Crowds of people, men, women, children and soldiers, were running with all they could carry, when the heat would become unbearable, and dropping all, they would flee for their lives, leaving everything but their bodies to burn.

Over the levee the sights and sounds were harrowing. Thousands of people, mostly women, children and old men, were wringing their hands as they stood by the little piles of what was left of all their worldly possessions. Thieves were everywhere, and some of them were soldiers. I saw one knocked down and left in the street, who had his arms full of stolen articles. The provost guards were everywhere, and, I am told, shot down everyone caught spreading the fire or stealing. Nearly all buildings were of wood; great patches of burning roofs would sail away, to drop and start a new fire.

By noon the thickly settled portion of Alexandria was a smoking ruin. The thousands of beautiful shade trees were as bare as in winter, and those that stood nearest the houses were themselves burning. An attempt was made to save one section by blowing up a church that stood in an open space, but the fuse went out and the powder did not explode until the building burned down to it, and then scattered the fire instead of stopping it, making the destruction more complete than if nothing of the kind had been attempted.

Having done all that could be done for the place and the people, the call sounded and, as soon as we could get together and call the roll, we came on to this place, where we hope to stay tonight, for we certainly are in need of a rest. It is said the ironclads got over the rapids this morning and that we are to start on our long tramp early tomorrow morning.

CHAPTER 15

The Red River Retreat

May 14, 1864.
Saturday.

Reveille at 3.30 a. m., breakfast at 4.00, and at 4.30 we were off. The road followed the river, which is very crooked, making it nearly double the distance it would be in a straight line. About 9 a. m. the cavalry got into a fight on our right. We halted, and for the first time had the men load their guns. The enemy had come out from the woods and charged a squadron of our cavalry as it was passing, and for a time it was hard to tell which was getting the best of it. One of our men was shot from his horse, but the horse kept his place in the line as if nothing of the kind had happened. When the Rebs were finally routed and driven through the woods, the riderless horse kept his place and distance as long as they were in sight.

Before leaving Alexandria I had traded my horse for a mule that had no brand on him, and I had let a man who was not feeling well ride until now. In the skirmish just noted one of the mules in the quartermaster's team got hit and the quartermaster took my mule to put in his place, putting his rider in the wagon. That left me to walk whether I wanted to or not, but as I had plenty of company I didn't so much care. We kept going at a lively gait until noon, when we halted for hard-tack and coffee. The men on the boats kept exchanging shots with the Rebs on the opposite shore, but with what result I don't know.

Soon after dinner we came to a sharp turn in the river where the road ran close up to the river bank, and while rounding this on a double-quick we got the first attention from the other side that had been paid to us direct. A volley came from a thicket on the other side, the most of which went over our heads. One shot, however, went through the haversack of the man next to me and spoiled his tin cup. The shot came as close to me as it did to him, but I have nothing to show for it, while he is prouder of his battered cup than he ever was before.

About 2 p. m. the advance had a sharp skirmish with the enemy, losing ten men killed and forty wounded. The wounded were put on a boat and a detail left to bury the dead, after which they must catch up as best they can. About dark we passed Wilson's Landing, said to be twenty-five miles from Alexandria. Soon after we overtook the pontoon train and halted for the night. We are detailed to guard the pontoon train on the trip and have nothing to do but keep up with it unless it is attacked. I found the 128th close by, and after comparing notes with the boys of Company B, crawled behind a log and went to sleep.

May 15, 1864.
Sunday.

I was lying behind the log this morning, rubbing my eyes open, when a horseman rode right over it. The horse missed me and that was about all, but a miss is just as good as a mile. I found we were right by the wreck of the *John Warner,* her burned hull showing above the water. The letters that Sim carried were scattered over the ground, the wind having distributed them over several acres. I looked for some of my own, but did not find any. Some of those I read were curiosities, and possibly mine were carried off as such.

The train did not start until noon, and without any startling adventures we reached Marksville at 8 p. m. I wondered if this is the Marksville mentioned in *Uncle Tom's Cabin.* At any rate, it doesn't seem to be much of a place. The Rebs are said to be at Avoyelles Plains[1] in force, only a little way from here. Sergeant Nace of the 176th New York appeared to me again, having lost his regiment, as he said. I thought it a queer thing for a sergeant to lose on a trip like this, and I made up my mind he was a shirk and was beating his way through. However, I invited him to share my bed and board for the night, and while he went after water I hunted for something to eat.

He soon after came back, lugging a big feather bed, which he said he found at the house where he went for water and brought it along for a keepsake. After supper we planted ourselves on it and slept so sound that nothing short of a general engagement could have roused us.

---

1. Better known as the Plains of Mansura.

May 16, 1864.
Monday.

Reveille at 3.30 did not. awaken the feather bed brigade. Colonel Parker pulled me off just in time to fall in line, and without a mouthful to eat or drink I started on another hard day's tramp. Passing through Marksville, which I found to be much more of a place than I thought last night, we found the artillery stationed on a rise of ground, beyond which was a hollow and thick woods beyond it. We passed the artillery and were in the hollow beyond when the Rebs opened fire from the woods, and soon a big gun fight was on, the shot and shells passing directly over us, but doing us no harm. We parked the train and formed in front of it. Soon after the lines were pushed forward, and again the enemy opened on us and the same performance was gone through with.

As we lay on the ground in front of the train, a goose, from no one knows where, came squawking down the line in front of us and I captured it. I cut its throat with my sword, and as it was the first blood drawn by the 90th I let the blood dry on. Aside from the goose, the only casualty I know of was the killing of four artillery horses. They were all killed instantly by the same shot. Two pairs happened to be standing side by side and broadside to the enemy, when what must have been a three-pounder went through three of them and stopped in the fourth one, dropping the four dead in their tracks. The men behaved splendidly. The shots that missed the rise of ground behind us went on in the direction from which thousands were coming, but I don't know what harm they did.

About noon the enemy was driven out of the woods and we went on, I picking my goose as we went. While going through the woods we came to a sluggish stream too deep to cross without a bridge and a halt was made for some pontoons to be put across. I gathered some kindlings and made a fire to cook my goose, and was swinging it around my head to let all see what a prize I had, when a cavalry officer riding past caught it by one leg and riding on, took me and the goose with him. The leg I had hold of finally pulled off and the rascal went on with all the rest of it While it was roasting, I washed my pocket handkerchief in the stream, and was holding it by two corners, dipping it up and down in the water to rinse it, when, as I pulled it up the head of a great big snake came up after it as if he wanted to get hold of it, or perhaps to see what it was. He went right back and I saw no more of him.

Just then "Attention" sounded and I grabbed the goose leg and tried to eat it. Hungry as I was, raw goose was too much for me. I went around begging a hard-tack here and there and in that way got quite a meal, and also got the goosey taste out of my mouth. I no longer begrudged the fellow that stole my goose, but did wish he had to eat it raw.

The troops were all across at 9 p. m. and the pontoons were soon emptied and loaded on the wagons. Then began such marching as we never before had done. No attention was paid to the files. Those that could keep up did so, and the rest fell out by the way. The whole army was ahead of us and we must get to the front for the next crossing. We went on until midnight and then halted for an hour. "Fall in" again sounded and away we went, passing the thousands upon thousands of sleeping men and beasts.

At 3 a. m. we reached Yellow Bayou, the biggest stream we had so far met with. Excepting in the travelled path, men were sleeping all over the ground. My blanket was on some wagon, but I was too tired to look for it. Crawling in between some men who were sleeping on a blanket, I made out to get my body out of the wet grass and was soon sound asleep. When I awoke the sun was shining in my face. My bed-fellows had gone and taken the bed with them. Whether they pulled me off the blanket or pulled it from under me, I shall never know. The heavy dew and the chill night air had gone through my clothing, which was already wet with sweat, and I found myself about helpless, so sore and stiff were my joints.

As soon as I got my stiffened joints working, I looked around for the 90th and found them across the bridge on the bank of the bayou. More than half our men were missing, having fallen out by the way and been left to sleep it off. A detail was at the bridge to pick up stragglers and direct them where to go. Tony was among the first to get in and was dreadful sorry he had missed me in the night. I started right in for another nap and was next awakened by Tony, who had found a chicken that the others had missed and had it cooked. As soon as that was disposed of, I continued my nap, sleeping until night, when I was sent to the bridge to pick out our men as they came straggling in.

I had five sergeants, and posting one at each end of the bridge, I went and sat down on a knoll to watch them work. I finally lay down and in spite of myself dropped off again and slept all night. The sergeants had relieved each other and had gathered in nearly or quite all of our missing men. The troops were still crossing the bridge in a steady stream and the end was not yet in sight. We of the 90th had nothing more to do but wait for the troops to pass and then hustle for the front again. But we were rested and ready for it, and put in the day talking about our first experience on a forced march. The opinion was that if the next was any worse than this had been we wouldn't all be there to tell about it.

May 18, 1864.
Wednesday.

The rear guard was just coming in sight this morning when, we heard firing at the rear. Soon *aides* came riding down the line, halting some and turning others out of the way. They raced across the bridge and in a little while troops were hurrying back across the bridge from the front. It beat all how soon the scene was changed. The firing in the rear kept increasing and grew plainer to hear. The 90th stood at attention on the bank, which overlooked the whole plain where the trouble seemed to be centring. Unless the bridge was attacked we had only to look on, and it was a sight worth a lifetime to see. The ground, except where worn down by the passing army, was covered with weeds and bushes, which hid the skirmish line from our view until they rose up and fired almost in each others' faces. Smoke soon hid the battleground. There was no wind and the smoke rose up like a cloud instead of spreading. The smoke came nearer and it began to look as if our turn would soon come, but by and by it stood still and then began to move back.

By noon it was plain to see that the fight was ours, for the smoke cloud went faster and the firing grew less. By 4 p. m. it was over and the troops began recrossing toward the front. The surgeons had their shop under a big tree near the bridge. I heard one of them say to another that he had never seen so few slight wounds among so many. Most of those that were hit were either killed outright or mortally wounded. Only a few legs or arms were cut off. The saddest sight I saw was the killing of a boy, son of a colonel somebody, whose name or regiment I could not get. I had often seen the boy while at Alexandria and wondered why such a child should be in such a place. He rode a handsome bay pony, and wore the infantry uniform, even to a little sword.

When the fight began he was somewhere in the advance, and came riding back at the head of his regiment by the side of his father. They went into the cloud of smoke and in a few minutes a man came leading the pony back with the little fellow stretched across the saddle, his hands and feet hanging down on either side. He was taken back toward the front and I suppose his body will be sent home. What must that father have felt, and what will the mother feel when she knows of his death! It was such a useless sacrifice from my point of view. Nothing bigger than bullets came our way and they either went over our heads or struck in the bank of the bayou below us.

May 19, 1864.
Thursday.
Our dead were picked up and brought to the bayou, where they were laid in rows on the ground. Those that were identified were buried in separate graves, and the others put crosswise in a wide ditch, with blankets spread under and over them. Our loss was estimated at 500 and that of the Rebs at 800. That must mean killed and wounded, for no such number was buried. The rebel dead were buried in the field, I suppose, for none of them were brought in.

Later. A couple of our men are sick and Dr. Warren called in another doctor to look at them. They called it smallpox, and the men were put in a wagon and carted off right away. When the team came back the driver said they were put in the first house they came to, and a man who has had the disease was left to give them medicine. By night everything but the rear guard was across the bridge, and we had orders to be ready to march. We settled down to get some sleep if we could, but the long roll soon sounded and we sprang to our places. No enemy appearing, we built fires and made coffee, and then sat round nodding our sleepy heads until 4 o'clock in the morning.

May 20, 1864.
Friday.
By 4 a. m. the troops were across and the pontoons loaded. We marched at quick time and at 6 o'clock were at Simmsport, where we stopped for breakfast of hard-tack and coffee. While at it a man rode in saying the Rebs were already bridging Yellow Bayou. Simmsport is on the Atchafalaya River, and the same Colonel Bailey who planned the dam at Alexandria had built a bridge of boats for us to cross over. Twenty-four steamboats were lashed together side by side, and reached from shore to shore. Across the bows of these the artillery, cavalry and wagons were passing in a continuous stream, and infantry was crossing through and among them as best they could.

Other boats were busy ferrying the troops, and such getting across a river I never saw. The *Liberty* took us across and we marched down the opposite side for an hour, and halted for the line to straighten out. And so the whole day went, first starting and then stopping again, but expecting every minute to set out for good. The time we were waiting, if all put together, would have given us a good rest, and the marching we did would have been good exercise. But as it was, we had a hard day of it. It was pitch dark when we finally started. We came to woods and the darkness could be felt.

The train got stalled in the narrow road and then another wait. I was so dead sleepy that twice I fell flat on the ground as I was walking along. The fall woke me up each time and I kept going some way. Men had given out and were sleeping all along beside the road like dead men. Daylight never seemed so long coming. We got through the woods and could see much better. My naps as we walked along, and the falls I had in consequence of them, helped to drive off the dreadful drowsiness and by daylight I was wide awake.

May 21, 1864.
Saturday.

When daylight came we were passing the mouth of the Atchafalaya and were again on the banks of the Red River. About sunrise we halted. Lieutenant Moody and I sat down and began to figure up how long we had been awake, when we both tumbled over on the ground and were sound asleep. The next thing I knew Moody was shaking me and asking if I was hurt. His face was bloody and I supposed he had been shot. But we soon found that a horse had ran over us, his hoofs striking between our heads and scraping the skin off Moody's forehead as he picked them up. We soon after started again, and at 8 o'clock stopped for breakfast, after which we took a livelier gait than ever. The day was hot. The horses and mules showed the strain as well as the men. Soon the men began to give out, dropping like dead men, and it was impossible to rouse them from the deathlike sleep that had overtaken them.

There was nothing to do but pull them out of the road and leave them, for every horse and vehicle was loaded with all it could carry. No stop was made for dinner. On we went, and by 6 o'clock men were lying all along by the roadsides. Teams gave out and were left panting, their sides showing how cruelly they had been whipped to get the very last effort out of them. My feet were blistered, I knew by the feeling, though I had no time to see or attend to them. The pain each step gave me was, I think, the only thing that kept me awake and going.

About sundown we passed a little village and turned from the road across the country, which was said to be the nearest way to the Mississippi. It was a beautiful country, much like the Teche country, which is sometimes called the "Garden of Louisiana." There were some cattle, and a drove of them was gathered and driven along for our supper. In passing round a body of water that came in our way, a huge snake lay floating on it and was shot by some of the passing throng. Several small snakes lay across the big one, and I suppose it was a mother and children taking a bath. Some thought the old one was twelve feet long, but it flopped about so it was hard to give a close guess. It was the nearest approach to my Port Hudson snake that I have seen.

At 9 p. m. we reached the Mississippi at Morgan's Bend, or Morganzia. The cattle had been shot down and were lying as they fell. It was everyone for himself. Chunks were cut out and were being eaten before the animal was done kicking. A pack of wolves never acted more ravenous and bloodthirsty. I managed to get my hand between the ribs of one and hold of the liver. I couldn't pull my hand out without straightening the fingers and so only got shreds, but I kept it up until I had taken the edge off my appetite and then lay over on my back and was sound asleep. I suppose a hundred men stepped over me and maybe on me, but nothing disturbed my slumbers. I slept like a dead man.

CHAPTER 16

Camp at Morganzia, La.

May 22, 1864.
Sunday.

The sun was shining bright, and the flies were crawling over my bloody face, and hands when I awoke. Tony had got in and had found some hard-tack and a piece of beef for my breakfast. The skeletons of the cattle were picked clean. The field looked like a battleground. Men were stretched on the ground everywhere and in every position, and others were picking their way about among them. But unlike a battlefield, the dead began to rise up and move about. At 8 o'clock the order "Fall in" came and soon after we started again. I had to walk on my heel, for something was grinding the ends of my toes off. No attention was paid to the order of our going; it was simply a question of going at all.

We only went about a mile, when we stopped in a grove of big trees between the road and the river, and preparations for camping were soon under way. Captain Laird appeared and took charge of his company. He said he had lost us while fighting fire in Alexandria. I joined the multitude in the river. The dirt our clothes and our bodies had picked up on the way was astonishing. Enough of it to make a garden was soon floating down the river. My feet were in terrible shape, one much worse than the other. The blisters had broken and bled and the dirt had formed a scab, which had acted like a grater on the raw flesh underneath.

A good swim in the river and a good beating of our clothes, together with a good dinner after it, made the world seem different to all of us. The hard tramp was over and we cared little what came next. The 90th had had the hardest time of all. We had to hustle from the rear to the front with the pontoons, marching mile after mile and hour after hour, while others were sleeping soundly by the way. Upon comparing notes I had the satisfaction of knowing I was the only white man in the regiment that had walked the entire distance. Every other one confessed to having ridden some part of the way. From the time we formed in line at Yellow Bayou until we stopped at Morgan's Bend was forty-one hours of hard marching, on scant rations and with less than an hour's sleep all put together. I had heard and read of forced marching, and now that I had taken part in one, I was ready to believe anything that was ever said or written on the subject.

Major Palon's prophecy that I would find plenty of filling for my diary had certainly come true. I have only skimmed over the account, but will never forget the rest. It would fill a book if written out, and then only give a faint idea of the reality. The sufferings of the horses and mules made me sick at heart. Men, when they could go no farther, said so and gave up trying, but the poor beasts' sufferings went right on until neither whip nor spur could get another move out of them.

May 23, 1864.
Monday.
The army of stragglers kept coming in. They were gathered in a bunch and then sorted out and sent to their respective commands. Our tents arrived and were put up, and we began to live like folks again. Smallpox had by this time begun to develop, and a tent was put up outside the camp and such as showed the symptoms sent to it. We have all been exposed and may all have it, but a trifle like that does not worry us after what we have lived through. Some of the men have had the disease and they are to be used in nursing the others.

A nice little shower came up toward night which washed the dust from the leaves and grass, leaving everything about us beautiful. The smallpox is the only enemy in sight now, and that we can neither shoot nor run away from. The best thing about it is that one stands just as good a chance as another, and no better.

May 24, 1864.
Tuesday.
Thomas Dorsey, one of the brightest of my company, is dead. Before I knew what ailed him, I had done all I could to make him comfortable, even to giving him my blanket to keep him off the ground. His death scared the others so they could not be got near his tent. As I had been exposed as much as it was possible to be, I rolled him up in his blanket and dragged him into a hole that had been dug outside

the tent and covered him up.

May 25, 1864.
Wednesday.
All hands have been vaccinated. All stood in line and as fast as the job was done the line moved up until all had had a dose. This is the fourth or fifth time I have been vaccinated in the army, and so far nothing has come of it. In the afternoon I borrowed the adjutant's horse and went with Sol and Gorton for a ride. They both have the shakes yet. Stragglers kept coming in, among them being Sergeant Nace, who has not yet found his regiment. When he found we had smallpox he cut short his visit. He is a dead beat, I thought so before and am sure of it now. I hope his regiment will find him, if he don't find it.

The picket lines are well out, and videttes are still farther out. This gives us a large territory to feel at home in. The enemy is said to be hovering around on the outside, but give us no trouble. Maybe they, too, are tired and are taking a rest.

May 26, 1864.
Thursday.
Nothing happened today worth telling of. I am detailed for picket duty tomorrow.

May 27, 1864.
Friday.
With a horse to ride and a company of men from a western regiment, I went out about one and a half miles to relieve a part of the picket line. Quite an army goes out every day, for the line about our present stopping-place is many miles in length. I had about half a mile, almost all the way through bushes and wet ground. An empty house near one end of the line was my headquarters, and from there I hobbled over the line every two hours, the line being too rough to ride. I was not called out once, everything being quiet along my line, and I heard no calls from those on either side of me. The officer of the day came round as often as he could ride the line, and at midnight the grand rounds came.

Sol and Gorton came out and brought me a supper and visited me until I had to go over the line. Orders were very strict at night to halt everything. An Irishman on one of the posts asked me if he should halt a pig if he came along, and I repeated the order to "halt everything." At midnight, when I went over the line with the grand rounds, there was fresh pork frying at that post, and as the orders were strictly against . foraging I said to the man, "You paid for the pig, didn't you?" "Yes, sor," said he; "it's only the loikes of them Indiana fellers that'll steal." That almost made me yell, for the grand officer was colonel of an Indiana regiment that were noted foragers. He grinned at the joke on him, and with that one adventure we reached the end of the line, where I turned him over to the next and came back. I got a generous slice of the stolen pig for my breakfast.

May 28, 1864.
Saturday.

The night wore away and at 9 a. m. the new guard came. After my line was relieved I marched them back to guard headquarters to discharge them. A new order, that no loaded guns be allowed in camp, had come out, and I took them to the river bank to fire off the guns. I noticed that the gun next to me did not go off and told the man of it. He tried it again and still it didn't go. I then pricked some powder in the tube and snapped it, and as it didn't go off I tried the ramrod to see if it was loaded. The gun was nearly half full of something, and upon taking it to the armourer, who took out the breach, found the first charge had the bullet end down. The man could not account for it, but probably in the excitement of the Yellow Bayou fight he had got rattled and kept loading every time he snapped the gun. It is said such things do happen in volley firing, but I never before saw anything of the kind. I was glad enough the first charge was wrong end up. There were six charges in the gun and something must have happened if the first charge had exploded. I then returned to our camp and slept till night.

May 29, 1864.
Sunday.

This was to be our pay day, and little else was thought of or talked about all the morning. A number of us were in Colonel Parker's tent when the adjutant congratulated me on getting full pay, with no reduction for the time I was absent without leave; that the rolls had been passed upon at headquarters and no reduction made. Colonel Parker said it could not be. The record had never been cleared, and if the paymaster was informed of the fact I wouldn't get any pay at all. After some talk, in which some took one view and some another, the matter was dropped and I thought no more about it until told by the paymaster, when I stepped up for my $415, that I could get no pay until an investigation was had and the rolls cleared.

I was mad clear through, and I was terribly disappointed, too. I first found out that the colonel had done it and then went and gave him a piece of my mind. He laughed the matter off, but he was just as mad as I. I forgot about his being my superior, and I wonder he didn't put me under arrest. I certainly gave him plenty of excuse for doing it. I had no right to talk as I did, but I had plenty of reason, and I have not yet got to the point where I am sorry for doing it. I reminded him that although I was absent from my regiment for a few days without leave, I was on duty in another, and earning my pay, while he and the rest of them were loafing in camp at Lakeport. I can't imagine why Colonel Parker has so suddenly turned against me. So far as I know he has no reason for it, and if he knows of one, he is not man enough to tell. So I must live on borrowed money for another two months, and affairs at home must get along the best way they can. Maybe it all comes from his hobby, "*The good of the service*," which he so often quotes.

May 30, 1864.
Monday.
I made an application for an investigation of my reasons for being absent without leave, and Colonel Parker endorsed and sent it to headquarters. The matter has blown over for the present. From all I can hear, the colonel is ashamed of the shabby trick he played me. If Colonel Bostwick had been here instead of at headquarters, I don't believe the thing would have been thought of. Colonel Parker is like some others I have seen. A little authority makes a fool of him.

A fort is being built just above here and our men are to work on it. We have a new doctor. Dr. Henry, Dr. Warren having been detached. He is doing all he can to stop the spread of smallpox, and as no new cases have developed in several days now Ave think the worst may be over.

May 31, 1864.
Tuesday.
Was in camp all day writing.

June 1, 1864.
Wednesday.
Moved camp up the river to where the fort is being built,—that is, all the well ones. Hallisy, our new sutler, came today with a full stock of goods. He belonged to the 6th Michigan; was wounded at Port Hudson. Shot through the arm and the wound would not heal and he

was discharged. Not wishing to go home, his comrades chipped in for a box of cigars, which he peddled out among the soldiers and was able to buy more and continue peddling. He was soon able to make trips to the city for anything needed by his comrades, and in a short time was doing quite a business. He is honest and trustworthy in every way, and when he asked to be appointed sutler for the 90th. he had all the recommendations the officers could give. He is a money-maker and will get rich if the war lasts long enough, yet he is so fair and square in all his dealings that no one ought to begrudge him the money he makes. He brought our mail and in the bundle were seven letters for me, and none of them had any bad news in them.

June 2, 1864.
Thursday.
Was on detail at the fort. Officers of the engineer corps have the work in charge. They have stakes stuck everywhere with marks on them that they may understand, but surely none of us can. A plan on paper shows it to be in the form of a star, with a wide and deep ditch running round it. The dirt from this ditch is being carefully piled up inside in a bank just like the ditch, so that every foot the ditch goes down, the bank rises another foot. There is no lack of men or teams. A detail is made every day of as many men as can work to advantage. On my section a curious snake or animal was dug out. He came out from a hole that was cut across as the ditch went down. It looked most like an eel at first, but a closer examination showed four short legs, not over an inch long, and armed with toes for digging. The men called it a Congo snake and seemed to have a superstitious dread of it, for they left the ditch as soon as it appeared and would not go back until I had killed it and thrown it out of their sight. A shower broke off the work in the afternoon and flooded the diggings.

June 3, 1864.
Friday.
Was notified that a commission had been appointed to investigate the stopping of my pay and would meet at brigade headquarters as soon as practicable. Then we will know. If Colonel Parker is right I shall apologize for the free speech I gave him. I wonder if he will do as much if I win out.

June 5, 1864.
Sunday.
Captain Laird, who has not been mustered yet, went to Port Hud-

son to see about it, today. I put in the day visiting and being visited. While in Sol's tent, and as we lay talking to each other, we heard a commotion in Colonel Parker's tent, which was close by. Just then a big black snake slid in under the tent, and stopped when right between us. His head was well up and he just slid over the ground like a sleigh crook. Sol's sword was within my reach and I crippled him before he got any further. Where on earth he could have come from and not be seen till he entered the colonel's tent is a mystery, for the ground is as bare as a board all through the camp, and' men are all the time moving about on it. We think he must have crawled under somebody's bunk in the night, and not liking the quarters had started for the country again.

June 6, 1864.
Monday.
Captain Laird came back, saying he was unable to get mustered, and says he shall throw up the job and go home. Major Palon, who has been to New Orleans, came on the same boat.

June 7, 1864.
Tuesday.
Was called before the commission to show cause why I should not be punished for being absent without leave. Colonel Fuller of the 73rd, Captain Morton, acting assistant comprised the board. I was not put under oath, but just told my story and was acquitted. The findings of the court, however, will have to go to Washington for approval. Colonel P. was the only one of the 90th who did not congratulate me. He appears more cranky than ever.

June 8, 1864.
Wednesday.
Borrowed $200 and sent home to pay on the place. Went down to visit the 128th and came near a sunstroke on the way. The weather is something awful in the middle of the day. I was completely used up when I got home.

June 9 1864.
Thursday.
I kept very quiet today for the heat is harder and harder for me to bear. Colonel Bostwick, Captain Hoyt, the quartermaster, Moody and Reynolds all came up from the city, where they have been for a visit. Orders were received for us to turn over the best drilled of our men

to Major Paine.

June 10, 1864.
Friday.
Captain Laird went home today, and Company D is mine to look after again. I have just been able to keep about today.

June 11, 1864.
Saturday.
On duty as officer of the guard today. The duty is nothing, but the wearing of uniform, with a sword, belt and sash, for twenty-four hours came near using me up. I thought I would have to beg off, but I lived through it. There were plenty ready to take my place but were not allowed to.

June 12, 1864.
Sunday.
A friend in the 128th got in trouble and was brought up to see me. I helped him all I could, but I can't say I pitied him.

June 13, 1864.
Monday.
Major Paine came and took no of our men. He took all of Company D, and I am out of a job unless Colonel Parker finds something for me to do, which I have no doubt he will. Company D made the best showing in the manual of arms and in marching. Captain Laird has either taken away or destroyed the company papers, and it took me all day to get the transfers made out.

June 14, 1864.
Tuesday.
On detail at the fort. General Sickles reviewed the troops in this department today, from which we judge another move will soon be made. General Sickles lost a leg at Gettysburg but he rides just as well as if he had both. An orderly carried his crutches for him, and a pocket built on the saddle, in which to rest the stump, answered the purpose of a stirrup.

June 15, 1864.
Wednesday.
Was busy settling up Captain Laird's company affairs, which is made much harder on account of the original papers being missing.

After the 15th of June the diary is missing. Whether it has been lost, or whether I no longer kept it going, I cannot now tell. From papers in my possession, and from quite a vivid recollection of the events that made up those last days of my army life, I am able to give a pretty good account of it up to my homecoming.

We remained at Morganzia until about the middle of July, attending to the routine duties of camp life, and helping at the fort that was building as we were called upon.

On the fourth of July we had an old-fashioned celebration: one that doubtless is recalled with pleasure by every survivor of the event. We borrowed planks from the fort and built a long and wide table with seats along the sides. Having plenty of both workmen and materials, we spared no pains to make it a very substantial affair. The regimental colours were placed in the middle of the table, flanked on either side with stacks of muskets, each of which had a flag flying from its top. Everything good to eat, drink or look upon that we could buy, beg or borrow, was piled upon it. Sutler Hallisy made a special trip to New Orleans for such things as we could not otherwise get. The planning for it and the carrying out of the plans took all our spare time for weeks before. Officers from headquarters and from many of the regiments near us were invited, and few, if any, failed to accept the invitation.

After the dinner, all that could, made speeches, and many of them were worth going a long way to hear. Lieutenant Bell distinguished himself, making what I thought was the best and most appropriate speech of all. All joined in singing patriotic songs, and many a good story was told. From start to finish the affair passed off without a hitch. Not a thing happened to mar the enjoyment of any one present. When it was over, the men took possession and finished up the eatables, after which they, too, had speeches and singing and wound up with a dance on the table. Their part was fully as entertaining as ours had been, and taken altogether, the day was one to live long in the memory of those present.

Soon after the review of the troops by General Sickles, the great army that covered the ground for miles about us began to melt away, some going up the river and some down to other fields of activity. The Red River campaign was over and nothing left to show for it but the great waste of men and money it had cost.

The 128th left Morganzia a few days before the fourth of July, thus missing our great dinner, at which there were mutual regrets. They went into camp at Algiers for a time and then came North and served out their time under Sheridan and Grant. The men in our camp that had not already been transferred were taken to fill up other regiments, and the officers ordered to New Orleans for muster-out. (See General Order No. 88, Department of the Gulf, dated July 11, 1864.)

The trouble with Colonel Parker kept sticking up its head and was the cause of my only unpleasant recollections of those days. I still suffered from the heat, and it seemed as if I was detailed for guard or fatigue duty on the hottest days that came. On the 28th of June the sun came up blazing hot, bidding fair to beat any record it had yet made. I felt the heat more than common that morning, having been on duty at the fort the day before, and was congratulating myself on having nothing to do but keep as cool as possible, when an order came for me to take Company B out for a two-hours' drill.

This was such a direct slap in the face that I made up my mind it was time for the worm to turn. As politely as. I knew how, I refused to obey the order, and was at once ordered in arrest and sent to my tent. It was the first time I had ever known of an officer being detailed for extra duty two days in succession. I believed I was right and was willing to await the outcome. In a little while the order for arrest came to me in writing. I have it yet and it reads:

Special order No. 27.   Morganzia, La., June 28, 1864.
2nd Lieut. Lawrance VanAlstyne, 90th U. S. C. Infantry is hereby ordered in arrest for disobedience of orders.
      By command of Lt. Col. George Parker,
John Mathers, Jr.,
1st Lt. & Adjutant.

The next was a copy of the charges and specifications, which soon after came and which reads:

Headquarters 90th U. S. C. I.
Morganzia, La., June 28, 1864.
Charges and specifications preferred by Lieut. Col. George Parker, against 2nd Lieut. Lawrence VanAlstyne, 90th U. S. C. I.
Charge first.
Disobedience of orders.
Specification. In this that he, the said Lieut. Lawrence VanAlstyne did when ordered by his commanding officer to drill Co. B, 90th U. S. C. I., refuse, saying "I refuse to do it," or words to that effect. This at Morganzia, on or about the 28th day of June 1864.

Charge 2nd.

Conduct to the prejudice of good order and military discipline. Specification. In this that he the said 2nd Lieut. Lawrence VanAlstyne did when ordered by his commanding officer to drill Co. B, 90th U. S. C. I. refuse, saying "I refuse to do it" or words to that effect. This in the hearing and presence of enlisted men. This at Morganzia, La. on or about the 28th day of June 1864.

Witnesses.   George Parker, Dr. Henry, Steward Drury,
                              Sam Lewis Corp. Co. B
                              Henry Jones, Serg't Co. B

The next was a note from the colonel, saying:

Lieut. VanAlstyne's attention is respectfully called to Par. 223, revised army regulations. Indulgences will be granted upon written application, but it can hardly be expected that a sick officer will ask for very large limits.

Respectfully,

George Parker,
Lt. Col. Comm'ng.

To none of these did I make reply. In the course of an hour I received an empty envelope on which was written.

Lieut. L. VanAlstyne has the limits of the camp.

George Parker,
Lt. Col. Commanding.

Nothing more happened until the 30th, when the following was received:

Headquarters 90th U. S. Coloured Infantry,
Morganzia, La., June 30th, 1864.

Special order
No ...
2nd Lieut. Lawrence VanAlstyne, 90th United States Coloured Infantry is hereby released from arrest.

By order of
George Parker,
Lt. Col. Com'dg
90th U. S. Col'd Inf'y.

John Mathers,
Jr., 1st Lt. and Adj't.

Thus the matter of arrest ended. The charges had been duly forwarded to headquarters in the field and had been sent back with the single word "Disapproved" written across the back. I never found out who explained the matter at the headquarters office, but someone must have done it, for the charge was a serious one and could hardly have been overlooked without an investigation.

From that on I suffered such petty persecutions as could be lawfully put upon me, but otherwise had little more to do with Colonel Parker.

CHAPTER 17

Our Last Camp in the South

Soon after the order to report at New Orleans for muster-out was received, we left Morganzia and went into camp in the outskirts of New Orleans. We unloaded our things on the levee one night after dark, and in the rain. We felt our way down the embankment, and without the least idea as to where we were, spread some tents on the ground and raising others over them crawled in and made ourselves as comfortable as we could. In the morning we arranged our camp in a more respectable order and sat down to await the pleasure of the mustering officer. The men we had with us were used for guards to keep up the semblance of a military organization. Those that could afford it went into the city to board, and the rest, I among the number, contented ourselves with army fare. I had many invitations from my brother officers to live with them, and did visit them frequently, sometimes staying for a day or two. So the time passed until the 24th of August, when we were called before the mustering officer and mustered out of the service.

We were to be paid in New York, and as I was in debt to many, I was about to sell my pay to a broker in order that I might pay such as were not ready to go home, when the quartermaster offered to lend me the money and wait for it until we reached New York, thus saving me the broker's commission. In due time we reached our homes and the eventful life of the soldier was exchanged for the less eventful life of the private citizen. The prophecy that the return of the soldiers would mark the beginning of a reign of lawlessness in the North, did not come true. As law-abiding citizens the returned soldiers have averaged well with those who remained at home.

I must not close the book without a word about Tony, from whom I parted with sincere regret. I am sorry I cannot recall his surname, which was that of his owner, a planter in the Teche country.

From Tony's own account, he had had a good home and a kind master, in fact, had had everything he could wish for except the one thing above all others that he longed for, "freedom." Both he and his wife were house servants, born and raised in "the house," not in "the quarters." He was always careful to make this distinction. He had never been whipped, and he had little sympathy for those who had, saying they most always deserved all they got.

My acquaintance with him began while we were at Brashear City. He came with others from the Teche country, and was looking for someone who would write a letter to his wife and tell her how and where he was. I wrote the letter and from that on he was all the time wanting to do something for me. When the examination came, Tony was thrown out on account of an injury once received from the kick of a horse. He then came for me to take him to wait on me. More out of pity for him than because I wanted any waiting on, I took him on, giving him the ration allowed me by the government for such a purpose. From that time he was my willing slave. My clothes were as clean and my boots as black as if I had been General Banks himself. He was never in the way, and yet was never out of the way when wanted.

I became more careful of my personal appearance by finding out that in Tony's estimation my only failing was a little carelessness in that direction. I accidentally overheard a conversation between Tony and his chums as to the good and bad qualities possessed by the officers of the 90th, and when I found how little I lacked of perfection, I resolved to be more careful. He was a very rapid talker, speaking both French and English, When he was angry or excited he would mix the two together in a way that was laughable. He loved horses and would talk to them as if they were people and understood all he said. I shall never forget a scolding he gave one while we were at Grand Ecore. Tony had taken a wounded horse into the river and washed him clean.

As he was leading him back to hard ground, the horse dropped in the sand and rolled his sore back full of grit. Tony looked at the horse in silence for a while, and then began hurling such a mixture of French and English in his face as no other horse ever heard. Everyone that heard it laughed. The horse looked sober enough, but may have understood, for when he was washed again he came through the sand without offering to lay down.

Tony was the best forager I ever knew. He could scent a chicken as well as a pointer dog, and many a one he picked up where no one else could find a feather. I never fully understood his devotion to me. It certainly was not on account of the pay he got, for much of the time we were together I was as poor as he. I have good reason to believe he would have stood between me and danger, and perhaps death itself if the opportunity had offered. It was little I could do for him beyond writing letters for him to his wife, and teaching him to read words of one or two syllables. I left him at New Orleans with money enough for immediate needs, and suppose he went back to his plantation home.